T0252408

Architecting HBase Applications
A Guidebook for Successful Development and Design

Jean-Marc Spaggiari and Kevin O'Dell

Beijing · Boston · Farnham · Sebastopol · Tokyo

Architecting HBase Applications

by Jean-Marc Spaggiari and Kevin O'Dell

Copyright © 2016 Jean-Marc Spaggiari and Kevin O'Dell. All rights reserved.

Printed in the United States of America.

Published by O'Reilly Media, Inc., 1005 Gravenstein Highway North, Sebastopol, CA 95472.

O'Reilly books may be purchased for educational, business, or sales promotional use. Online editions are also available for most titles (*http://safaribooksonline.com*). For more information, contact our corporate/institutional sales department: 800-998-9938 or *corporate@oreilly.com*.

Editor: Marie Beaugureau	**Indexer:** WordCo Indexing Services, Inc.
Production Editor: Nicholas Adams	**Interior Designer:** David Futato
Copyeditor: Jasmine Kwityn	**Cover Designer:** Karen Montgomery
Proofreader: Amanda Kersey	**Illustrator:** Rebecca Demarest

August 2016:   First Edition

Revision History for the First Edition

2016-07-14:   First Release

See *http://oreilly.com/catalog/errata.csp?isbn=9781491915813* for release details.

The O'Reilly logo is a registered trademark of O'Reilly Media, Inc. *Architecting HBase Applications*, the cover image, and related trade dress are trademarks of O'Reilly Media, Inc.

While the publisher and the authors have used good faith efforts to ensure that the information and instructions contained in this work are accurate, the publisher and the authors disclaim all responsibility for errors or omissions, including without limitation responsibility for damages resulting from the use of or reliance on this work. Use of the information and instructions contained in this work is at your own risk. If any code samples or other technology this work contains or describes is subject to open source licenses or the intellectual property rights of others, it is your responsibility to ensure that your use thereof complies with such licenses and/or rights.

978-1-491-91581-3

[LSI]

To my father. I wish you could have seen it...

—Jean-Marc Spaggiari

To my mother, who I think about every day; my father, who has always been there for me; and my beautiful wife Melanie and daughter Scotland, for putting up with all my complaining and the extra long hours.

—Kevin O'Dell

Table of Contents

Part III. Troubleshooting

Foreword

Throughout my 25 years in the software industry, I have experienced many disruptive changes: the Internet, the World Wide Web, mainframes, the client–server model, and more. I once worked on a team that was implementing software to make oil refineries safer. Our 40-person team shared a single DEC VAX—a machine no more powerful than the cell phone I use today.

I still remember a day in the early 90s when we were scheduled to receive new machines. The machines being replaced were located on the third floor, and were large, heavy, washing machine–sized behemoths. A bunch of us waited inside the "machine room" to see how they would heave the new machines up all those flights of stairs. We imagined a giant crane, the street outside being blocked off…in short, a big operation!

But what actually happened was quite different. A man entered the room carrying a small box under his arm. He placed it on top of one of the old "washing machines," switched some cables around, did some tests, and left. That was it? Wow. Things change!

That is the joy of being part of the tech industry: if we are willing to learn new things and move with it, we will never be bored, and will never cease to be amazed. What seemed impossible just a few years ago is suddenly commonplace.

Big data is such a change. Big data is everywhere. The revolution started by Google with the Google File System and BigTable has now reached almost every tech company, bank, government, and startup. Directly or indirectly, for better or for worse, these systems touch the lives of almost every human being on the planet.

Apache HBase, like BigTable before it, has a unique place in this ecosystem: it provides an updatable view into essentially unlimited datasets stored in an immutable, distributed filesystem. As such, it bridges the gap between pure file storage and OLTP/OLAP databases.

HBase is everywhere: Facebook, Apple, Salesforce.com, Adobe, Yahoo!, Bloomberg, Huawei, The Gap, and many other companies use it. Google adopted the HBase API for its public cloud BigTable offering, a testament to the popularity of HBase.

Despite its ubiquity, HBase is not plug and play. Distributed systems are hard. Terms such as *partition tolerance*, *consistency*, and *availability* inevitably creep into every discussion, soon followed by even more esoteric terms such as *hotspotting* and *salting*. Scaling to hundreds or thousands of machines requires painful trade-offs, and these trade-offs make it harder to use these systems optimally. HBase is no exception.

In my years in the HBase and Hadoop communities, I have experienced these challenges firsthand. Use cases must be designed and architected carefully in order to play to the strengths of HBase.

This book, written by two insiders who have been on the ground supporting customers, is a much needed guide that details how to architect applications that will work well with HBase and that will scale to thousands of machines.

If you are building or are planning to build new applications that need highly scalable and reliable storage, this book is for you. Jean-Marc and Kevin have seen it all: the use cases, the mistakes people make, the assumptions from single-server systems that no longer hold. But most importantly, they know what works well, how to fix what doesn't, and how to make sense of it all

> — *Lars Hofhansl,*
> *Committer and member of the HBase*
> *Project Management Committee*
> *Apache Foundation member VP at*
> *Salesforce.com*

Preface

As Hadoop has grown into mainstream popularity, so has its vibrant ecosystem, including widely used tools such as Hive, Spark, Impala, and HBase. This book focuses on one of those tools: Apache HBase, a scalable, fault-tolerant, low-latency data store that runs on top of the Hadoop Distributed Filesystem (HDFS). HBase merges Hadoop scalability with real-time data serving. At scale, HBase allows for millions of read and write operations per second from a single cluster, while still maintaining all of Hadoop's availability guarantees. HBase quickly grew in popularity and now powers some of the largest Hadoop deployments on the planet—it is used by companies such as Apple, Salesforce.com, and Facebook.

However, getting started with HBase can be a daunting task. While there are numerous resources that can help get a developer started (including mailing lists, an online book, and Javadocs), information about architecting, designing, and deploying real-world applications using Apache HBase is quite limited. That's where this book comes in.

The goal of the book is to bring to life real-world HBase deployments. Each use case discussed in this book has been deployed and put into production. This doesn't mean there isn't room for improvement, or that you won't need to modify for your particular task, but it does show how things have actually been done.

The book also includes robust coverage of troubleshooting (Part III). Our goal is to help you avoid common deployment mistakes. Part III will also offer insight into often overlooked tuning such as garbage collection and region allocations.

Who Should Read This Book?

Architecting HBase Applications is designed for architects, developers, and those looking to get a better idea of big data application deployment in general. You should have basic knowledge about Hadoop, including the components needed for setting up and installing a successful Hadoop cluster. We will not spend time on Hadoop configurations or NodeManager actions. Architects reading this book are not required to have a full working knowledge of Java, but it will be necessary to fully grasp the deployment chapters. The book is designed to cover multiple vertical use cases and designed to assist enterprises and startups alike.

Architects will appreciate the detail-oriented use case chapters, which outline the individual components being deployed and how they are all tied together. The development chapters offer developers a quick look at detailed code examples to speed up production deployments. The deployment chapters will offer insight into the specific APIs being used, along with performance enhancement tips that can save hours of troubleshooting. Those curious about big data will find both the architecture and deployment chapters useful, and also gather insight into the HBase ecosystem and what it takes to deploy HBase.

How This Book Is Organized

Architecting HBase Applications is organized into three parts: Part I, the introduction to HBase, covers topics such as what HBase is, what its ecosystem looks like, and how to deploy it. Part II, which covers the use cases, is the heart of the book. We hope this will be the part you refer back to most frequently, as it contains tips and tricks that will prove useful to you. Finally, Part III discusses troubleshooting—you should refer to this part frequently. We hope this will be the second-most referenced section (in a proactive manner, not a reactive one). This part offers insights about controlling your region count, properly tuning garbage collection, and avoiding hotspots.

Additional Resources

This book is not designed to cover the internals of HBase. Our good friend Lars George has taken HBase internals to a whole new level with *HBase: The Definitive Guide* (O'Reilly, 2011). We recommend reading his book as a precursor to ours. It will help you better understand some terminology that we only gloss over with a paragraph or two.

While we spend a fair bit of time discussing the details of deploying HBase, our book will not cover much of the theory behind deploying HBase. Nick Dimiduk and Amandeep Khurana's *HBase in Action* (Manning, 2013) covers the practicalities of deploying HBase. Their book is less focused on the total application development and spends more time on production best practices.

Conventions Used in This Book

The following typographical conventions are used in this book:

Italic

Indicates new terms, URLs, email addresses, filenames, and file extensions.

`Constant width`

Used for program listings, as well as within paragraphs to refer to program elements such as variable or function names, databases, data types, environment variables, statements, and keywords.

`Constant width bold`

Shows commands or other text that should be typed literally by the user.

`Constant width italic`

Shows text that should be replaced with user-supplied values or by values determined by context.

 This element signifies a tip or suggestion.

 This element signifies a general note.

 This element indicates a warning or caution.

Using Code Examples

Supplemental material (code examples, exercises, etc.) is available for download at *https://github.com/ArchitectingHBase/examples*.

This book is here to help you get your job done. In general, if example code is offered with this book, you may use it in your programs and documentation. You do not need to contact us for permission unless you're reproducing a significant portion of the code. For example, writing a program that uses several chunks of code from this book does not require permission. Selling or distributing a CD-ROM of examples from O'Reilly books does require permission. Answering a question by citing this book and quoting example code does not require permission. Incorporating a significant amount of example code from this book into your product's documentation does require permission.

We appreciate, but do not require, attribution. An attribution usually includes the title, author, publisher, and ISBN. For example: "*Architecting HBase Applications* by Jean-Marc Spaggiari and Kevin O'Dell (O'Reilly). Copyright 2016 Jean-Marc Spaggiari and Kevin O'Dell, 978-1-491-91581-3."

If you feel your use of code examples falls outside fair use or the permission given above, feel free to contact us at *permissions@oreilly.com*.

Safari® Books Online

 *Safari Books Online* is an on-demand digital library that delivers expert content in both book and video form from the world's leading authors in technology and business.

Technology professionals, software developers, web designers, and business and creative professionals use Safari Books Online as their primary resource for research, problem solving, learning, and certification training.

Safari Books Online offers a range of plans and pricing for enterprise, government, education, and individuals.

Members have access to thousands of books, training videos, and prepublication manuscripts in one fully searchable database from publishers like O'Reilly Media, Prentice Hall Professional, Addison-Wesley Professional, Microsoft Press, Sams, Que, Peachpit Press, Focal Press, Cisco Press, John Wiley & Sons, Syngress, Morgan Kaufmann, IBM Redbooks, Packt, Adobe Press, FT Press, Apress, Manning, New Riders, McGraw-Hill, Jones & Bartlett, Course Technology, and hundreds more. For more information about Safari Books Online, please visit us online.

How to Contact Us

Please address comments and questions concerning this book to the publisher:

O'Reilly Media, Inc.
1005 Gravenstein Highway North
Sebastopol, CA 95472
800-998-9938 (in the United States or Canada)
707-829-0515 (international or local)

707-829-0104 (fax)

We have a web page for this book, where we list errata, examples, and any additional information. You can access this page at *http://bit.ly/architecting-hbase-applications*.

To comment or ask technical questions about this book, send email to *bookques-tions@oreilly.com*.

For more information about our books, courses, conferences, and news, see our website at *http://www.oreilly.com*.

Find us on Facebook: *http://facebook.com/oreilly*

Follow us on Twitter: *http://twitter.com/oreillymedia*

Watch us on YouTube: *http://www.youtube.com/oreillymedia*

Acknowledgments

Kevin and Jean-Marc would like to thank everyone who made this book a reality for all of their hard work: our amazing editor Marie Beaugureau; the exceptional staff at O'Reilly Media; Lars Hofhansl for composing the foreword; our primary reviewers Nate Neff, Suzanne McIntosh, Jeff "Jeffrey" Holoman, Prateek Rungta, Jon Hsieh, Sean Busbey, and Nicolae Popa; fellow authors for their unending support and guidance; Ben Spivey, Joey Echeverria, Ted Malaska, Gwen Shapira, Lars George, Eric Sammer, Amandeep Khurana, and Tom White. We would also like to thank Linden Hillenbrand, Eric Driscoll, Ron Beck, Paul Beduhn, Matt Jackson, Ryan Blue, Aaron "ATM" Meyers, Dave Shuman, Ryan Bosshart (thank you for all the hoops you jumped through), Jean-Daniel "JD" Cryans, St. Ack, Elliot Clark, Harsh J Chouraria, Amy O'Connor, Patrick Angeles, and Alex Moundalexis. Finally, we'd like to thank everyone at Cloudera and Rocana for their support, advice, and encouragement along the way.

From Kevin

I would like to thank my best friends and brothers for the lifetime of support and encouragement: Matthew "Kabuki" Langrehr, Scott Hopkins, Paul Bernier, Zack Myers, Matthew Ring, Brian Clay, Chris Holt, Cole Sillivant, Viktor "Shrek" Skowronek, Kyle Prawdzik, and Master Captain Matt Jones. I would also like to thank my friends, coworkers, partners, and customers who helped along the way: Ron Kent, John "Over the Top" Lynch, Brian Burton, Mark Schnegelberger, David Hackett, Sekou McKissick, Scott Burkey, David Rahm, Steve Williams, Nick Preztak, Steve "Totty" Totman, Brock Noland, Josh "Nooga" Patterson, Shawn Dolley, Stephen Fritz, Richard Saltzer, Ryan P, and Sam Heywood. A special thanks to everyone who helped by publishing their use case or consulting on content: Kathleen DeValk, Kevin

Farmer, Raheem Daya, Tomas Mazukna, Chris Ingrassia, Kevin Sommer, and Jeremy Ulstad.

A special thanks goes to Mike Olson and Angus Klein for taking a chance and hiring me at Cloudera. Eric Sammer, Omer Trajman, and Marc "Boat Ready" Degenkolb for bringing me onto Rocana. A begrudging thanks to Don "I am a millennial-hating baby" Brown. One final thank you to Jean-Marc, I can't thank you enough for asking me to be your coauthor.

From Jean-Marc

I would like to thank everyone who supported me over the journey.

Introduction to HBase

Welcome to Part I of *Architecting HBase Applications*. Before we dive into architecting and deploying production use cases, it is important to level set on general HBase knowledge. Part I will be a high-level review for anyone who has read either of the amazing books *HBase: The Definitive Guide* (O'Reilly) or *HBase In Action* (Manning). If it has been awhile since reading these books, or if *Architecting HBase Applications* is your first foray into HBase, it is recommended that you read Part I.

We will start with a high-level overview of general HBase principles. Next, we will look at the surrounding HBase ecosystem. The goal is not to cover every HBase related technology, but to give you an understanding of the options and integration points surrounding HBase. After the ecosystem, we will cover one of the harder topics surrounding HBase: sizing and tuning of a general HBase cluster. The goal is to help you avoid upfront mistakes around improper node sizing, while providing tuning best practices to prevent performance issues before they happen. Finally, we will wrap up with an HBase deployment overview. This will allow you to set up your own standalone HBase instance to follow along with the examples in the books.

## CHAPTER 1

What Is HBase?

Back in the 1990s, Google started to index the Web, and rapidly faced some challenges.

The first challenge was related to the size of the data to store: the Web was quickly growing from a few tens of millions of pages to the more than one billion pages we have today. Indexing the Web was becoming harder and harder with each passing day.

This led to the creation of the Google File System (GFS), which Google used internally, and in 2006, the company published "Bigtable: A Distributed Storage System for Structured Data," (*http://bit.ly/1BDktk9*) a white paper on GFS. The open source community saw an opportunity and within the Apache Lucene search project started to implement a GFS equivalent filesystem, Hadoop. After some months of development as part of the Apache Lucene project, Hadoop became its own Apache project.

As Google began to store more and more data, it soon faced another challenge. This time it was related to the indexing of mass volumes of data. How do you store a gigantic index spread over multiple nodes, while maintaining high consistency, failover, and low-latency random reads and random writes? Google created an internal project known as BigTable to meet that need.

Yet again, the Apache open source community saw a great opportunity for leveraging the BigTable white paper and started the implementation of HBase. Apache HBase was originally started as part of the Hadoop project.

Then, in May 2010, HBase graduated to become its own top-level Apache project. And today, many years after its founding, the Apache HBase project continues to flourish and grow.

According to the Apache HBase website, HBase "is the Hadoop database, a distributed, scalable, big data store." This succinct description can be misleading if you have a lot of experience with databases. It's more accurate to say it is a columnar store instead of a database.

This book should help to clarify expectations forming in your head right now.

To get even more specific, HBase is a Java-based, open source, NoSQL, non-relational, column-oriented, distributed database built on top of the Hadoop Distributed Filesystem (HDFS), modeled after Google's BigTable paper. HBase brings to the Hadoop eccosystem most of the BigTable capabilities.

HBase is built to be a fault-tolerant application hosting a few large tables of sparse data (billions/trillions of rows by millions of columns), while allowing for very low latency and near real-time random reads and random writes.

HBase was designed with availability over consistency and offers high availability of all its services with a fast and automatic failover.

HBase also provides many features that we will describe later in this book, including:

- Replication
- Java, REST, Avro, and Thrift APIs
- MapReduce over HBase data framework
- Automatic sharding of tables
- Load balancing
- Compression
- Bloom filters
- Server-side processing (filters and coprocessors)

Another major draw for HBase is the ability to allow creation and usage of a flexible data model. HBase does not force the user to have a strong model for the columns definition, which can be created online as they are required.

In addition to providing atomic and strongly consistent row-level operations, HBase achieves consistency partition tolerance for the entire dataset.

However, you also need to be aware of HBase's limitations:

- HBase is not an SQL RDBMS replacement.
- HBase is not a transactional database.
- HBase doesn't provide an SQL API.

Column-Oriented Versus Row-Oriented

As previously stated, HBase is a column-oriented database, which greatly differs from legacy, row-oriented relational database management systems (RDBMSs). This difference greatly impacts the storage and retrieval of data from the filesystem. In a column-oriented database, the system stores data tables as sparse columns of data rather than as entire rows of data. The columnar model was chosen for HBase to allow next-generation use cases and datasets to be quickly deployed and iterated on. Traditional relational models, which require data to be uniform, do not suit the needs of social media, manufacturing, and web data. This data tends to be sparse in nature, meaning not all rows are created equal. Having the ability to quickly store and access sparse data allows for rows with 100 columns to be stored next to rows with 1,000 columns without being penalized. HBase's data format also allows for loosely defined tables. To create a table in HBase, only the table name and number of column families are needed. This enables dynamic column allocation during write, which is invaluable when dealing with nonstatic and evolving data.

Leveraging a column-oriented format impacts aspects of applications and use case design. Failing to properly understand the limitations can lead to degrading performance of specific HBase operations, including reads, writes, and check and swap (CAS) operations. We will allude to these nuances as we explain properly leveraging the HBase API and schema design around successful deployments.

Implementation and Use Cases

HBase is currently deployed at different scales across thousands of enterprises worldwide. It would be impossible to list them all in this book. As you begin or refine your HBase journey, consider the following large-scale, public HBase implementations:[1]

- Facebook's messaging platform
- Yahoo!
- eBay

In Part II, we will focus on four real-world use cases currently in production today:

- Using HBase as an underlying engine for Solr
- Using HBase for real-time event processing
- Using HBase as a master data management (MDM) system

---

[1] For in-depth discussions of these implementations, see "The Underlying Technology of Messages," (*http://bit.ly/28XZZFq*) "Apache HBase at Yahoo! – Multi-Tenancy at the Helm Again," (*http://yhoo.it/291rVKH*) and "HBase: The Use Case in eBay Cassini," (*http://bit.ly/291rShM*) respectively.

- Using HBase as a document store replacement

As HBase has evolved over time, so has its logo. Today's HBase logo has adopted a simplified and modern text representation. Since all other projects in the Hadoop eccosystem have adopted a mascot, HBase recently voted to choose an orca representation (Figure 1-1).

Figure 1-1. HBase logos from past to present, including the mascot

## CHAPTER 2

HBase Principles

In the previous chapter, we provided a general HBase overview, and we will now go into more detail and look at HBase principles and internals. Although it is very important to understand HBase principles in order to create a good design, it is not mandatory to know all of the internals in detail. In this chapter, we will focus the discussion on describing those HBase internals that will steer you toward good design decisions.

Table Format

Like traditional databases, HBase stores data in tables and has the concept of row keys and column names. Unlike traditional databases, HBase introduces the concept of column families, which we will describe later. But compared to RDBMSs, while the nomenclature is the same, tables and columns do not work the same way in HBase. If you're accustomed to traditional RDBMSs, most of this might seem very familiar, but because of the way it is implemented, you will need to hang up your legacy database knowledge and put your preconceptions aside while learning about HBase.

In HBase, you will find two different types of tables: the system tables and the user tables. *Systems tables* are used internally by HBase to keep track of meta information like the table's access control lists (ACLs), metadata for the tables and regions, namespaces, and so on. There should be no need for you to look at those tables. *User tables* are what you will create for your use cases. They will belong to the `default` namespace unless you create and use a specific one.

Table Layout

An HBase table is composed of one or more column families (CFs), containing columns (which we will call columns qualifiers, or CQ for short) where values can be stored. Unlike traditional RDBMSs, HBase tables may be sparsely populated—some columns might not contain a value at all. In this case, there is no *null* value stored in anticipation of a future value being stored. Instead, that column for that particular row key simply does not get added to the table. Once a value is generated for that column and row key, it will be stored in the table.

 The HBase world uses many different words to describe different parts: rows, columns, keys, cells, values, KeyValues, timestamps, and more. To make sure we talk about the same thing, here is a clarification: a row is formed of multiple columns, all referenced by the same key. A specific column and a key are called a cell. It is possible to have multiple versions of the same cell, all differentiated by the timestamp. A cell can also be called a KeyValue pair. So a row, referenced by a key, is formed of a group of cells, each being a specific column for the given row.

Only columns where there is a value are stored in the underlying filesystem. Also, even if column families need to be defined at the table creation, there is no need to define the column names in advance. They can be dynamically generated as data is inserted into the column family. Therefore, it is possible to have millions of columns with dynamically created names, where columns names are different between all the rows.

To allow a faster lookup access, keys and columns are alphabetically sorted within a table but also in memory.

 HBase orders the keys based on the byte values, so "AA" will come before "BB". If you store numbers as character chains, keep in mind that "1234" will come before "9". If you have to store numbers, then to save on space and to keep the ordering, you will need to store their byte representation. In this model, the integer 1234 will be stored as 0x00 0x00 0x04 0xD2, while 9 will be 0x00 0x00 0x00 0x09. Sorting those two values, we can see that 0x00 0x00 0x00 0x09 will come before 0x00 0x00 0x04 0xD2.

The easiest way to understand how an HBase table is structured is to look at it. Figure 2-1 shows a standard data representation for a table where some columns for some rows are populated and some others are not.

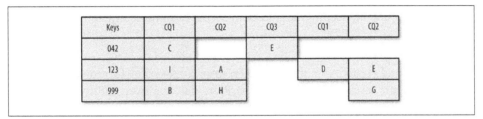

Keys	CQ1	CQ2	CQ3	CQ1	CQ2
042	C		E		
123	I	A		D	E
999	B	H			G

Figure 2-1. Logical representation of an HBase table

Because they will be used to create files and directories in the filesystem, the table name and the column family names need to use only printable characters. This restriction doesn't apply to the column qualifiers, but if you are using external applications to display table content, it might be safer to also use only printable characters to define them.

Table Storage

There are multiple aspects of the table storage. The first aspect is how HBase will store a single value into the table. The second aspect is related to how all those cells are stored together in files to form a table.

As shown in Figure 2-2, from the top to the bottom, a table is composed of one to many regions, composed of one to many column families, composed of a single store, composed of a unique memstore plus one to many HFiles, composed of blocks composed of cells.

On a RegionServer, you will have as many memstores as you have regions multiplied by the number of column families receiving writes, all sharing the same reserved memory area.

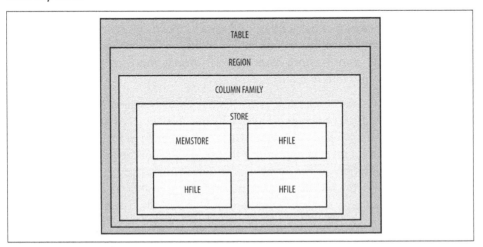

Figure 2-2. Storage layers

The following subsections provide a quick overview of all those different layers.

Regions

All the rows and related columns, together, form a table. But to provide scalability and fast random access, HBase has to distribute the data over multiple servers. To achieve this, tables are split into regions where each region will store a specific range of data. The regions are assigned to RegionServers to serve each region's content. When new regions are created, after a configured period of time, the HBase load balancer might move them to other RegionServers to make sure the load is evenly distributed across the cluster. Like presplitting, there are many good practices around regions. All of these points are addressed in subsequent chapters.

Each region will have a start key and an end key that will define its boundaries. All this information will be stored within the files into the region but also into the `hbase:meta` table (or `.META.`, for versions of HBase prior to 0.96), which will keep track of all the regions. When they become too big, regions can be split. They can also be merged if required.

Column family

A column family is an HBase-specific concept that you will not find in other RDBMS applications. For the same region, different column families will store the data into different files and can be configured differently. Data with the same access pattern and the same format should be grouped into the same column family. As an example regarding the format, if you need to store a lot of textual metadata information for customer profiles in addition to image files for each customer's profile photo, you might want to store them into two different column families: one compressed (where all the textual information will be stored), and one not compressed (where the image files will be stored). As an example regarding the access pattern, if some information is mostly read and almost never written, and some is mostly written and almost never read, you might want to separate them into two different column families. If the different columns you want to store have a similar format and access pattern, regroup them within the same column family.

The write cache memory area for a given RegionServer is shared by all the column families configured for all the regions hosted by the given host. Abusing column families will put pressure on the memstore, which will generate many small files, which in turn will generate a lot of compactions that might impact the performance. There is no technical limitation on the number of column families you can configure for a table. However, over the last three years, most of the use cases we had the chance to work on only required a single column family. Some required two column families, but each time we have seen more than two column families, it has been possible and recommended to reduce the number to improve efficiency. If your design includes more than three column families, you might want to take a deeper look at it and see if all those families are really required; most likely, they can be regrouped. If you do not have any consistency constraints between your two columns families and data will arrive into them at a different time, instead of creating two column families for a single table, you can also create two tables, each with a single column family. This strategy is useful when it comes time to decide the size of the regions. Indeed, while it was better to keep the two column families almost the same size, by splitting them accross two different tables, it is now easier to let me grow independently.

Chapter 15 provides more details regarding the column families.

Stores

We will find one store per column family. A store object regroups one memstore and zero or more store files (called HFiles). This is the entity that will store all the information written into the table and will also be used when data needs to be read from the table.

HFiles

HFiles are created when the memstores are full and must be flushed to disk. HFiles are eventually compacted together over time into bigger files. They are the HBase file format used to store table data. HFiles are composed of different types of blocks (e.g., index blocks and data blocks). HFiles are stored in HDFS, so they benefit from Hadoop persistence and replication.

Blocks

HFiles are composed of blocks. Those blocks should not be confused with HDFS blocks. One HDFS block might contain multiple HFile blocks. HFile blocks are usually between 8 KB and 1 MB, but the default size is 64 KB. However, if compression is configured for a given table, HBase will still generate 64 KB blocks but will then compress them. The size of the compressed block on the disk might vary based on the data and the compression format. Larger blocks will create a smaller number of index values and are good for sequential table access, while smaller blocks will create more index values and are better for random read accesses.

 If you configure block sizes to be very small, it will create many HFiles block indexes, which ultimately will put some pressure on the memory, and might produce the opposite of the desired effect. Also, because the data to compress will be small, the compression ratio will be smaller, and data size will increase. You need to keep all of these details in mind when deciding to modify the default value. Before making any definitive changes, you should run some load tests in your application using different settings. However, in general, it is recommended to keep the default value.

The following main block types can be encountered in an HFile (because they are mostly internal implementation details, we will only provide a high-level description; if you want to know more about a specific block type, refer to the HBase source code):

Data blocks

A data block will contain data that is either compressed, or uncompressed, but not a combination of both. A data block includes the `delete` markers as well as the puts.

Index blocks

When looking up a specific row, index blocks are used by HBase to quickly jump to the right location in an HFile.

Bloom filter block

These blocks are used to store bloom filter index related information. Bloom filter blocks are used to skip parsing the file when looking for a specific key.

Trailer block

This block contains offsets to the file's other variable-sized parts. It also contains the HFile version.

Blocks are stored in reverse order. It means that instead of having the index at the beginning of the file followed by the other blocks, the blocks are written in reverse order. Data blocks are stored first, then the index blocks, then the bloom filter blocks; the trailer blocks are stored at the end.

Cells

HBase is a column-oriented database. That means that each column will be stored individually instead of storing an entire row on its own. Because those values can be inserted at different time, they might end up in different files in HDFS.

Figure 2-3 represents how HBase will store the values from Figure 2-1.

042	CF1	CQ1	C
042	CF1	CQ3	E
123	CF1	CQ1	I
123	CF1	CQ2	A
123	CF2	CQ1	D
123	CF2	CQ2	E
999	CF1	CQ1	B
999	CF1	CQ2	H
999	CF2	CQ2	G

Figure 2-3. Physical representation of an HBase table

As you can see, only columns with values are stored. All columns where no value is defined are ignored.

Internally, each row will be stored within a specific format. Figure 2-4 represents the format of an individual HBase cell.

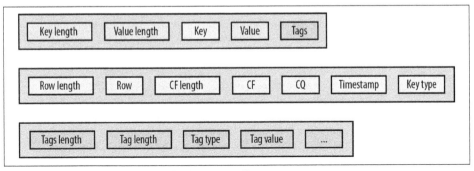

Figure 2-4. Format of an individual HBase cell

Figure 2-5 represents how the first cell from the table shown in Figure 2-3 will be stored by HBase. The tags are optional and are available only with version 3 of the HFiles format. When a cell doesn't require any tag, they are simply not stored.

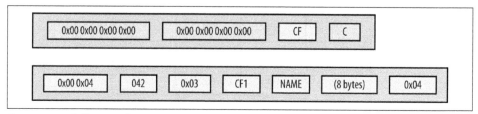

Figure 2-5. Cell example

The "key type" field represents the different possible HBase operations among the following:

- Put
- Delete
- DeleteFamilyVersion
- DeleteColumn
- DeleteFamily

The way HBase stores the data will greatly impact the design of the HBase schema. From the preceding example, we can see that to store 1 byte, HBase had to add an extra 31 bytes. This overhead varies depending on the CQ name, the CF name, and some other criteria, but it is still very significant.

HBase implements some mechanisms to perform key compression. At a high level, only the delta between the current and the previous key is stored. For tall tables, given large and lexicographically close keys like URLs, this can provide some good space saving. However, it creates a small overhead, as the current key needs to be rebuilt from the previous one. Because columns are stored separately, this kind of compression also works well with wide tables that have many columns for the same key, as the key needs to be repeated frequently. The size of the key will be reduced, which will reduce the overall size of the entire row. This feature is called block encoding and will be discussed in more detail in "Data block encoding" on page 86.

Because of its storage format, HBase has some limitations regarding the size of those different fields (to simplify the understanding of those limitations, the reference in parentheses corresponds to Figure 2-4):

- The maximum length for the row key plus the column family and the column qualifier is stored as four bytes and is $2^{31} - 1 - 12$ or, 2,147,483,635 (key length).

- The maximum length for the value is stored as four bytes and is $2^{31} - 1$ or 2,147,483,647 (value length).

- The maximum length for the row key is stored as two signed bytes and is 32,767 (row length).

- Because it is stored in one signed byte, the maximum length for the column family is 127 (CF length).

- The maximum length for all the tags together is stored as two bytes and is 65,535 (tags length).

Internal Table Operations

HBase scalability is based on its ability to regroup data into bigger files and spread a table across many servers. To reach this goal, HBase has three main mechanisms: compactions, splits, and balancing. These three mechanisms are transparent for the user. However, in case of a bad design or improper usage, it might impact the performance of servers. Therefore, it is good to know about these mechanisms to understand server reactions.

Compaction

HBase stores all the received operations into its memstore memory area. When the memory buffer is full, it is flushed to disk (see "Memory" on page 192 for further details about the memstore and its flush mechanisms). Because this can create many small files in HDFS, from time to time, and based on specific criteria that we will see later, HBase can elect files to be compacted together into a bigger one. This will benefit HBase in multiple ways. First, the new HFile will be written by the hosting Region-Server, ensuring the data is stored locally on HDFS. Writing locally will allow the RegionServer local lookups for the file rather than going over the network. Second, this will reduce the number of files to look at when a user is requesting some data. That will allow HBase to do faster lookups and will reduce the pressure on HDFS to keep track of all the small files. Third, it allows HBase to do some cleanup on the data stored into those files. If the time to live (TTL) causes some cells to expire, they will not be rewritten in the new destination file. The same applies for the deletes under certain conditions that are detailed momentarily.

There exist two types of compactions.

Minor compaction

A compaction is called minor when HBase elects only some of the HFiles to be compacted but not all. The default configurable threshold triggers HBase compaction when there are three files (HFiles) or more in the current region. If the compaction is triggered, HBase will elect some of those files based on the compaction policy. If all the files present in the store are elected, the compaction will be promoted into a major compaction.

Minor compactions can perform some cleanup on the data, but not everything can be cleaned. When you perform a delete of a cell, HBase will store a marker to say that all identical cells older than that one have been deleted. Therefore, all the cells with the same key but a previous timestamp should be removed. When HBase performs the compaction and finds a delete marker, it will make sure that all older cells for the same key and column qualifier will be removed. However, because some cells might still exist in other files that have not been elected for compaction, HBase cannot remove the marker itself, as it still applies and it cannot make sure no other cells need to be removed. The same thing is true if the delete marker is present on a file that has not been elected for compaction. If that's the case, cells that should have been deleted because of the marker will still remain until a major compaction is performed. Expired cells based on the TTL defined on the column family level will be deleted because they don't depend on the content of the other non-elected files, except if the table has been configured to keep a minimal number of versions.

 It is important to understand the relationship of cell version count and compactions. When deciding the number of versions to retain, it is best to treat that number as the minimum version count available at a given time. A great example of this would be a table with a single column family configured to retain a maximum version count of 3. There are only two times that HBase will remove extra versions. The first being on flush to disk, and the second on major compaction. The number of cells returned to the client are normally filtered based on the table configuration; however, when using the RAW => true parameter, you can retrieve all of the versions kept by HBase. Let's dive deeper into a few scenarios:

- Doing four puts, followed immediately by a scan without a flush, will result in four versions being returned regardless of version count.

- Doing four puts, followed by a flush and then a scan, will result in three versions being returned.

- Doing four puts and a flush, followed by four puts and a flush, and then a scan, will result in six versions being returned.

- Doing four puts and a flush, followed by four puts and a flush, and then a major compaction followed by a scan, will result in three versions being returned.

Major compaction

We call it a major compaction when all the files are elected to be compacted together. A major compaction works like a minor one except that the delete markers can be removed after they are applied to all the related cells and all extra versions of the same cell will also be dropped. Major compactions can be manually triggered at the column family level for a specific region, at the region level, or at the table level. HBase is also configured to perform weekly major compactions.

 Automatic weekly compactions can happen at any time depending on when your cluster was started. That means that it can be overnight when you have almost no HBase traffic, but it also means that it can be exactly when you have your peak activity. Because they need to read and rewrite all the data, major compactions are very I/O intensive and can have an impact on your cluster response time and SLAs. Therefore, it is highly recommended to totally disable those automatic major compactions and to trigger them yourself using a cron job when you know the impact on your cluster will be minimal. We also recommend that you do not compact all the tables at the same time. Instead of doing all the tables once a week on the same day, spread the compactions over the entire week. Last, if you really have a very big cluster with many tables and regions, it is recommended to implement a process to check the number of files per regions and the age of the oldest one and trigger the compactions at the region level only if there are more files than you want or if the oldest one (even if there is just one file) is older than a configured period (a week is a good starting point). This will allow to keep the region's data locality and will reduce the I/O on your cluster.

Splits (Auto-Sharding)

Split operations are the opposite of compactions. When HBase compacts multiple files together, if not too many values are dropped over the compaction process, it will create a bigger file. The bigger the input files, the more time it takes to parse them, to compact them, and so on. Therefore, HBase tries to keep them under a configurable maximum size. In HBase 0.94 and older, this default maximum size was 1 GB. Later, this value was increased to 10 GB. When one of the column families of a region reaches this size, to improve balancing of the load, HBase will trigger a split of the given region into two new regions. Because region boundaries apply to all the column families of a given region, all the families are split the same way even if they are much smaller than the configured maximum size. When a region is split, it is transformed into two new smaller regions where the start key of the first one is the start key of the original region, and the end key of the second one is the end key of the original region. The keys for the end of the first region and the beginning of the second one are decided by HBase, which will choose the best mid-point. HBase will do its best to select the middle key; however we don't want this to take much time, so it is not going to split within an HFile block itself.

There are a few things you need to keep in mind regarding the splits. First, HBase will never split between two columns of the same row. All the columns will stay together in the same region. Therefore, if you have many columns or if they are very big, a single row might be bigger than the maximum configured size and HBase will not be able to split it. You want to avoid this situation where an entire region will serve only a single row.

You also need to remember that HBase will split all the column families. Even if your first column reached the 10 GB threshold but the second one contains only a few rows or kilobytes, both of them will be split. You might end up with the second family having only very tiny files in all the regions. This is not a situation you want to find yourself in, and you might want to review your schema design to avoid it. If you are in this situation and you don't have a strong consistency requirement between your two column families, consider splitting them into two tables.

Finally, don't forget that splits are not free. When a region is balanced after being split, it loses its locality until the next compaction. This will impact the read performance because the client will reach the RegionServer hosting the region, but from there, the data will have to be queried over the network to serve the request. Also, the more regions you have, the more you put pressure on the master, the hbase:meta table, and the region services. In the HBase world, splits are fine and normal, but you might want to keep an eye on them.

Figure 2-6 shows a two-column family table before and after a split. As you will note in the figure, one CF is significantly bigger than the other.

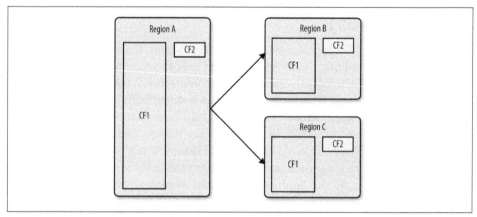

Figure 2-6. A two-column family table, before and after a split

Balancing

Regions get split, servers might fail, and new servers might join the cluster, so at some point the load may no longer be well distributed across all your RegionServers. To help maintain a good distribution on the cluster, every five minutes (default configured schedule time), the HBase Master will run a load balancer to ensure that all the RegionServers are managing and serving a similar number of regions.

HBase comes with a few different balancing algorithms. Up to version 0.94, HBase used the `SimpleLoadBalancer`, but starting with HBase 0.96, it uses the `StochasticLoadBalancer`. Although it is recommended to stay with the default configured balancer, you can develop you own balancer and ask HBase to use it.

 When a region is moved by the balancer from one server to a new one, it will be unavailable for a few milliseconds, and it will lose its data locality until it gets major compacted.

Figure 2-7 shows how the master reassigns the regions from the most loaded servers to the less loaded ones. Overloaded servers receive the instruction from the master to close and transition the region to the destination server.

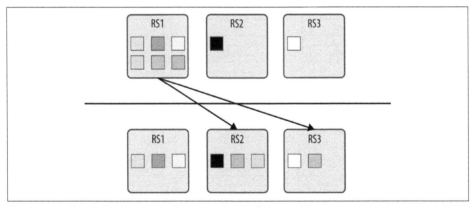

Figure 2-7. Example migration from overworked RegionServer

Dependencies

To run, HBase only requires a few other services and applications to be available. Like HDFS, HBase is written in Java and will require a recent JDK to run. As we have seen, HBase relies on HDFS. However, some work has been done in the past to run it on top of other filesystems, including Amazon S3.

HBase will need HDFS to run on the same nodes as the HBase nodes. It doesn't mean that HBase needs to run on all the HDFS nodes, but it is highly recommended, as it might create very unbalanced situations. HBase also relies on ZooKeeper to monitor the health of its servers, to provide high-availability features, and to keep track of information such as replication progress, current active HBase Master, the list of existing tables, and so on.

There is work in progress in HBase 2.0 to reduce its dependency on ZooKeeper.

HBase Roles

HBase is composed of two primary roles: the master (also sometime called HBase Master, HMaster, or even just HM) and the RegionServers (RS). It is also possible to run Thrift and REST servers to access HBase data using different APIs.

Figure 2-8 shows how the different services need to be collocated on the different types of servers. Recent HDFS versions allow more than two NameNodes. It allows all the master servers to have a consistent list of services running (HMaster, NameNode, and ZooKeeper). Running with only two NameNodes instead of three is also totally fine.

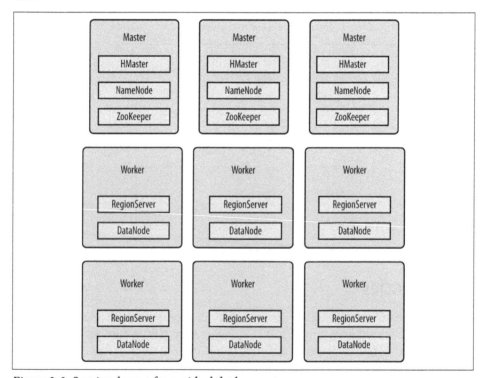

Figure 2-8. Services layout for an ideal deployment

Master Server

The HBase master servers are the head of the cluster and are responsible for few a operations:

- Region assignment
- Load balancing
- RegionServer recovery
- Region split completion monitoring
- Tracking active and dead servers

For high availability, it is possible to have multiple masters in a single cluster. However, only a single master will be active at a time and will be responsible for those operations.

Unlike HBase RegionServers, the HBase Master doesn't have much workload and can be installed on servers with less memory and fewer cores. However, because it is the brain of your cluster, it has to be more reliable. You will not lose your cluster if you lose two RegionServers, but losing your two Masters will put you at high risk. Because of that, even though RegionServers are usually built without disks configured as RAID or dual power supplies, etc., it is best to build more robust HBase Masters. Building HBase Masters (and other master services like NameNodes, ZooKeeper, etc.) on robust hardware with OS on RAID drives, dual power supply, etc. is highly recommended. To improve overall cluster stability, there is work in progress in HBase 2.0 to let the master track some of the information currently tracked by Zookeeper.

A cluster can survive without a master server as long as there is no RegionServer failing nor regions splitting.

RegionServer

A RegionServer (RS) is the application hosting and serving the HBase regions and therefore the HBase data. When required (e.g., to read and write data into a specific region), calls from the Java API can go directly to the RegionServer. This is to ensure the HBase master or the active ZooKeeper server are not bottlenecks in the process.

A RegionServer will decide and handle the splits and the compactions but will report the events to the master.

Even if it is technically doable to host more than one RegionServer on a physical host, it is recommended to run only one server per host and to give it the resources you will have shared between the two servers.

When a client tries to read data from HBase for the first time, it will first go to ZooKeeper to find the master server and locate the hbase:meta region where it will locate the region and RegionServer it is looking for. In subsequent calls from the same client to the same region, all those extra calls are skipped, and the client will talk directly with the related RegionServer. This is why it is important, when possible, to reuse the same client for multiple operations.

Thrift Server

A Thrift server can be used as a gateway to allow applications written in other languages to perform calls to HBase. Even if it is possible to use Java to call HBase through the Thrift server, it is recommended to directly call the Java API instead. HBase provides the Apache Thrift schema that you will have to compile for the language you want to use. There are currently two versions of the Thrift schema. Version 1 is the legacy schema and is kept for compatibility for external applications built against it. Version 2 is the new version and includes an updated schema. The two schemas can be found in the HBase code under the following locations:

Version 1 (legacy)
> *hbase-thrift/src/main/resources/org/apache/hadoop/hbase/thrift/Hbase.thrift*

Version 2
> *hbase-thrift/src/main/resources/org/apache/hadoop/hbase/thrift2/hbase.thrift*

Unlike the Java client that can talk to any RegionServer, a C/C++ client using a Thrift server can talk only to the Thrift server. This can create a bottleneck, but starting more than one Thrift server can help to reduce this point of contention.

Not all the HBase Java API calls might be available through the Thrift API. The Apache HBase community tries to keep them as up to date as possible, but from time to time, some are reported missing and are added back. If the API call you are looking for is not available in the Thrift schema, report it to the community.

REST Server

HBase also provides a REST server API through which all client and administration operations can be performed. A REST API can be queried using HTTP calls directly from client applications or from command-line applications like curl. By specifying the Accept field in the HTTP header, you can ask the REST server to provide results in different formats. The following formats are available:

- `text/plain` (consult the warning note at the end of this chapter for more information)
- `text/xml`
- `application/octet-stream`
- `application/x-protobuf`
- `application/protobuf`
- `application/json`

Let's consider a very simple table created and populated this way:

```
create 't1', 'f1'
put 't1', 'r1', 'f1:c1', 'val1'
```

Here is an example of a call to the HBase REST API to retrieve in an XML format the cell we have inserted:

```
curl -H "Accept: text/xml" http://localhost:8080/t1/r1/f1:c1
```

This will return the following output:

```
<?xml version="1.0" encoding="UTF-8" standalone="yes"?>
<CellSet>
  <Row key="cjE=">
    <Cell column="ZjE6YzE=" timestamp="1435940848871">dmFsMQ==</Cell>
  </Row>
</CellSet>
```

where values are base64 encoded and can be decoded from the command line:

```
$ echo "dmFsMQ==" | base64 -d
val1
```

If you don't want to have to decode XML and based64 values, you can simply use the `octet-stream` format:

```
curl -H "Accept: application/octet-stream" http://localhost:8080/t1/r1/f1:c1
```

which will return the value as it is:

```
val1
```

Even if the HBase code makes reference to the `text/html` format, it is not implemented and cannot be used.

Because it is not possible to represent the responses in all the formats, some of the calls are implemented for only some of the formats. Indeed, even if you can call the */version* or the */t1/schema* URLs for the `text/plain` format, it will fail with the */t1/r1/f1:c1* call. Therefore, before choosing a format, make sure all the calls you will need work with it.

## CHAPTER 3

HBase Ecosystem

As we know, HBase is designed as part of the Hadoop ecosystem. The good news is that when creating new applications, HBase comes with a robust ecosystem. This should come as no surprise, as HBase is typically featured in a role of serving production data or powering customer applications. There are a variety of tools surrounding HBase, ranging from SQL query layers, ACID compliant transactional systems, management systems, and client libraries. In-depth coverage of every application for HBase will not be provided here, as the topic would require a book in and of itself. We will review the most prominent tools and discuss some of the pros and cons behind them. We will look at a few of the most interesting features of the top ecosystem tools.

Monitoring Tools

One of the hottest topics around Hadoop, and HBase in general, is management and monitoring tools. Having supported both Hadoop and HBase for numerous years, we can testify that any management software is better than none at all. Seriously, take the worst thing you can think of (like drowning in a vat of yellow mustard, or whatever scares you the most); then double it, and that is debugging a distributed system without any support. Hadoop/HBase is configured through XML files, which you can create manually. That said, there are two primary tools for deploying HBase clusters in the Hadoop ecosystem. The first one is Cloudera Manager, and the second is Apache Ambari. Both tools are capable of deploying, monitoring, and managing the full Hadoop suite shipped by the respective companies. For installations that choose not to leverage Ambari or Cloudera Manager, deployments typically use automated configuration management tools such as Puppet or Chef in combination with monitoring tools such as Ganglia or Cacti. This scenario is most commonly seen where there is an existing infrastructure leveraging these toolsets. There is also an interesting visualization out there called Hannibal that can help visualize HBase internals after a deployment.

Cloudera Manager

The first tool that comes to mind for managing HBase is Cloudera Manager (yeah, we might be a little biased). Cloudera Manager (CM) is the most feature-complete management tool available. Cloudera Manager has the advantage of being first to market and having a two-year lead on development over Apache Ambari. The primary downside commonly associated with CM is its closed source nature. The good news is that CM has numerous amazing features, including a point-and-click install interface that makes installing a Hadoop cluster trivial. Among the most useful features of Cloudera Manager are parcels, the Tsquery language, and distributed log search.

Parcels are an alternative method for installing Cloudera Distribution of Apache Hadoop (CDH). Parcels, in their simplest form, are "glorified tarballs." What is implied by tarballs is that Cloudera packages up all the necessary start/stop scripts, libs/jars, and other files necessary for CM functions. Cloudera Manager will use this setup to easily manage the deployed services. Figure 3-1 shows an example of Cloudera Manager listing available and installed packages. Parcels allow for full stack rolling upgrades and restarts without having to incur downtime between minor releases. They also contain the necessary dependencies to make deploying Hadoop cleaner than using packages. CM will take advantage of the unified directory structure to generate and simplify classpath and configuration management for the different projects.

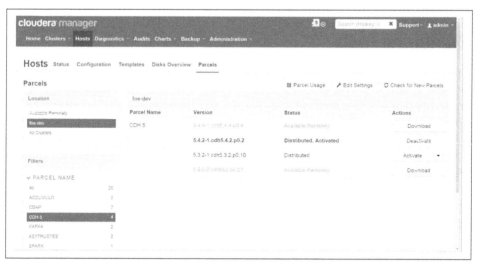

Figure 3-1. Listing of available and currently deployed parcels

Monitoring is key to any successful Hadoop or HBase deployment. CM has impressive monitoring and charting features built in, but it also has an SQL-like language known as "Tsquery." As shown in Figure 3-2, administrators can use Tsquery to build and share custom charts, graphs, and dashboards to monitor and analyze clusters' metrics.

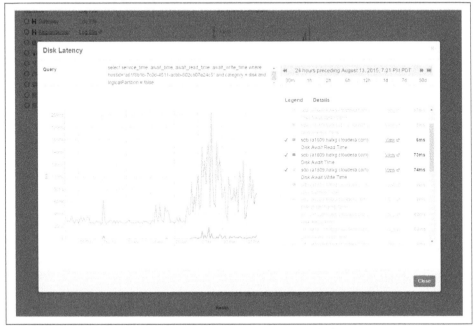

Figure 3-2. Executed query showing average wait time per disk

Finally, troubleshooting in distributed systems like Hadoop is frustrating, to say the least. Logs are stored on different systems by different daemons, and searching through these logs can quickly escalate from tedious to pure insanity. CM has a distributed-log search feature (Figure 3-3) that can search and filter logs based on hostname, service, error level, and other parameters. Administrators can use CM's log search to quickly locate and identify related errors that occur on different machines.

Figure 3-3. Distributed log search, spanning numerous nodes and services looking for ERROR-level logs

For more information, visit the Cloudera website (*http://bit.ly/298yluQ*).

Apache Ambari

Apache Ambari is Cloudera Manager's open source counterpart. Ambari is part of the Apache Foundation and became a top-level project in December 2013. Ambari is equipped with all of the management tool features you would expect; it is capable of deploying, managing, and monitoring a Hadoop cluster. Ambari has some very interesting features that help it stand out as a first-class management tool. The primary differentiating features for Ambari are the support of deployment templates called Blueprints, extensible frameworks like Stacks, and user views for Tez.

The Blueprints architecture is an interesting concept for cluster deployment. Blueprints allow a user to deploy a cluster by specifying a Stack (more on this momentarily), basic component layout, and the configurations for the desired Hadoop cluster instance. Blueprints leverages the REST API, and allows deployment without having to run an install wizard. Blueprints allows users to create their own templates from scratch or by exporting the configuration of a previous cluster. Having seen numerous job failures when promoting from development to quality assurance to production, or from testing disaster recovery plans, being able to export a cluster configuration for deployment is an amazing feature. Blueprints is designed to be utilized without UI interaction; the screenshot in Figure 3-4 shows the Ambari UI in action.

Figure 3-4. Easy YARN scheduler deployment with convenient overview, slide bars, and toggles

Ambari offers an extensible framework called Stacks. Stacks allows users to quickly extend Ambari to leverage custom services. Stacks allows for the addition of custom services and custom client services to be added to the Ambari server for management. This is an amazing feature that can make running services outside the core HDP (Hortonworks Data Platform) release much simpler by unifying the management source. A couple examples of this could be Pivotal HAWQ or Apache Cassandra. Our friends over at ZData Inc. have done a lot of work with Stacks and sent over this example of adding Greenplum to Ambari.

Looking at Figure 3-5, starting in the top left and going clockwise: the first image is creating a configuration, the second image is creating the service, and the final image creating the start/stop script.

```xml
<configuration>
    <property>
        <name>gp.installer.zip.file.location</name>
        <value></value>
        <description>The absolute file path of where the Greenplum installer zip file is on the master host.</description>
    </property>
    <property>
        <name>gp.installation.path</name>
        <value>/usr/local</value>
        <description>The absolute path to the install location. You must have write permissions to the location you specify.</description>
    </property>
    <property>
        <name>gp.admin.user</name>
        <value>gpadmin</value>
        <description>The Greenplum system user used to administer the Greenplum Database. The user will be created on all Greenplum hosts.</description>
    </property>
    <property>
        <name>gp.admin.password</name>
        <value></value>
        <description>The password for gp.admin.user.</description>
    </property>
    <property>
        <name>use.mirrors</name>
        <value>false</value>
        <description>Create segment mirrors</description>
    </property>
</configuration>
```

```python
import sys
from resource_management import *
class Slave(Script):
  def install(self, env):
    print 'Install the Sample Srv Slave';
  def stop(self, env):
    print 'Stop the Sample Srv Slave';
  def start(self, env):
    print 'Start the Sample Srv Slave';
  def status(self, env):
    print 'Status of the Sample Srv Slave';
  def configure(self, env):
    print 'Configure the Sample Srv Slave';
if __name__ == "__main__":
  Slave().execute()
```

```xml
<service>
    <name>GREENPLUM</name>
    <displayName>Greenplum</displayName>
    <comment>Pivotal Greenplum Database</comment>
    <version>0.1</version>

    <components>
      <component>
        <name>GREENPLUM_MASTER</name>
        <displayName>Greenplum Master</displayName>
        <category>MASTER</category>
        <cardinality>1</cardinality>
        <commandScript>
          <script>scripts/master.py</script>
          <scriptType>PYTHON</scriptType>
          <timeout>4800</timeout>
        </commandScript>
      </component>

      <component>
        <name>GREENPLUM_SLAVE</name>
        <displayName>Greenplum Segment</displayName>
        <category>SLAVE</category>
        <cardinality>1+</cardinality>
        <commandScript>
          <script>scripts/segment.py</script>
          <scriptType>PYTHON</scriptType>
          <timeout>600</timeout>
        </commandScript>
```

Figure 3-5. Example configuration for adding Greenplum

In Figure 3-6, the top screenshot is of the services installed and heartbeating into the Ambari server. The bottom screenshot is selecting the custom Stack to install, which has been provided through the custom configurations.

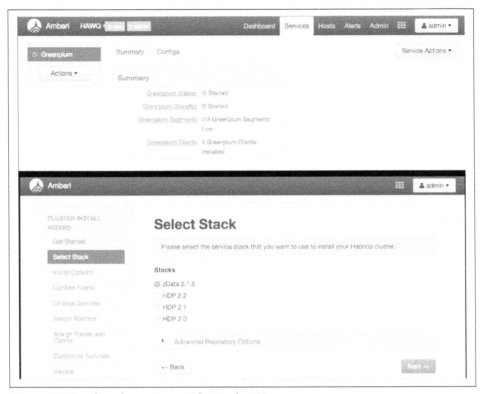

Figure 3-6. Loading the custom stack into the UI

User Views are a particularly exciting way to visualize data. Like Stacks, Ambari Views offers an ability to plug in third-party UI sources to manage data and services not included in stock Ambari. Also, Ambari is kind enough to bundle in a couple out-of-the box DAG flow tools in User Views to get you started. Ambari ships with Capacity Scheduler View and Tez View. Of all the Ambari features, Tez View is by far the coolest, and it showcases what will be possible down the line (Figure 3-7). Tez View offers a visual of the DAGs that have been run. Each job that has been run can be drilled down into a visualization layer that quickly shows how many tasks are running for each part of the job to allow for quick optimizations against skews. Before this feature was available, it took drilling into numerous jobs and logs to attempt to optimize these jobs.

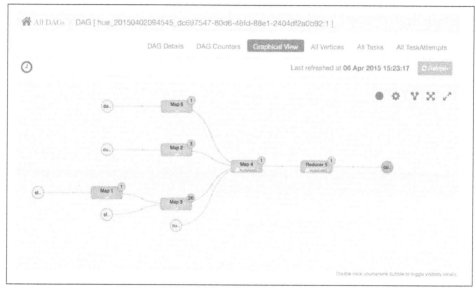

Figure 3-7. Ability to view physical execution of Tez jobs

For more information, visit the Apache Ambari website (*https://ambari.apache.org/*).

Hannibal

The last management tool we want to mention is not a standalone tool and complements any environment regardless if it is CM, Ambari, or a standalone Puppet/Chef infrastructure. Hannibal is a tool for visualizing different aspects of the HBase internals such as region distribution, region size per table, and region evolution over time. This is extremely powerful information to visualize. All of the information Hannibal presents is available in the HBase logs and quite difficult to parse manually. Hannibal really shines when following best practices, such as manual splitting of regions, as it allows the end user to quickly visualize the largest regions in the table and determine when is the best time to split the region. Region history is also a very fascinating feature, as it allows you to look at the behavior of a region (e.g., HFile count, sizes, and memstore sizes) over a period of time. This is very helpful when adding additional load or nodes to the cluster to verify you are getting the expected behavior. Now for the bad news: it appears that Hannibal is no longer being developed. However, because Hannibal still works with HBase 0.98 and earlier, we felt it was still worthy of inclusion here.

For more information, visit the Hannibal GitHub (*https://github.com/sentric/hanni bal*).

SQL

One of hottest topics for Big Data is SQL on Hadoop. HBase, with numerous offerings, is never one to be left out of the mix. The vast majority of the tools that bring SQL functionality to the Hadoop market are mostly aimed at providing business intelligence functionality. With HBase, there are a few tools that focus on business intelligence, but on an arguably more interesting side, there are a few that focus on full-blown transactional systems. There are three main solutions we will look at: Apache Phoenix, Trafodion, and Splice Machine.

Apache Phoenix

Apache Phoenix was contributed by our friends at Salesforce.com. Phoenix is designed as a relational database layer set on top of HBase designed to handle SQL queries. It is important to note that Phoenix is for business intelligence rather than absorbing OLTP workloads. Phoenix is still a relatively new project (it reached incubator status in December 2013 and recently graduated to a top-level project in May 2014). Even with only a couple years in the Apache Foundation, Phoenix has seen a nice adoption rate and is quickly becoming the de facto tool for SQL queries. Phoenix's main competitors are Hive and Impala for basic SQL on HBase. Phoenix has been able to establish itself as a superior tool through tighter integration by leveraging HBase coprocessors, range scans, and custom filters. Hive and Impala were both built for full file scans in HDFS, which can greatly impact performance because HBase was designed for single point gets and range scans.

Phoenix offers some interesting out-of-the-box functionality. Secondary indexes are probably the most popular request we receive for HBase, and Phoenix offers three different types: functional indexing, global indexing, and local indexing. Each index type targets a different type of workload; whether it is read heavy, write heavy, or needs to be accessed through expressions, Phoenix has an index for you. Phoenix will also help to handle the schema, which is especially useful for time series records. You just have to specify the number of salted buckets you wish to add to your table. By adding the salted buckets to the key and letting Phoenix manage the keys, you will avoid very troublesome hot spots that tend to show their ugly face when dealing with time series data.

For more information, visit the Apache Phoenix website (*https://phoenix.apache.org/*).

Apache Trafodion

Trafodion is an open source tool and transactional SQL layer for HBase being designed by HP and currently incubating in Apache. Unlike Phoenix, Trafodion is more focused on extending the relational model and handling transactional processes. The SQL layer offers the ability to leverage consistent secondary indexes for faster data retrieval. Trafodion also offers some of its own table structure optimizations with its own data encoding for serialization and optimized column family and column names. The Trafodion engine itself has implemented specific technology to support large queries as well as small queries. For example, during large joins and grouping, that Trafodion will repartition the tables into *executor server processes* (ESPs), outside of the HBase RegionServers, then the queries will be performed in parallel. An added bonus is Trafodion will optimize the SQL plan execution choices for these types of queries. Another interesting feature is the ability to query and join across data sources like Hive and Impala with HBase. Like Phoenix, Trafodion does not offer an out-of-the-box UI, but expects BI tools or custom apps built on ODBC/ JDBC to connect to Trafodion.

For more information, visit the Apache Trafodion website (*http://trafo dion.apache.org/*).

Splice Machine

Splice Machine is a closed source offering targeting the OLTP market. Splice Machine has leveraged the existing Apache Derby framework for its foundation. Splice Machine's primary goal is to leverage the transaction and SQL layer to port previous relational databases on to HBase. Splice Machine has also developed its own custom encoding format for the data which heavily compresses the data and lowers storage and retrieval costs. Similar to the previously discussed SQL engines, the parallel transaction guarantees are handled through custom coprocessors, which enables the high level of throughput and scalability these transactional systems are able to achieve. Like Trafodion, Splice Machine can also just leverage the SQL layer for business reporting from not just HBase, but Hive and Impala as well.

For more information, visit Splice Machine's website (*http://www.splicema chine.com/*).

Honorable Mentions (Kylin, Themis, Tephra, Hive, and Impala)

There are also numerous other systems out there to bring SQL and transaction functionality to HBase:

- Apache Kylin (originally contributed by eBay) is designed for multidimensional online analytical processing (MOLAP) and relational online analytical processing (ROLAP). Kylin is interesting because the data cubes have to be pre-created in Hive and then pushed over to HBase. Kylin is designed for large-scale reporting as opposed to real-time ingest/serving systems.

- Themis is a cross row/cross table transaction built on top of HBase sponsored by XiaoMi.

- Tephra is another transaction system brought to us by the team at Cask.

- Finally, Hive and Apache Impala are storage engines both designed to run full table or partitioned scans against HDFS. Hive and Impala both have HBase storage handlers allowing them to connect to HBase and perform SQL queries. These systems tend to pull more data than the other systems, which will greatly increase query times. Hive or Impala make sense when a small set of reference data lives in HBase, or when the queries are not bound by SLAs.

Frameworks

Another interesting aspect of the HBase ecosystem is frameworks. There are many different types of frameworks available on the market for HBase. Some frameworks specialize in handling time series data, while others focus on codifying best practices, handling the use of different languages, or moving to an asynchronous client model. We will take a deeper look at the OpenTSDB framework, which is really almost a standalone application, before moving on to discuss Kite, HappyBase, and AsyncHBase.

OpenTSDB

OpenTSDB is one of the most interesting applications we will talk about. OpenTSDB is not a framework itself, but it takes the place of a custom framework for handling time series data. OpenTSDB is designed as a time series database on top of HBase. It has a full application layer integrated for querying and presenting the data, as well as frameworks written on top of it for ingesting the time series data. It is a pretty straightforward system, where individual, stateless collectors called *time series daemons* (TSDs) receive the time series data from the servers. Those TSDs then act as clients and write the data to HBase using a schema designed for fetching the series data over a period of time in an efficient manner. The end user never directly accesses HBase for any of the data. All necessary calls are funneled through the TSDs. OpenTSDB also has a basic UI (Figure 3-8) built into it for graphing the different metrics from the time series data. The TSDs can also expose an HTTP API for easily querying data to be consumed by third-party monitoring frameworks or reporting dashboards.

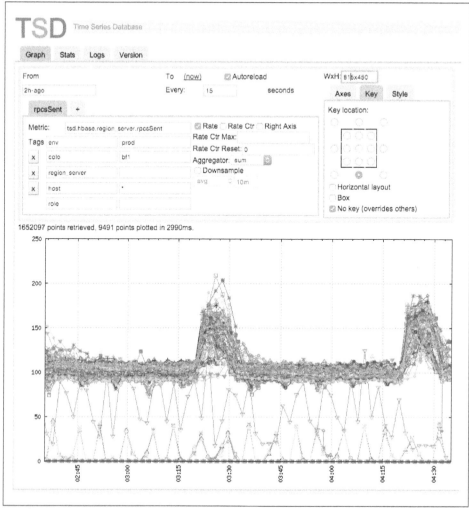

Figure 3-8. OpenTSDB offers a fully functional UI out of the box

For more information, visit OpenTSDB's website (*http://opentsdb.net/*).

Kite

There are quite a few different frameworks that either replace or alter the HBase client's behavior. Kite is a whole SDK designed to codify Hadoop best practices. Kite also comes with a prebuilt transformation, aggregation, and extract library set called Morphlines. Kite on HBase is relatively new and still flagged as experimental. The portion of Kite designed for HBase is in heavy use in Cloudera for its Customer Operations Tools Team. It is being based on the internal library known as HBase-common. The goal is to codify how the records should be stored in HBase columns to optimize for storage and performance efficiency. Kite offers the ability to map specific HBase columns, and has many different flexible options. The column mapping is stored in JSON and is used to write the Avro records into the HBase table structure. Kite also offers a simple way to load data into the cluster. Once the configuration has been stored, all Kite writers know exactly how to put the data into the dataset without having to reconfigure each writer. Kite also leverages the concept of datasets. The dataset used can be Hadoop, Hive, or HBase. By pre-creating these datasets, Kite knows how and where to write the data into Hadoop, thus saving many hours of direct coding.

For more information, visit Kite's website (*http://kitesdk.org/docs/current/*).

HappyBase

The HappyBase framework is designed to allow the end user to leverage the HBase client through the use of Python. HappyBase is designed to allow Python to access the HBase system by leveraging the Thrift gateway. HappyBase supports the vast majority of functions an HBase application needs in order to flourish, right down to atomic counters and batch mutations. HappyBase is great for getting an application up and running, but leveraging the Thrift interface brings a few different issues to light. You should consider how you are going to load balance and handle failovers (pro tip: HAProxy is your friend), and the thrift interface will be slower than the direct Java API.

For more information visit the HappyBase website (*http://bit.ly/290tM0s*).

AsyncHBase

Finally, the AsyncHBase project (which happens to be part of OpenTSDB) is one we run into out in the field constantly. AsyncHBase is a client replacement that offers better throughput and performance if your data can be processed asynchronously. One of the coolest features of AsyncHBase is the ease of deploying a multithreaded application using the single client. You should keep in mind that it is not a trivial matter to switch back and forth between the clients, as they require almost a complete rewrite. This is a very popular library for handling time series data without fully deploying OpenTSDB.

For more information, visit the OpenTSDB's GitHub (*https://github.com/OpenTSDB/ asynchbase*).

## CHAPTER 4

HBase Sizing and Tuning Overview

The two most important aspects of building an HBase appplication are sizing and schema design. This chapter will focus on the sizing considerations to take into account when building an application. We will discuss schema design in Part II.

In addition to negatively impacting performance, sizing an HBase cluster incorrectly will reduce stability. Many clusters that are undersized tend to suffer from client time-outs, RegionServer failures, and longer recovery times. Meanwhile, a properly sized and tuned HBase cluster will perform better and meet SLAs on a consistent level because the internals will have less fluctuation, which in turn means fewer compactions (major and minor), fewer region splits, and less block cache churn.

Sizing an HBase cluster is a fine art that requires an understanding of the application needs prior to deploying. You will want to make sure to understand both the read and the write access patterns before attempting to size the cluster. Because it involves taking numerous aspects into consideration, proper HBase sizing can be challenging. Before beginning cluster sizing, it's important to analyze the requirements for the project. These requirements should be broken down into three categories:

Workload
> This requires understanding general concurrency, usage patterns, and ingress/ egress workloads.

Service-level agreements (SLAs)
> You should have an SLA that guarantees fully quantified read and write latencies, and understanding the tolerance for variance.

Capacity
> You need to consider how much data is ingested daily, the total data retention time, and total data size over the lifetime of the project.

After fully understanding these project requirements, we can move on to cluster sizing. Because HBase relies on HDFS, it is important to take a bottom-up approach when designing an HBase cluster. This means starting with the hardware and then the network before moving on to operating system, HDFS, and finally HBase.

Hardware

The hardware requirements for an HBase-only deployment are cost friendly compared to a large, multitenant deployment. HBase currently can use about 16–24 GB of memory for the heap, though that will change with Java 7 and the G1GC algorithm. The initial testing with the G1GC collector has shown very promising results with heaps over 100 GB is size. This becomes especially important when attempting to vertically scale HBase, as we will see later in our discussion of the sizing formulas.

When using heaps larger than 24 GB of allocated heap space, garbage collection pauses will become so long (30 seconds or more) that RegionServers will start to time out with ZooKeeper causing failures. Currently, stocking the DataNodes with 64–128 GB of memory will be sufficient to cover the RegionServers, DataNodes, and operating system, while leaving enough space to allow the block cache to assist with reads. In a read-heavy environment looking to leverage bucketcache, 256 GB or more of RAM could add significant value. From a CPU standpoint, an HBase cluster does not need a high core count, so mid-range speed and lower-end core count is quite sufficient. As of early 2016, standard commodity machines are shipping with dual octacore processors on the low end, and dual dodecacore processors with a clock speed of about 2.5 GHz. If you are creating a multitenant cluster (particularly if you plan to utilize MapReduce), it is beneficial to use a higher core count (the exact number will be dictated by your use case and the components used). Multitenant use cases can be very difficult, especially when HBase is bound by tight SLAs, so it is important to test with both MapReduce jobs as well as an HBase workload. In order to maintain SLAs, it is sometimes necessary to have a batch cluster and a real-time cluster. As the technology matures, this will become less and less likely. One of the biggest benefits of HBase/Hadoop is that a homogenous environment is not required (though it is recommended for your sanity). This allows for flexibility when purchasing hardware, and allows for different hardware specifications to be added to the cluster on an ongoing basis whenever they are required.

Storage

As with Hadoop, HBase takes advantage of a JBOD disk configuration. The benefits offered by JBOD are two-fold: first, it allows for better performance by leveraging short-circuit reads (SCR) and block locality; and second, it helps to control hardware costs by eliminating expensive RAID controllers. Disk count is not currently a major factor for an HBase-only cluster (where no MR, no Impala, no Solr, or any other applications are running). HBase functions quite well with 8–12 disks per node. The HBase writepath is limited due to HBase's choice to favor consistency over availability. HBase has implemented a write-ahead log (WAL) that must acknowledge each write as it comes in. The WAL records every write to disk as it comes in, which creates slower ingest through the API, REST, and thrift interface, and will cause a write bottleneck on a single drive. Planning for the future drive count will become more important with the work being done in HBASE-10278, which is is an upstream JIRA to add multi-WAL support; it will remove the WAL write bottleneck and share the incoming write workload over all of the disks per node. HBase shares a similar mentality with Hadoop where SSDs are currently overkill and not necessary from a deployment standpoint. When looking to future-proof a long-term HBase cluster, a purchase of 25%–50% of the storage could be beneficial. This is accounting for multi-WAL and archival storage.

Archival Storage

For more information about archival storage, check out The Apache Software Foundation's guide to archival storage, SSD, and memory (*http://bit.ly/28TeqgR*).

We would only recommend adding the SSDs when dealing with tight SLAs, as they are still quite expensive per GB.

Networking

Networking is an important consideration when designing an HBase cluster. HBase clusters typically employ standard Gigabit Ethernet (1 GbE) or 10 Gigabit Ethernet (10 GbE) rather than more expensive alternatives such as fiber or InfiniBand. While the minimum recommendation is bonded 1 GbE, 10 GbE is ideal for future scaling. The minimum recommended is bonded 1 GbE with either two or four ports. Both hardware and software continue to scale up, so 10 GbE is ideal (it's always easier to plan for the future now). 10 GbE really shines during hardware failures and major compactions. During hardware failures, the underlying HDFS has to re-replicate all of the data stored on that node. Meanwhile, during major compactions, HFiles are rewritten to be local to the RegionServer that is hosting the data. This can lead to remote reads on clusters that have experienced node failures or many regions being rebalanced. Those two scenarios will oversaturate the network, which can cause performance impacts to tight SLAs. Once the cluster moves to multiple racks, top-of-rack (TOR) switches will need to be selected. TOR switches connect the nodes and bridge multiple racks. For a successful deployment, the TOR switches should be no slower than 10 GbE for inter-rack connections (Figure 4-1). Because it is important to eliminate single points of failure, redundancy between racks is highly recommended. Although HBase and Hadoop can survive a lost rack, it doesn't make for a fun experience. If the cluster gets so large that HBase begins to cross multiple aisles in the data-center, core/aggregation switches may need to be introduced. These switches should not run any slower than 40 GbE, and again, redundancy is recommended. The cluster should be isolated on its own network and network equipment. Hadoop and HBase can quickly saturate a network, so separating the cluster on its own network can help ensure HBase does not impact any other systems in the datacenter. For ease of admin-istration and security, VLANs may also be implemented on the network for the cluster.

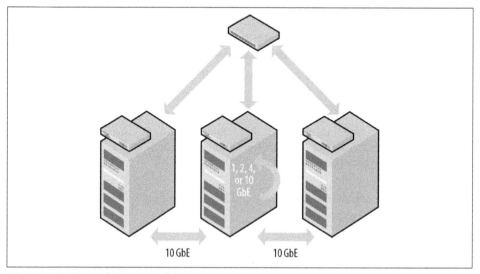

Figure 4-1. Networking example

OS Tuning

There is not a lot of special consideration for the operating system with Hadoop/HBase. The standard operating system for a Hadoop/HBase cluster is Linux based. For any real deployment, an enterprise-grade distribution should be used (e.g., RHEL, CentOS, Debian, Ubuntu, or SUSE). Hadoop writes its blocks directly to the operating system's filesystem. With any of the newer operating system versions, it is recommended to use EXT4 for the local filesystem. XFS is an acceptable filesystem, but it has not been as widely deployed for production environments. The next set of considerations for the operating system is swapping and swap space. It is important for HBase that swapping is not used by the kernel of the processes. Kernel and pro-cess swapping on an Hbase node can cause serious performance issues and lead to failures. It is recommended to disable swap space by setting the partition size to 0; process swapping should be disabled by setting vm.swappiness to 0 or 1.

Hadoop Tuning

Apache HBase 0.98+ only supports Hadoop2 with YARN. It is important to understand the impact that YARN (MR2) can have on an HBase cluster. Numerous cases have been handled by Cloudera support where MapReduce workloads were causing HBase to be starved of resources. This leads to long pauses while waiting for resources to free up.

Hadoop2 with YARN adds an extra layer of complexity, as resource management has been moved into the YARN framework. YARN also allows for more granular tuning of resources between managed services. There is some work upstream to integrate HBase within the YARN framework (HBase on YARN, or HOYA), but it is currently incomplete. This means YARN has to be tuned to allow for HBase to run smoothly without being resource starved. YARN allows for specific tuning around the number of CPUs utilized and memory consumption. The three main functions to take into consideration are:

`yarn.nodemanager.resource.cpu-vcores`
> Number of CPU cores that can be allocated for containers.

`yarn.nodemanager.resource.memory-mb`
> Amount of physical memory, in megabytes, that can be allocated for containers. When using HBase, it is important not to over allocate memory for the node. It is recommended to allocate 8–16 GB for the operating system, 2–4 GB for the DataNode, 12–24 GB for HBase, and the rest for the YARN framework (assuming there are not other workloads such as Impala or Solr).

`yarn.scheduler.minimum-allocation-mb`
> The minimum allocation for every container request at the RM, in megabytes. Memory requests lower than this won't take effect, and the specified value will get allocated at minimum. The recommended value is between 1–2 GB of data.

When performing the calculations, it is important to remember that the vast majority of servers use an Intel chip set with hyper-threading enabled. Hyper-threading allows the operating system to present two virtual or logical cores for every physical core present. Here is some back-of-the-napkin tuning for using HBase with YARN (this will vary depending on workloads—your mileage may vary):

> physicalCores * 1.5 = total v-cores

We also must remember to leave room for HBase:

> Total v-cores – 1 for HBase – 1 for DataNode – 1 for NodeManager – 1 for OS ... – 1 for any other services such as Impala or Solr

For an HBase and YARN cluster with a dual 10-core processor, the tuning would look as follows:

20 * 1.5 = 30 virtual CPUs
30 – 1 – 1 – 1 – 1 = 26 total v-cores

Some sources recommend going one step further and dividing the 26 v-cores in half when using HBase with YARN. You should test your application at production levels to determine the best tuning.

HBase Tuning

As stated at the beginning of the chapter, HBase sizing requires a deep understanding of three project requirements: workload, SLAs, and capacity. Workload and SLAs can be organized into three main categories: read, write, or mixed. Each of these categories has its own set of tunable parameters, SLA requirements, and sizing concerns from a hardware-purchase standpoint.

The first one to examine is the write-heavy workload. There are two main ways to get data into HBase: either through an API (Java, Thrift, or REST) or by using bulk load. This is an important distinction to make, as the API will use the WAL and memstore, while bulk load is a short-circuit write and bypasses both. As mentioned in "Hardware" on page 40, the primary bottleneck for HBase is the WAL followed by the memstore. There are a few quick formulas for determining optimal write performance in an API-driven write model.

To determine region count per node:

HBaseHeap * memstoreUpperLimit = availableMemstoreHeap
availableMemstoreHeap / memstoreSize = recommendedActiveRegionCount

(This is actually column family based. The formula is based on one CF.)

To determine raw space per node:

recommendedRegionCount * maxfileSize * replicationFactor = rawSpaceUsed

To determine the number of WALs to keep:

availableMemstoreHeap / (WALSize * WALMultiplier) = numberOfWALs

Here is an example of this sizing using real-world numbers:

    HBase heap = 16 GB
    Memstore upper limit = 0.5*
    Memstore size = 128 MB
    Maximum file size = 20 GB
    WAL size = 128 MB
    WAL rolling multiplier = 0.95

First, we'll determine region count per node:

    16,384 MB * 0.5 = 8,192 MB
    8,192 MB / 128 MB = 64 activeRegions

Next, we'll determine raw space per node:

    64 activeRegions * 20 GB * 3 = 3.75 TB used

Finally, we need to determine the number of WALs to keep:

    8,192 GB / (128 MB * 0.95) = 67 WALs

When using this formula, it is recommended to have no more than 67 regions per RegionServer while keeping a total of 67 WALs. This will use 3.7 TB (with replication) of storage per node for the HFiles, which does not include space used for snapshots or compactions.

Bulk loads are a short-circuit write and do not run through the WAL, nor do they use the memstore. During the reduce phase of the MapReduce jobs, the HFiles are created and then loaded using the completebulkload tool. Most of the region count limitations come from the WAL and memstore. When using bulkload, the region count is limited by index size and response time. It is recommended to test read response time scaling up from 100 regions; it is not unheard of for successful deployments to have 150–200 regions per RegionServer. When using bulk load, it is important to reduce the upper limit (hbase.regionserver.global.memstore.upper limit) and lower limit (hbase.regionserver.global.memstore.lower limit) to 0.11 and 0.10, respectively, and then raise the block cache to 0.6–0.7 depending on available heap. Memsore and block cache tuning will allow HBase to keep more data in memory for reads.

 It is important to note these values are percentages of the heap devoted to the memstore and the block cache.

The same usable space from before per node calculation can be used once the desired region count has been determined through proper testing.

Again, the formula to determine raw space per node is as follows:

recommendedRegionCount * maxfileSize * replicationFactor = rawSpaceUsed

Using this formula, we'd calculate the raw space per node as follows in this instance:

150 activeRegions * 20 GB * 3 = 9 TB used

Capacity is the easiest portion to calculate. Once the workload has been identified and properly tested (noticing a theme with testing yet?), it is a simple matter of dividing the total amount of data by capacity per node. It is important to leave scratch space available (the typical recommendation is 20%–30% overhead). This space will be used for MapReduce scratch space, extra space for snapshots, and major compactions. Also, if using snapshots with high region counts, testing should be done to ensure there will be enough space for the desired backup pattern, as snapshots can quickly take up space.

Different Workload Tuning

For primary read workloads, it is important to understand and test the SLA requirements. Rigorous testing is required to determine the best settings. The primary settings that need to be tweaked are the same as write workloads (i.e., lowering memstore settings and raising the block cache to allow for more data to be stored in memory). In HBase 0.96, bucket cache was introduced. This allows for data to be stored either in memory or on low-latency disk (SSD/flash cards). You should use 0.98.6 or higher for this feature due to HBASE-11678.

In a mixed workload environment, HBase bucket cache becomes much more interesting, as it allows HBase to be tuned to allow more writes while maintaining a higher read response time. When running in a mixed environment, it is important to overprovision your cluster, as doing so will allow for the loss of a RegionServer or two. It is recommended to allow one extra RegionServer per rack when sizing the cluster. This will also give the cluster better response times with more memory for reads and extra WALs for writes. Again, this is about finding the perfect balance to fit the workload, which means tuning the number of WALs, memstore limits, and total allocated block cache.

HBase can run into multiple issues when leveraging other Hadoop components. We will cover deploying HBase with Impala, Solr, and Spark throughout Part II. Unfortunately, there really isn't a great answer for running HBase with numerous components. The general concerns that arise include the following:

- CPU contention
- Memory contention
- I/O contention

The first two are reasonably easy to address with proper YARN tuning (this means running Spark in YARN mode) and overprovisioning of resources. What we mean here is if you know your application needs W GB for YARN containers, Impala will use X memory, HBase heap needs Y to meet SLAs, and I want to save Z RAM for the OS, then my formula should be:

$$W + X + Y + Z = totalMemoryNeeded$$

This formula makes sense at first glance, but unfortunately it rarely works out to be as straightforward. We would recommend upgrading to have at least 25%–30% free memory. The benefits of this approach are twofold: first, when it's time to purchase additional nodes, it will give you room to vertically grow until those new nodes are added to the cluster; and second, the OS will take advantage of the additional memory with OS buffers helping general performance across the board.

The I/O contention is where the story really starts to fall apart. The only viable answer is to leverage control groups (cgroups) in the Linux filesystem. Setting up cgroups can be quite complex, but they provide the ability to assign specific process such as Impala, or most likely YARN/MapReduce, into specific I/O-throttled groups.

Most people do not bother with configuring cgroups or other throttle technologies. We tend to recommend putting memory limits on Impala, container limits on YARN, and memory and heap limits on Solr. Then properly testing your application at scale will allow for fine-tuning of the components working together.

Our colleague Eric Erickson, who specializes in all things Solr, has trademarked the phrase "it depends" when asked about sizing. He believes that back-of-the-napkin math is a great starting point, but only proper testing can verify the sizing estimates. The good news with HBase and Hadoop is that they provide linear scalability, which allows for testing on a smaller level and then scaling out from there. The key to a successful HBase deployment is no secret—you need to utilize commodity hardware, keep the networking simple using Ethernet versus more expensive technologies such as fiber or InfiniBand, and maintain detailed understanding of all aspects of the workload.

## CHAPTER 5

Environment Setup

To be able to test locally and see how HBase behaves, we will install and configure a standalone HBase environment that will be used to run the given examples. HBase can run in three modes, each of which offers different behaviors (the first two modes are mainly for testing purposes, while the last one is the mode you will use for your production HBase cluster):

Standalone mode

This mode starts all of the HBase processes in a single virtual machine (VM). Standalone mode uses the local disk for HBase storage and does not require any specific configuration. Data will be stored in the current user-configured temporary folder (usually */tmp*) in a folder named *hbase-$USERNAME*. Removing this folder when HBase is down will remove all HBase data. This is the simplest mode for running HBase, and it's the one we will use for our testing. Using this mode allows the end user to easily clear all HBase content and restart with a blank installation. This mode doesn't require running any other external service (e.g., ZooKeeper or HDFS).

Pseudodistributed mode

In pseudodistributed mode, HBase will run the same processes as in fully distributed mode, but as a single node cluster. HBase will start the ZooKeeper process and both the HBase Master and RegionServer processes.

Fully distributed mode

Last, fully distributed mode is when HBase runs on multiple machines with all required services (ZooKeeper, Hadoop, etc.).

System Requirements

Whether you are choosing a standalone, pseudo-distributed, or fully distributed deployment, the choices made around the environment will be key for its success. There will be choices around using bare metal or VMs for the core infrastructure; which OS should you install; what Hadoop distribution you should use; the Java version to deploy on; and the most important question, what system resources are going to be needed for success. The following sections will help guide and answer these questions for you.

Operating System

All example outputs provided in this book are captured from a Linux shell terminal using HBase 1.0.1 (some on Debian, some on CentOS). In order to reproduce our results, try to use the same Linux version that we have used. The examples can be run in a Linux environment running on either a physical or virtual machine. Commands might also work in other environments (Windows, Mac OS X, etc.) or on Cygwin (*http://cygwin.com/*), but we have not tested them.

If you want to install a Linux environment, you can download and install one of the following distributions:

- Debian 7+ (*http://debian.org*)
- Ubuntu 14.04+ (*http://ubuntu.com*)
- RedHat 6.6+ (*http://redhat.com*)
- CentOS 6.6 (*http://centos.org*)

This is a nonexhaustive list—there are many other distributions and versions available today, and any of them should work. You should choose and install the one you are most comfortable working with. If you decide to use an Apache Hadoop distribution, make sure to validate which Linux distribution and version it is compatible with.

Virtual Machine

As described in the following subsections, there are multiple ways to use a VM to run a pseudodistributed HBase environment. Let's take a look at each of these options.

VM modes

Local VM
> You can install a virtual machine support (e.g., VirtualBox) on your local computer and then create a Linux VM into which you can install HBase and run it in either standalone or pseudodistributed mode.

Public cloud

This is similar to the previous option, except that you create the Linux VM (instance) on a public cloud such as Amazon EC2. You then install the HBase software and run it in standalone or pseudodistributed mode. You can also provision multiple virtual nodes and run HBase in a fully distributed mode. Be careful with running a production HBase cluster in a public cloud, as some specific configuration might be required.

Local virtual distribution

Install a virtual machine support (e.g., VirtualBox) on your local computer and instead of installing software manually, simply download the Cloudera Quick-Start VM, which includes a fully functional HBase installation in pseudodistributed mode (no manual installation required).

Linux environment

If you don't have a computer available on which to install a Linux distribution, you can run one on your local environment by running it in a local VM. The following applications will help you to run a Linux environment in a local VM:

- VirtualBox (*https://www.virtualbox.org*)
- VMWare (*http://www.vmware.com*)
- KVM (*http://www.linux-kvm.org*)

Hadoop distribution

This book covers HBase application design and development, but to be fully implemented, some use cases might require other external applications, such as Solr or Flume. Installing, configuring, and running those tools is outside the scope of this book. If you want to implement those integration examples, you will need to have a VM with an entire Hadoop distribution already installed. A Hadoop distribution is a bundle, usually packaged by a Hadoop vendor, including most if not all of the Hadoop-related applications. This is usually easier to install, as all the applications are configured to work together and they usually come with some setup scripts to prepare them all.

For simplicity and because it already contains all the applications we need (HDFS, HBase, Solr, Flume, etc.), you can use the Cloudera QuickStart VM (*http://bit.ly/292jimP*). We used version 5.4.2 of this VM to build all those use cases, and all the examples are tested with it. If you are not familiar with Linux or HBase and Hadoop installation, it might be easier for you to follow the same path and use the QuickStart VM.

All of the examples in the book are built for HBase 1.0.1. If you choose to use another Hadoop distribution in a virtual environment or if you decide to install HBase locally, you'll need to make sure that the distribution you choose comes with the same HBase version. While the examples might work with more recent versions, most of them will fail with older ones.

If you choose to use a Hadoop distribution, we still recommend reading the following sections so that you can become familiar with HBase, its constraints, and its installation.

In order to make the most of HBase's capabilities, all of the examples in this book are tested against a local Linux standalone HBase server and the Cloudera QuickStart VM. If you have access to a Hadoop test cluster (physical or virtual), you can also use it. That will allow you to choose the environment with which you are the most comfortable to run your tests.

Resources

The necessary resources are an important choice when choice when starting down the HBase path. Having enough resources will decide early success or failure.

Memory

Whether you are working in your local environment or on a VM, you need enough memory for provide to HBase and the other services to run. A standalone HBase environment running locally will require a minimum of 1 GB memory. However, if possible, we recommend allocating more memory, as doing so will allow you to run the tests on bigger datasets and to have a better view of the results and the behaviors of the application. If you are testing the examples directly in a Hadoop distribution running in a virtual environment, you should allocate a minimum of 4 GB to the VM. Here again, giving more memory to the environment will allow you to have a better response time from your applications and to run on bigger datasets. That's why we recommend allocating at least 8 GB to your virtual machine.

You should allocate as much memory as possible to your virtual machine. If you have 32 GB or more in your environment, make sure to allocate as much as you can to your VM. We ran most of the examples on a 12 GB VirtualBox virtual environment.

Disk space

The HBase installation file takes less than 100 MB (and the examples require just a few megabytes), so you can run all of the examples with less than 1 GB of available disk space. However, if you want to see all of the features in the examples pushed further, you'll need to create bigger datasets—and that requires more space for you to test. Therefore, we recommend allowing for at least 10 GB of available disk space.

If you want to run in a virtual environment, you will need at least 4 GB of available disk space to download the VM and another 4 GB to extract it. The Cloudera Quick-Start VM is configured to allow its virtual disk to grow up to 64 GB. Creating big datasets and running HBase for a long period will create a lot of data in your virtual environment. As a result, you will easily use up to 50 GB of disk space. Although it's possible to start with less, we recommend that you to have this space available before you start.

Java

HBase is written in Java and therefore it depends on specific versions of the JDK. It supports version 7 since HBase 0.94 and version 8 since HBase 0.99, while Java 6 support has been dropped starting with HBase 1.0. To run your local HBase version and the given examples, we recommend using the most up-to-date Java 7 version available. The VM we used for the examples runs with Java 1.7.0_67, so you should use that version to ensure that you will get the same results.

 Be careful when choosing your JVM version—you need to make sure it is bug free. As an example, JDK 1.7.0_75 has some issues with the jps command when running it in sudo mode.

Version	Recommended JDK	Other JDKs
1.x	JDK 7	JDK 8
0.98	JDK 7	JDK 6, JDK 8
0.96	JDK 7	JDK 6
0.94	JDK 6	JDK 7

HBase Standalone Installation

This section will describe the steps necessary for installing HBase on metal or on a VM running Linux.

Running a standalone HBase installation should be a straightforward process—you simply need to download the HBase binary, extract it, and finally, run it.

At the time of this writing, the last stable Apache HBase version from the stable branch is version 1.0.1. We recommend using a mirror to download the release. Once you have found the best mirror to download the HBase release, the file to download should be named something like *hbase-1.0.x-bin.tar.gz*, where *x* is the last subrelease number. Take the downloaded file and extract it to the directory of your choice using `tar -xzf` from the command line. The instructions that follow will assume that

HBase has been extracted or is accessible from the ~/hbase directory and that the *hbase/bin* folder has been added to the user path.

Using the Unix command line, the steps just described can be achieved as follows:

```
#:~$ cd ~
#:~$ wget \
"http://www.us.apache.org/dist/hbase/hbase-1.0.1/hbase-1.0.1-bin.tar.gz"
#:~$ tar -xzf hbase-1.0.1-bin.tar.gz
#:~$ ln -s hbase-1.0.1 hbase
#:~$ rm hbase-1.0.1-bin.tar.gz
#:~$ cd hbase
#:~/hbase$ export PATH=$PATH:~/hbase/bin
```

Because this is based on HBase release 1.0.1, the download of the binaries might fail if this release is replaced by a more recent one. Go to *http://www.apache.org/dyn/closer.cgi/hbase/* to check for the last available version, and update the preceding command if necessary.

The next step is to specify which JDK should be used to run HBase (we recommend configuring the same JDK that will be used in the development environment). Once you've specified the JDK, you will need to let HBase know about the location of your JDK. First, identify the version and the location using the java -version and which java commands. When you have identified the location of your JDK, you can export the JAVA_HOME variable. Here are two examples of potential Java locations:

```
#:~$ export JAVA_HOME=/usr # If using your Linux distribution JDK
#:~$ export JAVA_HOME=/usr/local/jdk1.7.0_60/ # If installed manually
```

When your JAVA_HOME variable has been defined correctly, the HBase standalone server can simply be started using the following command:

```
#:~$ start-hbase.sh
```

Instead of exporting the JAVA_HOME variable each time you start the server, you can also edit the *conf/hbase-env.sh* file to get this value automatically defined when the HBase command is launched.

At this point, the HBase environment should be running locally. There are multiple ways to verify that HBase is functioning correctly. In the later examples, we will see how to do that using Java code. As a matter of simplicity, we will use the HBase shell for now.

To start the HBase shell, run the following command:

```
#:~$ hbase shell
```

The output should look something like this:

```
HBase Shell; enter 'help<RETURN>' for list of supported commands.
Type "exit<RETURN>" to leave the HBase Shell
Version 1.1.5, r239b8045640b2e562a5568b5c744252e,\
Sun May  8 20:29:26 PDT 2016

hbase(main):001:0>
```

 You might encounter some informational messages with warnings about deprecated properties or missing native libraries. For this example, it is safe to ignore them (and for brevity, we removed them from the code displayed here). The warnings could impact performance in a fully distributed system, but for a standalone HBase server they are not a cause for concern.

While in the HBase shell, simply run the `status` command to see HBase statistics:

```
hbase(main):001:0> status
1 servers, 0 dead, 2.0000 average load
```

The output from the `status` command explains that there is one HBase server running, with an average of two HBase regions per RegionServer. At this point, if your environment is not running correctly, refer to "Troubleshooting" on page 59.

 Even if you just installed HBase, it already contains two regions: one for the `hbase:meta` table (which contains all information for all other table regions) and another for the `hbase:namespace` table (which contains the details of the available namespaces). Those two tables are HBase system tables and therefore belong to the `hbase` namespace (for more information regarding namespaces, refer to "HBase Filesystem Layout" on page 213).

The HBase standalone server is now available for the next set of tests. tests. If anything is not as expected, refer to "Troubleshooting" on page 59.

Now that the environment is running, it can be accessed by its web interface at *http://localhost:16010* or you can replace localhost by the local machine hostname or IP.

The HBase cluster can be stopped by calling the *stop-hbase.sh* script as follows:

```
#:~$ stop-hbase.sh
stopping hbase..........
```

Depending on server performance and the state of the environment, it might take some time for HBase to properly shut down.

HBase in a VM

To install and run a virtual machine, you first need to have a virtualization environment (e.g, VirtualBox, KVM, or VMWare) installed and running locally. Because the computer we used to build the examples runs on Debian, and because it is available as a Debian distribution package, we used VirtualBox for our tests. The next step is to download the QuickStart VM file and extract it where you have enough space available. Then import it into your virtualization environment. For VirtualBox users, this can be done by navigating to the File menu and selecting "Import virtual application" (it can take some time to complete the import). The last step is to configure your newly imported virtual environment to have enough memory.

When all of those steps are completed, you can start your environment. The first time you run it, it will take some time to perform initialization steps that are not required for subsequent restarts. When the VM is started and ready to be used, a browser should automatically open and be visible in the VM with some useful links and information on the home page.

To validate that HBase is already correctly installed, configured, and running, simply open a terminal and proceed with the same steps as the standalone installation.

Open the HBase shell:

```
#:~$ hbase shell
```

And use the `status` command to make sure it is running:

```
hbase(main):001:0> status
1 servers, 0 dead, 2.0000 average load
```

Then you can close the terminal you just opened. Congratulations! You have a pseudodistributed (cluster features but with a single node) HBase, HDFS, YARN, etc. installation running.

If HBase is not running but was running correctly before, it might have been killed because you paused your VM. You can use the `sudo jps` command to list all of the running Java processes:

```
[cloudera@quickstart ~]$ sudo jps
3097 HMaster
2820 ResourceManager
1915 DataNode
2270 SecondaryNameNode
5199
4914 Bootstrap
5225
1844 QuorumPeerMain
2137 NameNode
4380 Worker
2050 JournalNode
```

```
3629 RunJar
4054 HistoryServer
6242 Jps
4151 Master
3445 RunJar
3346 ThriftServer
5171 Bootstrap
2397 Bootstrap
3213 RESTServer
4278 HRegionServer
4026 Bootstrap
2452 JobHistoryServer
2547 NodeManager
```

This lists all of the Java processes currently running on your environment. What we are looking for here is 3097 `HMaster` and 4278 `HRegionServer`. The former is the HBase master server process, while the latter is the RegionServer process. The number before the process name is the process ID, which might change after each restart. If you don't see either of those processes running, restart your HBase server using the *hbase-start.sh* command or your manager web interface.

Local Versus VM

If you are still are still deciding which mode to run (e.g., local mode, a virtual Linux environment, or a QuickStart VM), consider the pros and cons for each. Keep in mind that whichever mode you decide to run HBase in, you can always move to another one by exporting the examples again.

Local Mode

This mode is the fastest to run, and requires the least amount of memory. However, if you are not running a Linux environment or if you are not savvy at the Linux shell, you might prefer to run another mode.

Pros

- Requires less than 1 GB of disk space and only a few gigabytes of memory
- Very fast to stop and start

Cons

- Does not allow running of complex use cases where other tools are required
- Needs to run on a Linux-like environment

Virtual Linux Environment

This mode is a good compromise between the local mode and the QuickStart VM mode. Choose this mode if you are not running a local Linux environment but are comfortable with the command line and don't need the other applications (Solr, etc.) to be running.

Pros

- Allows you to easily run HBase on non-Linux systems
- Avoid conflicts with already-installed applications

Cons

- Requires at least 3 GB of memory (2 GB for the operating system and 1 GB for HBase)
- Slower to start compared to the local mode

QuickStart VM (or Equivalent)

This is the most resource-demanding mode. It will start slowly and will use more disk space and memory. However, it comes preconfigured with all of the applications you will need to fully run the examples in this book. If you want to skip all of the installation steps but still have a powerful enough environment, choose this option—it's the one we used to develop this book's examples.

Pros

- Allows you to easily run HBase and other related applications (Solr, HDFS, YARN, etc.)
- Avoid conflicts with already installed applications

Cons

- Requires more memory than the two other modes (4 GB minimum, with 8+ GB recommended)
- Slowest mode to start/restart

Troubleshooting

When HBase is not starting correctly or is showing some issues, the first place to look is the logs directory. Three types of files can be found in this directory:

- The HBase scripts log files ending with the *.out* extension containing the start process output
- The security logs in the *SecurityAuth.audit* file, which should be empty
- And finally, the most important one for us, the HBase application log files ending with *.log*

In standalone mode, the one you will look at is *hbase-$USERNAME-master-$HOSTNAME.log*. In pseudodistributed mode, you will look at *hbase-$USERNAME-regionserver-$HOSTNAME.log* in addition to *hbase-$USERNAME-master-$HOSTNAME.log*

Next, we discuss some options that may cause failures if not configured correctly.

IP/Name Configuration

The */etc/hosts* file allows you to define an IP address for the localhost. The localhost entry is usually assigned to 127.0.0.1 and the local IP to the hostname. Verify that the */etc/hosts* file looks something like the following:

```
127.0.0.1      localhost
192.168.1.3    myhostname
```

In standalone mode, because HBase will start multiple processes by doing remote connections, it is required to have passwordless SSH authentication to the localhost.

Access to the /tmp Folder

In standalone mode and pseudodistributed mode, when HBase HDFS *root.dir* is not configured, HBase will store all of its data into the */tmp/hbase-USERNAME* folder. If write access to this folder is not available or if this device is full, HBase will fail to start. Using the following commands, verify that files can be created in this directory:

```
mkdir /tmp/hbase-$USERNAME
touch /tmp/hbase-$USERNAME/test.txt
rm -rf /tmp/hbase-$USERNAME
```

If any of those three commands fail, verify the rights in the */tmp* folder.

Environment Variables

Different Hadoop or HBase-related tools might have already been tested, and might have required some environment variable to be defined. They most probably will cause issues for HBase to start. Make sure that neither HADOOP_HOME nor HBASE_HOME are defined in your environment. To list all Hadoop and HBase-related variables, use the following commands:

```
export -p | egrep -i "(hadoop|hbase)"
```

The unset command can be used to remove those variables, but this might have an impact on the other running applications.

Available Memory

By default, HBase will let the JVM assign a maximum heap size to all HBase processes. On a 16 GB machine, the 1.7 JDK will allow a Java process to use up to 4 GB of memory. The following command will print how much memory is allocated for a Java process when no memory parameters are specified:

```
java -XX:+PrintFlagsFinal -version | grep MaxHeapSize
```

This applies to the standalone HBase process, but also to RegionServer and Master services when running in pseudo or fully distributed mode. It is not recommended to run HBase with less than 1 GB; it is important to make sure you have enough memory available for it. It is possible to modify this limit in the *hbase-env.sh* file by modifying the HBASE_HEAPSIZE variable, but this variable impacts all HBase roles.

If you want to modify the Java heap size for a specific role only, add the Java -Xmx parameter to the HBASE_*service*_OPTS option where *service* represents the service you want to configure (e.g., MASTER, REGIONSERVER, THRIFT, ZOOKEEPER, or REST).

Don't use these options at the same time, as they might conflict. If you decide to modify each process configuration using the HBASE_service_OPTS approach, then keep the HBASE_HEAPSIZE commented and specify the required amount of memory you want to use for each of the processes. If you decide to use the HBASE_HEAPSIZE property to allocate the same amount of memory for all the services, don't use the HBASE_service_OPTS approach.

In the following example, we allocate 2 GB of memory for the Master role and 8 GB for the RegionServer role:

```
# export HBASE_HEAPSIZE=1000
export HBASE_MASTER_OPTS="$HBASE_MASTER_OPTS $HBASE_JMX_BASE -Xmx2g\
        -Dcom.sun.management.jmxremote.port=10101"
export HBASE_REGIONSERVER_OPTS="$HBASE_REGIONSERVER_OPTS $HBASE_JMX_BASE -Xmx8g\
        -Dcom.sun.management.jmxremote.port=10102"
```

Make sure you have at least 1 GB heap size allocated to HBase (however, note that we recommend 4 GB for the examples in this book).

First Steps

Now that HBase is running, let's perform a few additional steps to get comfortable working with it. We will run some very basic HBase commands, download and install the book examples, and then run some of those examples. All of the examples described in the following sections are available via the book's GitHub page (*https:// github.com/ArchitectingHBase/examples*). Once you get the hang of things, feel free to make modifications to see the result and impacts of the different available options.

Basic Operations

Because the HBase shell will be used throughout all the development chapters, let's go back and run some basic operations to get familiar with it. If you find yourself lost at any time, you can always type `exit` or press Ctrl-C to come back to the Unix command line and restart the shell by running `hbase shell` or `bin/hbase shell`. When running in a standalone environment, if your HBase instance enters a bad state, you can stop it, remove the contents of the */tmp/hbase-$USERNAME* folder, and restart. For the VM environment, you will need to stop HBase, remove */hbase* content from HDFS, remove */hbase* content from ZooKeeper, and restart.

The following commands might help you to achieve this:

```
hadoop fs -rm -r /hbase
echo "rmr /hbase" | grep hbase zkcli
```

The last command involves the ZooKeeper client. Depending on how your environment has been installed, the client might have to be called in a different way.

We conclude this section by demonstrating a few basic commands to display HBase help, create a table, and then list all of the current nonsystem tables.

help

The `help` command lists all of the available HBase shell commands. Because the output of the `help` command in the book as it is quite lengthy, we won't repeat it here; however, over the next few chapters, we will issue most of the commands reported by `help`.

create

The `create` command helps to create a new HBase table. The following command creates a table called `t1` with a single column family called `f1`, all with the default parameters:

```
hbase(main):002:0> create 't1', 'f1'
0 row(s) in 1.2860 seconds

=> Hbase::Table - t1
```

list

The list command shows the newly created table:

```
hbase(main):003:0> list
TABLE
t1
1 row(s) in 0.0100 seconds

=> ["t1"]
hbase(main):004:0>
```

list only reports user tables. User tables are nonsystem tables (i.e., they are tables that are explicitly created by the user).

If everything has been installed and is running correctly, you should have been able to run those three commands with outputs very similar to what has been reported.

Import Code Examples

The examples presented in this book are available in full via the book's GitHub repository (*https://github.com/ArchitectingHBase/examples*). For the sake of brevity and to focus on the most important parts of the code, the examples presented here have been condensed. The names of the examples used in the book match the names of the files in the GitHub repository. Package names correspond to this book's chapter numbering. This naming convention will allow you to easily and quickly find the code you are looking for in the example repository. For example, the TestInstallation sample code that we will use in Example 5-1 is available in package *com.architecting.ch05* under the name *TestInstallation.java*.

 Also, because many examples depend on others (e.g., scan depends on table creation and data generation), some examples will reuse other examples, and some helper classes are used to prepare the environment and make results predictable. You are invited to modify those helpers and those examples to create different environments and test different scenarios, such as generating more data, bigger values, or even corrupted information to test failure handling.

To download, build, and modify the examples, you will need the following tools to be installed and configured (if you are running the examples in the QuickStart VM, all those tools are already installed for you; if you are running the examples in a Linux

VM, you will need to use package management tools such as APT or yum to install them):

Text editor

To look at the examples and modify them, you will need a text editor. It can be vi in a terminal, xemacs, or any other kind of editor you want as long as you are comfortable with it. For simplicity, we built all the examples and code using Eclipse (*https://www.eclipse.org/*).

Git (http://git-scm.com/)

As stated on its website, "Git is a free and open source distributed version control system designed to handle everything from small to very large projects with speed and efficiency." You will need Git to retrieve the source code for the examples. It is available on all major Linux distributions.

This book's examples are hosted on GitHub, which provides an online public Git service. You can also access and download the examples using a web browser.

Maven (http://maven.apache.org/)

The Apache website defines Maven as "a software project management and comprehension tool. Based on the concept of a project object model (POM), Maven can manage a project's build, reporting and documentation from a central piece of information." The *Architecting HBase Applications* source code is configured to build using Maven. The instructions for building and packaging the examples are provided in the following subsections.

 If you choose to use the Cloudera QuickStart VM 5.4.0 or older to develop, you will need to use the command line to retrieve the Git repository. Indeed, the Eclipse version provided with the VM is not compatible with the Eclipse m2e-egit plugin. If you prefer to use Eclipse in the VM and use the import wizard, you will need to upgrade it to a more recent version.

Download from command line

The first thing we need to do is download the source repository. As we explained in the previous section, examples are hosted on a Git repository. If you prefer to use Eclipse for all those operations, refer to "Download and build using Eclipse" on page 65.

The following Git command will download a copy of the examples into a local folder:

```
git clone https://github.com/ArchitectingHBase/examples.git ~/ahae
```

This will create a directory called *architecting-hbase-applications-examples*, which looks like this:

```
#:~/ahae$ ll
total 32K
drwxr-xr-x 2 jmspaggiari jmspaggiari  4096 Sep 11 21:09 conf
-rw-r--r-- 1 jmspaggiari jmspaggiari 11324 Sep 11 21:09 LICENSE
-rwxr-xr-x 1 jmspaggiari jmspaggiari  5938 Sep 11 21:09 pom.xml
-rw-r--r-- 1 jmspaggiari jmspaggiari    38 Sep 11 21:09 README.md
drwxr-xr-x 3 jmspaggiari jmspaggiari  4096 Sep 11 21:09 src
```

If you are using Eclipse from the VM, you can now import the project into Eclipse using the Import command and the "Maven/Existing maven projects" entry.

Build from command line

Now that you have the sources available, you can build them using Maven with the following command:

```
#:~/ahae$ mvn package
```

This will download all of the required dependencies, compile the sources into binaries, and package them. You should see something like this in your console:

```
#:~/ahae$ mvn package
[INFO] Scanning for projects...
[INFO]
[INFO] ------------------------------------------------------------------------
[INFO] Building architecting-hbase-applications-examples 1
[INFO] ------------------------------------------------------------------------
Downloading: http://onejar-maven-plugin.googlecode.com/svn/mavenrepo/org/apache/\
maven/plugins/maven-resources-plugin/2.3/maven-resources-plugin-2.3.pom
Downloading: http://repo.maven.apache.org/maven2/org/apache/maven/plugins/\
maven-resources-plugin/2.3/maven-resources-plugin-2.3.pom
Downloaded: http://repo.maven.apache.org/maven2/org/apache/maven/plugins/\
maven-resources-plugin/2.3/maven-resources-plugin-2.3.pom (5 KB at 18.1 KB/sec)
Downloading: http://onejar-maven-plugin.googlecode.com/svn/mavenrepo/org/apache/\
maven/plugins/maven-resources-plugin/2.3/maven-resources-plugin-2.3.jar
Downloading: http://repo.maven.apache.org/maven2/org/apache/maven/plugins/\
maven-resources-plugin/2.3/maven-resources-plugin-2.3.jar
   .
   .
   .
[INFO] Building jar: /home/cloudera/ahae/target/ahae.jar
[INFO] ------------------------------------------------------------------------
[INFO] BUILD SUCCESS
[INFO] ------------------------------------------------------------------------
[INFO] Total time: 51.574s
[INFO] Finished at: Thu Sep 11 21:16:10 EDT 2014
[INFO] Final Memory: 40M/916M
[INFO] ------------------------------------------------------------------------
```

The first time you run the build command, depending on the speed of your Internet connection and the dependencies to be downloaded, this operation can take a few minutes. Dependencies will be stored in a local Maven cache folder and will not have to be downloaded again unless they change. When completed, you should find the examples packaged under the target directory with the name *ahae-1.jar*. This is the file we will use to run all of our examples.

Download and build using Eclipse

If you want to use Eclipse to look at the examples, you will need to make sure that you have the m2e Eclipse Maven plugin and the required EGit connectors installed. Using Eclipse will allow you to run the examples in the step-by-step mode to inspect the different variables and results. This is the way we recommend to run the examples.

Import the examples into the Eclipse Java Browsing perspective by selecting the Import option from the File menu. Eclipse will prompt you with a list of all the different kinds of projects it can import. Under the Maven section, select "Check out Maven Projects from SCM" and press Next. This option will be available only if you have correctly installed the m2e plugin or if your Eclipse version comes with the plugin already installed.

As illustrated in Figure 5-1, select "git" in the SCM URL drop-down menu, and enter the Git repository URL in the text area: *https://github.com/ArchitectingHBase/exam ples*. If the "git" option is not available, make sure you have the correct connector installed. You can use the "m2e Marketplace" link in the same window to install the connector. When all of this is completed, simply press Finish to get the project imported. This will close the window, download all the dependencies defined into the project, and import the source code into your Eclipse workshop into a project called *architecting-hbase-applications-examples*. This operation can take a few minutes, so now is a good time to grab a coffee or go for a walk—by the time you get back, the project should be available in your workspace.

Figure 5-1. Eclipse MVN import window

We are also going to use Maven to build the application using Eclipse. To do so, right-click on the newly imported project, select the "Run As" option, and then "Maven Build…". This will open a window to configure the way you want to build this project. The only part you need to modify is the "Goals" text field where you need to enter "package". Once you've completed these steps, simply click on the "Apply" button, and then the "Run" button. In the "Console" view, you will see Maven building and packaging the examples for you. The output should be the same as in "Build from command line" on page 64.

To simplify all of the command lines, create a symbolic link to the project folder in your home directory:

```
ln -s ~/workspace/architecting-hbase-applications-examples ~/ahae
```

Testing the Examples

Now that you have both a running HBase standalone server instance and all the examples downloaded and built locally in your system, we will try to run a simple test to make sure everything is configured correctly.

HBase configuration information is stored in the *hbase-site.xml* file under the *conf* folder. When running in standalone mode, you can keep this file empty, so you can run with or without this file in the classpath. However, if you make changes to this file, you need to make sure it is accessible in the classpath in order for the modifications to be used. The steps for adding the configuration files into the classpath depend on whether you are using the command line or Eclipse to run the examples.

From command line

When running the examples from the command line, you need to make sure that all HBase binaries and configuration files are in the classpath. HBase provides you its classpath when you issue the HBase `classpath` command. In addition to the example packaged binaries, those are the paths you will need to give to Java to correctly run the examples.

The following command will run the `TestInstallation` example from the *com.architecting.ch05* package:

```
#:~/ahae$ java -classpath ~/ahae/target/ahae.jar:`hbase classpath`\
                                      com.architecting.ch05.TestInstallation
```

`TestInstallation` is a simple piece of Java code that will try to call HBase to determine whether it is running (see Example 5-1).

Example 5-1. Using TestInstallation to check if HBase is running (Java)

```java
public class TestInstallation {
  private static final Log LOG = LogFactory.getLog(TestInstallation.class);

  public static void main(String[] args) {
    Configuration conf = HBaseConfiguration.create();
    try {
      LOG.info("Testing HBase connection...");
      HBaseAdmin.checkHBaseAvailable(conf);
      LOG.info("HBase is running correctly...");
    } catch (MasterNotRunningException e) {
      LOG.error("Unable to find a running HBase instance", e);
    } catch (ZooKeeperConnectionException e) {
      LOG.error("Unable to connect to ZooKeeper", e);
    } catch (ServiceException e) {
      LOG.error("HBase service unavailable", e);
    } catch (IOException e) {
      LOG.error("Error when trying to get HBase status", e);
    }
  }
}
```

This command calls the hbase classpath command to get the current HBase class-path, then it appends the example's JAR and runs one of the programs in the JAR. This command will produce a lot of output from the different HBase classes. What you need to look at is the output from the example itself, which should look like the following snippet (note that some lines have been removed or shortened for the sake of brevity; also, you can export the classpath variable into your running environment to avoid having to specify it for each of the Java commands you will run):

```
export CLASSPATH= ~/ahae/target/ahae.jar:`hbase classpath`

2014-09-14 INFO [main] ch05.TestInstallation: Testing HBase connection... ❶
2014-09-14 WARN [main] util.NativeCodeLoader: Unable to load native-hadoop\
    library for your platform... using builtin-java classes where applicable
2014-09-14 INFO [main] zk.RecoverableZooKeeper: Process identifier=hconnection-\
    0x783c342b connecting to ZooKeeper ensemble=localhost:2181
2014-09-14 INFO [main] zk.ZooKeeper: Client environment:zookeeper.\
    version=3.4.6-1565, built on 02/20/2014 09:09 GMT
2014-09-14 INFO [main] zk.ZooKeeper: Client environment:host.name=t430s
2014-09-14 INFO [main] zk.ZooKeeper: Client environment:java.version=1.7.0_60
2014-09-14 INFO [main] zk.ZooKeeper: Client environment:java.io.tmpdir=/tmp
2014-09-14 INFO [main] zk.ZooKeeper: Client environment:java.compiler=<NA>
2014-09-14 INFO [main] zk.ZooKeeper: Client environment:os.name=Linux
2014-09-14 INFO [main] zk.ZooKeeper: Initiating client connection,\
    connectString=localhost:2181 sessionTimeout=90000 watcher=hconnection-\
    0x783c342b, quorum=localhost:2181, baseZNode=/hbase
2014-09-14 INFO [main-SendThread(localhost:2181)] zookeeper.ClientCnxn: Socket\
    connection established to localhost/0:0:0:0:0:0:0:1:2181, initiating session
2014-09-14 INFO [main] client.HConnectionManager$HConnectionImplementation:\
```

```
                Closing master protocol: MasterService
      2014-09-14 INFO [main] client.HConnectionManager$HConnectionImplementation:\
          Closing zookeeper sessionid=0x1487467e621000a
      2014-09-14 INFO [main] zk.ZooKeeper: Session: 0x1487467e621000a closed
      2014-09-14 INFO [main-EventThread] zookeeper.ClientCnxn: EventThread shut down
      2014-09-14 INFO [main] ch05.TestInstallation: HBase is running correctly... ❷
```

❶ and ❷ are two lines printed by the example.

If you don't see the "HBase is running correctly..." line, you'll need to make sure your HBase server is running correctly and examples have been built as expected.

From Eclipse

To run an example from Eclipse, you simply need to right-click on it, select "Run As" and then "Java Application". Output of the same `TestInstallation` example run from Eclipse should be shorter and should include the HBase outputted logs. You should see the following lines printed in the console:

```
      2014-09-14 18:45:34 INFO ch05.TestInstallation: Testing HBase connection...
      ...
      2014-09-14 18:45:35 INFO ch05.TestInstallation: HBase is running correctly...
```

When running examples from Eclipse, the *hbase-site.xml* file that was used for the configuration is the default one embedded in the dependencies. Modifications of your local configuration file will not be used by your examples running in Eclipse unless you specifically add your HBase configuration directory into your project classpath. You can do this in your project properties. In the Java Build Path section, go to the Libraries tab, click on "Add External Class Folder..." and add the directory where your *hbase-site.xml* file is. If you installed HBase in standalone mode, the file should be under *~/hbase/conf*; otherwise, the file should be under */etc/hbase/conf/*. We also recommend doing the same thing for the Hadoop configuration files.

Pseudodistributed and Fully Distributed

Running and managing an HBase cluster in distributed mode is beyond the scope of this book and will not be discussed here. To better understand how to configure and run HBase in this mode, we recommend referring to the Apache HBase Reference Guide (*https://hbase.apache.org/book.html*). We will, however, provide a few configuration hints for running in pseudo- distributed mode.

To configure your HBase instance to run in pseudodistributed or distributed mode, add the following required configuration parameters into the *conf/hbase-site.xml*:

```
<property>
  <name>hbase.cluster.distributed</name>
  <value>true</value>
  <description>The mode the cluster will be in. Possible values are
    false: standalone and pseudodistributed setups with managed ZooKeeper
    true: fully distributed with unmanaged ZooKeeper Quorum (see hbase-env.sh)
  </description>
</property>
```

Unless you are running ZooKeeper separately, you will also need to tell HBase to manage it for you. To do that, open the *hbase/hbase-env.sh* file and update the following entry to set it to `true`:

```
# Tell HBase whether it should manage its own instance of ZooKeeper or not.
export HBASE_MANAGES_ZK=true
```

Finally, also in the *hbase/hbase-env.sh* file, configure `JAVA_HOME` to point to your local Java installation.

If you encounter any issues with these steps, refer to "Troubleshooting" on page 59 above or to the Apache HBase Reference Guide.

PART II

Use Cases

It is important to have a solid understanding of HBase principles before jumping into the use-case section. After reviewing Part I, we can start to look at how HBase can be used in real-life use cases. We will be looking at four core uses for HBase: using HBase with Solr, near real-time serving system with HBase, using HBase for Master Data Management, and using HBase as a document store.

Throughout Part II we will describe the business need, the way data is coming in, the way data is retrieved, and how it is processed. We will also provide draft solutions and code examples to implement those use cases. The goal here is to greatly reduce time to value for HBase applications by enabling you through detailed code examples. When specific aspects are approached, we will also detail how they impact the use case and why, while diving deeper into HBase internals when required.

It is impossible to cover all HBase use cases in a single book, so we have selected what we think covers the majority of HBase usage. We hope by going through all the described scenarios, you will attain a sense of HBase best practices, and then you will be able to apply the same thinking to your specific use case.

## CHAPTER 6

Use Case: HBase as a System of Record

The first use case that we will examine is from Omneo (a division of Camstar, a Siemens Company). Omneo is a big data analytics platform that assimilates data from disparate sources to provide a 360-degree view of product quality data across the supply chain. Manufacturers of all sizes are confronted with massive amounts of data, and manufacturing datasets comprise the key attributes of big data. These datasets are high volume, rapidly generated, and come in many varieties. When tracking products built through a complex, multitier supply chain, the challenges are exacerbated by the lack of a centralized data store and because there is no unified data format. Omneo ingests data from all areas of the supply chain, such as manufacturing, test, assembly, repair, service, and field.

Omneo offers this system to its end customers as a software-as-a-service (SaaS) model. This platform must provide users the ability to investigate product quality issues, analyze contributing factors, and identify items for containment and control. The ability to offer a rapid turnaround for early detection and correction of problems can result in greatly reduced costs and significantly improved consumer brand confidence. Omneo starts by building a unified data model that links the data sources so users can explore the factors that impact product quality throughout the product lifecycle. Furthermore, Omneo provides a centralized data store, and applications that facilitate the analysis of all product quality data in a single, unified environment.

Omneo evaluated numerous NoSQL systems and other data platforms. Its parent company, Camstar, has been in business for over 30 years, giving Omneo a well-established IT operations system. When Omneo was created, the team was given carte blanche to build its own system. Knowing the daunting task of handling all of the data at hand, Omneo decided against building a traditional EDW. Although other big data technologies such as Cassandra and MongoDB were considered, Hadoop was ultimately chosen as the foundation for the Omneo platform. The primary reason for this decision came down to ecosystem or lack thereof from the other technologies. The fully integrated ecosystem that Hadoop offered with MapReduce, HBase, Solr, and Impala allowed Omneo to handle the data in a single platform without the need to migrate the data between disparate systems.

The solution must be able to handle the data of numerous products and customers being ingested and processed on the same cluster. This can make handling data volumes and sizing quite precarious, as one customer could provide 80%–90% of the total records. At the time of writing, Omneo hosts multiple customers on the same cluster for a rough record count of 6+ billion records stored in ~50 nodes. The total combined set of data in the HDFS is approximately 100 TBs. Importantly, as we get into the overall architecture of the system, we will note where duplicating data is mandatory and where savings can be introduced by using a unified data format.

Omneo has fully embraced the Hadoop ecosystem for its overall architecture, and also takes advantage of Hadoop's Avro data serialization system. Avro is a popular file format for storing data in the Hadoop world. Avro allows for a schema to be stored with data, making it easier for different processing systems (e.g., MapReduce, HBase, and Impala/Hive) to easily access the data without serializing and deserializing the data over and over again.

The high-level Omneo architecture consists of the following phases:

- Ingest/pre-processing
- Processing/serving
- User experience

Ingest/Pre-Processing

The ingest/pre-processing phase includes acquiring the flat files, landing them in HDFS, and converting the files into Avro. As illustrated in Figure 6-1, Omneo currently receives all files in a batch manner. The files arrive in a CSV format or in an XML file format. The files are loaded into HDFS through the HDFS API. Once the files are loaded into Hadoop, a series of transformations are performed to join the relevant datasets together. Most of these joins are done based on a primary key in the data (in the case of electronic manufacturing, this is normally a serial number to identify the product throughout its lifecycle). These transformations are all handled through the MapReduce framework. Omneo wanted to provide a graphical interface for consultants to integrate the data rather than code custom MapReduce. To accomplish this, Omneo partnered with Pentaho to expedite time to production. Once the data has been transformed and joined together, it is then serialized into the Avro format.

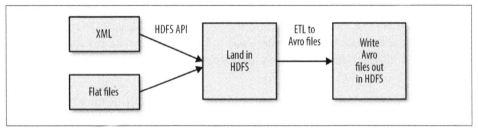

Figure 6-1. Batch ingest using HDFS API

Processing/Serving

Once the data has been converted into Avro, it is loaded into HBase (as illustrated in Figure 6-2). Because the data is already being presented to Omneo in batch, we take advantage of this and use bulk loads. The data is loaded into a temporary HBase table using the bulk loading tool. The previously mentioned MapReduce jobs output HFiles that are ready to be loaded into HBase. The HFiles are loaded through the `completebulkload` tool, which works by passing in a URL that the tool uses to locate the files in HDFS. Next, the bulk load tool will load each file into the relevant region being served by each RegionServer. Occasionally, a region has been split after the HFiles were created, and the bulk load tool will automatically split the new HFile according to the correct region boundaries.

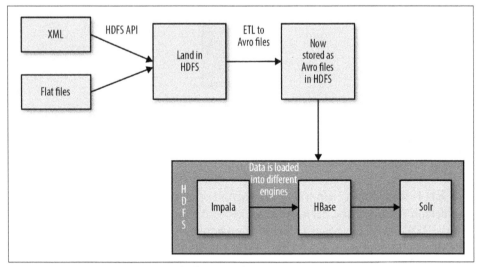

Figure 6-2. Using Avro for a unified storage format

Once the data is loaded into the staging table, it is then pushed out into two of the main serving engines, Solr and Impala. Omneo uses a staging table to limit the amount of data read from HBase to feed the other processing engines. The reason behind using a staging table lies in the HBase key design. One of the cool things about this HBase use case is the simplicity of the schema design. Normally, many hours will be spent figuring out the best way to build a composite key that will allow for the most efficient access patterns, and we will discuss composite keys in later chapters.

However, in this use case, the row key is a simple MD5 hash of the product serial number. Each column stores an Avro record. The column name contains the unique ID of the Avro record it stores. The Avro record is a de-normalized dataset containing all attributes for the record.

After the data is loaded into the staging HBase table, it is then propagated into two other serving engines. The first serving engine is Cloudera Search (Solr) and the second is Impala. Figure 6-3 illustrates the overall load of data into Solr.

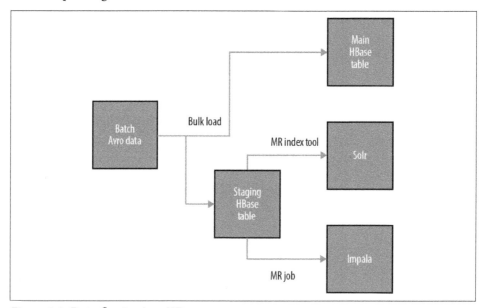

Figure 6-3. Data flowing into HBase

The data is loaded into Search through the use of a custom `MapReduceIndexerTool`. The default nature of the `MapReduceIndexerTool` is to work on flat files being read from HDFS. Given the batch aspect of the Omneo use case, the team modified the indexer tool to read from HBase and write directly into the Solr collection through the use of MapReduce. Figure 6-4 illustrates the two flows of the data from HBase into the Solr collections. There are two collections in play for each customer—in this case, there is collection A (active), collection B (backup)—and an alias that links to the "active" collection. During the incremental index, only the current collection is updated from the staging HBase table through the use of the `MapReduceIndexerTool`.

As shown in Figure 6-4, the HBase staging table loads into collection A and the alias points to the active collection (collection A). This approach—that is, using dual collections in addition to an alias—offers the ability to drop all of the documents in a single collection and reprocess the data without suffering an outage. This gives Omneo the ability to alter the schema and push it out to production without taking more downtime.

The bottom half of Figure 6-4 illustrates this action; the `MapReduceIndexerTool` is re-indexing the main HBase table into collection B while the alias is still pointing to collection A. Once the indexing step completes, the alias will be swapped to point at collection B and incremental indexing will be pointed at collection B until the dataset needs to be re-indexed again.

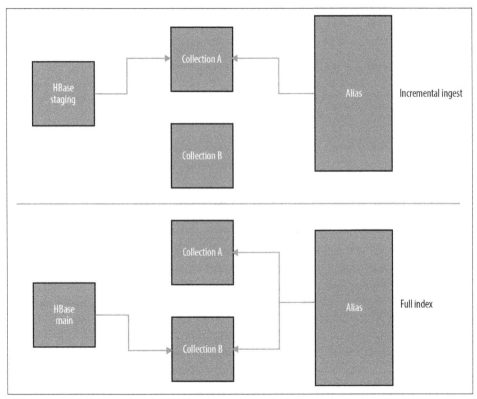

Figure 6-4. Managing full and incremental Solr index updates

This is where the use case really gets interesting. HBase serves two main functions in the overall architecture. The first one is to handle the master data management (MDM), as it allows updates. In this case, HBase is the system of record that Impala and Solr use. If there is an issue with the Impala or Solr datasets, they will rebuild them against the HBase dataset. In HBase, attempting to redefine the row key typically results in having to rebuild the entire dataset. Omneo first attempted to tackle faster lookups for secondary and tertiary fields by leveraging composite keys. It turns out the end users enjoy changing the primary lookups based on the metrics they are looking at. For example, they may look up by part time, test, date, or any other arbitrary field in the data. This is one of the reasons Omneo avoided leveraging composite keys, and used Solr to add extra indexes to HBase. The second and most important piece is HBase actually stores all of the records being served to the end user. Let's look at a couple sample fields from Omneo's Solr *schema.xml*:

```
<schema name="example" version="1.5">
<fields>
    <field name="id" type="string" indexed="true" stored="true" required="true"
                                                 multiValued="false" />
    <field name="rowkey"  type="binary" indexed="false" stored="true"
                                        omitNorms="true" required="true"/>
    <field name="eventid" type="string" indexed="true"  stored="false"
                                        omitNorms="true" required="true"/>
    <field name="docType" type="string" indexed="true" stored="false"
                                                      omitNorms="true"/>
    <field name="partName" type="lowercase" indexed="true" stored="false"
                                                      omitNorms="true"/>
    <field name="partNumber" type="lowercase" indexed="true" stored="false"
                                                      omitNorms="true"/>

    ...
    <field name="_version_" type="long" indexed="true" stored="true"/>
</fields>
```

Looking at some of the fields in this *schema.xml* file, we can see that Omneo is only flagging the HBase row key and the required Solr fields (id and _version_) as Stored, which will directly write these results to HDFS. The other fields are flagged as Indexed; which will store the data in a special index directory in HDFS. The indexed attribute makes a field searchable, sortable, and facetable; it is also stored in memory. The stored attributes make the fields retrievable through search and persisted to HDFS. Omneo ingests records that can have many columns present, ranging from hundreds to thousands of fields depending on the product being ingested. For the purposes of faceting and natural language searching, typically only a small subset of those fields are necessary. The amount of fields indexed will vary per customer and use case. This is a very common pattern, as the actual data results displayed to the customer are being served from the application calling scans and multigets from HBase based on the stored data. Just indexing the fields serves multiple purposes:

- All of the facets are served out of memory from Solr, offering tighter and more predictable SLAs.
- The current state of Solr Cloud on HDFS writes the data to HDFS per shard and replica. If HDFS replication is set to the default factor of 3, then a shard with two replicas will have nine copies of the data on HDFS. This will not normally affect a

search deployment, as memory or CPU is normally the bottleneck before storage, but it will use more storage.

- Indexing the fields offers lightning-fast counts to the overall counts for the indexed fields. This feature can help to avoid costly SQL or pre-HBase MapReduce-based aggregations

The data is also loaded from HBase into Impala tables from the Avro schemas and converted into the Parquet file format. Impala is used as Omneo's data warehouse for end users. The data is populated in the same manner as the Solr data, with incremental updates being loaded from the HBase staging table and full rebuilds being pulled from the main HBase table. As the data is pulled from the HBase tables, it is denormalized into a handful of tables to allow for an access pattern conducive to Impala. As shown in Figure 6-5, the data model used is part of Omneo's secret sauce.

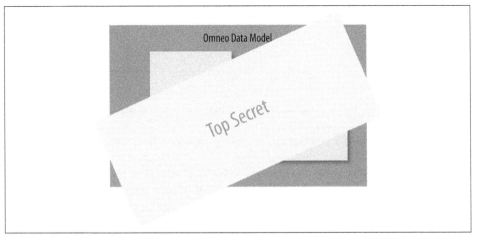

Figure 6-5. Nah, we can't share that. Get your own!

User Experience

Normally we do not spend a ton of time looking at end applications, as they tend to be quite different per application. However, in this case, it is important to discuss how everything comes together. As shown in Figure 6-6, combining the different engines into a streamlined user experience is the big data dream. This is how companies move from playing around to truly delivering a monumental product.

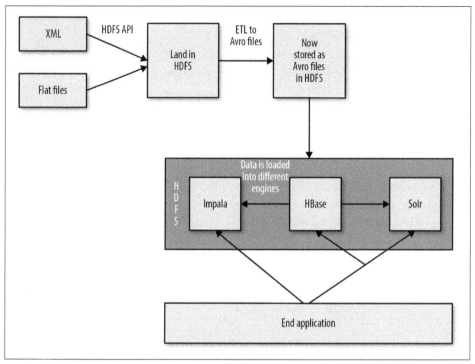

Figure 6-6. Overall data flow diagram, including the user interaction

The application makes use of all three of the serving engines in a single interface. This is important for a couple of key reasons: first, it allows for increased productivity from the analyst, as it's no longer necessary for the analyst to switch between different UIs or CLIs; second, the analyst is able to use the right tool for the right job. One of the major issues we see in the field is customers attempting to use one tool to solve all problems. By allowing Solr to serve facets and handle natural language searches, HBase to serve the full fidelity records, and Impala to handle the aggregations and SQL questions, Omneo is able to offer the analyst a 360-degree view of the data.

Let's start by looking at the Solr/HBase side of the house. These are the two most intertwined services of the Omneo application. As mentioned before, Solr stores the actual HBase row key and indexes the vast majority of other fields that the users like to search and facet against. In this case, as the user drills down or adds new facets (Figure 6-7), the raw records are not served back from Solr, but rather pulled from HBase using a multiget of the top 50 records. This allows the analyst to see the full fidelity record being produced by the facets and searches. The same thing holds true if the analyst wishes to export the records to a flat file; the application will call a scan of the HBase table and write out the results for end user.

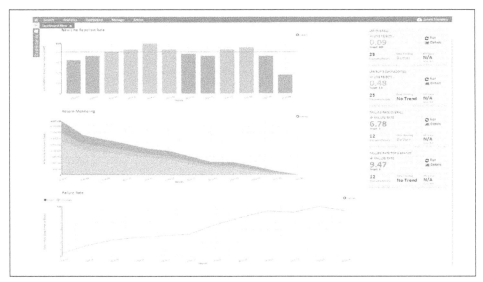

Figure 6-7. Check out this Solr goodness

On the Impala side of the house, also known as performance analytics, models are built and managed to handle SQL-like workloads. These are workloads that would normally be forced into HBase or Solr. Performance analytics was designed to run a set of pre-packed application queries that can be run against the data to calculate key performance indicators (KPIs), as shown in Figure 6-8. The solution does not allow for random free-form SQL queries to be utilized, as long-running rogue queries can cause performance degradation in a multitenant application. In the end, users can select the KPIs they want to look at, and add extra functions to the queries (sums, avg, max, etc.).

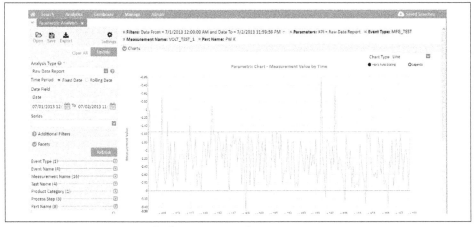

Figure 6-8. Leveraging Impala for custom analytics

## CHAPTER 7

Implementation of an Underlying Storage Engine

In the previous chapter, we described how Omneo uses the different Hadoop technologies to implement its use case. In this chapter, we will look more closely at all the different parts involving HBase. We will not discuss each and every implementation detail, but will cover all the required tools and examples to help you understand what is important during this phase.

As usual when implementing an HBase project, the first consideration is the table schema, which is the most important part of every HBase project. Designing an HBase schema can be straightforward, but depending on the use case, can also be quite complex and require significant planning and testing. It is a good practice to always start with this task, keeping in mind how data is received from your application (write path) and how you will need to retrieve it (read path). Read and write access patterns will dictate most of the table design.

Table Design

As we said and we will continue to say all over the book, table design is one of the most important parts of your project. The table schema, the key you will choose to use, and the different parameters you will configure will all have an impact on not only the performances of your application but also on the consistency. This is why for all the use cases we will describe, we are going to spend a lot of time on the table's design. After your application is running for weeks and storing terabytes of data, moving back from a bad table design to a good one will require duplicating the entire dataset, a lot of time, and usually an update to the client application. Those are all costly operations that you might want to avoid by spending the right amount of time in this phase.

Table Schema

Table design for the Omneo use case is pretty easy, but let's work through the steps so you can apply a similar approach to your own table schema design. We want both read and write paths to be efficient. In Omneo's case, data is received from external systems in bulk. Therefore, unlike other ingestion patterns where data is inserted one single value at a time, here it can be processed directly in bulk format and doesn't require single random writes or updates based on the key. On the read side, the user needs to be able to retrieve all the information for a specific sensor very quickly by searching on any combination of sensor ID, event ID, date, and event type. There is no way we can design a key to allow all those retrieval criteria to be efficient. We will need to rely on an external index, which given all of our criteria, will return a key that we will use to query HBase. Because the key will be retrieved from this external index and we don't need to look up or scan for it, we can simply use a hash of the sensor ID, with the column qualifier being the event ID. You can refer to "Generate Test Data" on page 88 to see a preview of the data format.

Sensors can have very similar IDs, such as 42, 43, and 44. However, sensor IDs can also have a wide range (e.g., 40,000–49,000). If we use the original sensor ID as the key, we might encounter hotspots on specific regions due to the keys' sequential nature. You can read more about hotspotting in Chapter 16.

Hashing keys

One option for dealing with hotspotting is to simply presplit the table based on those different known IDs to make sure they are correctly distributed accross the cluster. However, what if distribution of those IDs changes in the future? In that case, splits might not be correct anymore, and we might again end up with hot spots on some regions. If today all IDs are between 40xxxx and 49xxxx, regions will be split from the beginning to 41, 41 to 42, 42 to 43, and so on. But if tomorrow a new group of sensors is added with IDs from 40xxx to 39xxx, they will end up in the first region. Because it is not possible to forecast what the future IDs will be, we need to find a solution to ensure a good distribution whatever the IDs will be. When hashing data, even two initially close keys will produce a very different result. In this example, 42 will produce 50a2fabfdd276f573ff97ace8b11c5f4 as its md5 hash, while 43 will produce f0287f33eba7192e2a9c6a14f829aa1a. As you can see, unlike the original sensor IDs 42 and 43, sorting those two md5 hashes puts them far from one another. And even if new IDs are coming, because they are now translated into a hexadecimal value, they will always be distributed between 0 and F. Using such a hashing approach will ensure a good distribution of the data across all the regions, while given a specific sensor ID, we still have direct access to its data.

The hash approach cannot be used when you need to scan your data keeping the initial order of the key, as the md5 version of the key disrupts the original ordering, distributing the rows throughout the table.

Column qualifier

Regarding the column qualifier, the event ID will be used. The event ID is a hash value received from the downstream system, unique for the given event for this specific sensor. Each event has a specific type, such as "alert", "warning", or "RMA" (which stands for return merchandise authorization). At first, we considered using the event type as a column qualifier. However, a sensor can encounter a single event type multiple times. Each "warning" a sensor encountered would overwrite the previous "warning", unless we used HBase's "versions" feature. Using the unique event ID as the column qualifier allows us to have multiple events with the same type for the same sensor being stored without having to code extra logic to use HBase's "versions" feature to retrieve all of a sensor's events.

Table Parameters

To get the best peformances possible, we have to look at all the parameters and make sure to set them as required depending on our need and usage. However, only the parameters that apply to this specific use case are listed in this section.

Compression

The first parameter we'll examine is the compression algorithm used when writing table data to disk. HBase writes the data into HFiles in a block format. Each block is 64 KB by default, and is not compressed. Blocks store the data belonging to one region and column family. A table's columns usually contain related information, which normally results in a common data pattern. Compressing those blocks can almost always give good results. As an example, it will be good to compress column families containing logs and customer information. HBase supports multiple compression algorithms: LZO, GZ (for GZip), SNAPPY, and LZ4. Each compression algorithm will have its own pros and cons. For each algorithm, consider the performance impact of compressing and decompressing the data versus the compression ratio (i.e., was the data sufficiently compressed to warrant running the compression algorithm?).

Snappy will be very fast in almost all operations but will have a lower compression ratio, while GZ will be more resource intensive but will normally compress better. The algorithm you will choose depends on your use case. It is recommended to test a few of them on a sample dataset to validate compression rate and performance. As an example, a 1.6 GB CSV file generates 2.2 GB of uncompressed HFiles, while from the exact same dataset, it uses only 1.5 GB with LZ4. Snappy compressed HFiles for the same dataset take 1.5 GB, too. Because read and write latencies are important for us, we will use Snappy for our table. Be aware of the availability of the various compression libraries on different Linux distributions. For example, Debian does not include Snappy libraries by default. Due to licensing, LZO and LZ4 libraries are usually not bundled with common Apache Hadoop distributions, and must be installed separately.

 Keep in mind that compression ratio might vary based on the data type. Indeed, if you try to compress a text file, it will compress much better than a PNG image. For example, a 143,976 byte PNG file will only compress to 143,812 bytes (a space savings of only 2.3%), whereas a 143,509 byte XML file can compress as small as 6,284 bytes (a 95.7% space savings!) It is recommended that you test the different algorithms on your dataset before selecting one. If the compression ratio is not significant, avoid using compression and save processor overhead.

Data block encoding

Data block encoding is an HBase feature where keys are encoded and compressed based on the previous key. One of the encoding options (FAST_DIFF) asks HBase to store only the difference between the current key and the previous one. HBase stores each cell individually, with its key and value. When a row has many cells, much space can be consumed by writing the same key for each cell. Therefore, activating the data block encoding can allow important space saving. It is almost always helpful to activate data block encoding, so if you are not sure, activate FAST_DIFF. The current use case will benefit from this encoding because a given row can have thousands of columns.

Bloom filter

Bloom filters are useful in reducing unnecessary I/O by skipping input files from HBase regions. A Bloom filter will tell HBase if a given key *might be* or *is not* in a given file. But it doesn't mean the key is definitively included in the file.

However, there are certain situations where Bloom filters are not required. For the current use case, files are loaded once a day, and then a major compaction is run on the table. As a result, there will almost always be only a single file per region. Also, queries to the HBase table will be based on results returned by Solr. This means read requests will always succeed and return a value. Because of that, the Bloom filter will always return true, and HBase will always open the file. As a result, for this specific use case, the Bloom filter will be an overhead and is not required.

Because Bloom filters are activated by default, in this case we will need to explicitly disable them.

Presplitting

Presplits are not really table parameters. Presplit information is not stored within the metadata of the table and is used only at the time of table creation. However, it's important to have an understanding of this step before moving on the implementation. Presplitting a table means asking HBase to split the table into multiple regions when it is created. HBase comes with different presplit algorithms. The goal of presplitting a table is to make sure the initial load will be correctly distributed across all the regions and will not hotspot a single region. Granted, data would be distributed over time as region splits occur automatically, but presplitting provides the distribution from the onset.

Implementation

Now that we have decided which parameters we want to set for our table, it's time to create it. We will keep all the default parameters except the ones we just discussed. Run the following command in the HBase shell to create a table called "sensors" with a single column family and the parameters we just discussed, presplit into 15 regions (NUMREGIONS and SPLITALGO are the two parameters used to instruct HBase to presplit the table):

```
hbase(main):001:0> create 'sensors', {NUMREGIONS => 15,\
                                       SPLITALGO => 'HexStringSplit'}, \
                                       {NAME => 'v', COMPRESSION => 'SNAPPY',\
                                       BLOOMFILTER => 'NONE',\
                                       DATA_BLOCK_ENCODING => 'FAST_DIFF'}
```

When your table is created, you can see its details using the HBase WebUI interface or the following shell command:

```
hbase(main):002:0> describe 'sensors'
Table sensors is ENABLED
sensors
COLUMN FAMILIES DESCRIPTION
{NAME => 'v', DATA_BLOCK_ENCODING => 'FAST_DIFF', BLOOMFILTER => 'NONE',
REPLICATION_SCOPE => '0', VERSIONS => '1', COMPRESSION => 'SNAPPY',
MIN_VERSIONS => '0', TTL => 'FOREVER', KEEP_DELETED_CELLS => 'FALSE',
BLOCKSIZE => '65536', IN_MEMORY => 'false', BLOCKCACHE => 'true'}
1 row(s) in 0.1410 seconds
```

The NUMREGIONS and SPLITALGO parameters are used for the table creation but are not stored within the metadata of the table. It is not possible to retrieve this information after the table has been created.

As you can see, the parameters we specified are listed in the output, along with the default table parameters. The default parameters might vary based on the HBase version you are using. However, BLOOMFILTER, DATA_BLOCK_ENCODING, and COMPRESSION should be configured as we specified here.

Now that we have our table ready, we can move forward with the data preparation.

Data conversion

To be able to implement and test the described use case, we will need to have ingest data into our system. Therefore, it will be required to generated some testing data that we will later process and transform.

Generate Test Data

The next goal is to generate a set of representative test data to run through our process and verify the results. The first thing we will create is some data files with test values. The goal is to have a dataset to allow you to run the different commands and programs.

In the examples, you will find a class called CSVGenerator, which creates data resembling the code shown here:

```
1b87,58f67b33-5264-456e-938a-9d2e9c5f4db8,ALERT,NE-565,0-0000-000,1,ECEGYFFL ...
3244,350cee9e-55fc-409d-b389-6780a8af9e76,RETURNED,NE-382,0-0000-000,1,OOQTY ...
727d,b97df483-f0bd-4f24-8ff3-6988d8eff88c,ALERT,NE-858,0-0000-000,1,MSWOCQXM ...
53d4,d8c39bf8-6f5f-4311-8ee5-9d3bce3e18d7,RETURNED,NE-881,0-0000-000,1,PMKMW ...
1fa8,4a0bf5b3-680d-4b87-8d9e-e55f06614ae4,ALERT,NE-523,0-0000-000,1,IYIZSHKA ...
```

Each line contains a random sensor ID comprised of four characters (0 to 65535, represented in hexadecimal), then a random event ID, document type, part name, part number, version, and a payload formed of random letters (64 to 128 characters in length). To generate a different workload, you can rerun the CSVGenerator code any time you want. Subsequent parts of the example code will read this file from the ~/ahae/resources/ch07 folder. This class will create files relative to where it's run; therefore we need to run the class from the ~/ahae folder. If you want to increase or reduce the size of the dataset, simply update the following line:

```
for (int index = 0; index < 1000000; index++) {
```

You can run this data generator directly from Eclipse without any parameter or from the shell into the ~/ahae folder using the following command:

```
hbase -classpath ~/ahae/target/ahae.jar com.architecting.ch07.CSVGenerator
```

This will create a file called *omneo.csv* in ~/ahae/resources/ch07/omneo.csv.

Create Avro Schema

Now that we have some data to start with, we need to define an Avro schema that will reflect the format of the data generated. Based on the search schema provided in the previous chapter, we will need the following Avro schema:

```
{"namespace": "com.architecting.ch07",
 "type": "record",
 "name": "Event",
 "fields": [
     {"name": "id", "type": "string"},
     {"name": "eventid",   "type": "string"},
     {"name": "docType",   "type": "string"},
     {"name": "partName",  "type": "string"},
     {"name": "partNumber", "type": "string"},
     {"name": "version",   "type": "long"},
     {"name": "payload",   "type": "string"}
 ]
}
```

You can find the schema in the *omneo.avsc* file, which is available in the *resources/ch07* directory. Because it has already been compiled and imported into the project, it is not required to compile it. However, if you want to modify it, you can recompile it using the following command:

```
java -jar ~/ahae/lib/avro-tools-1.7.7.jar compile schema omneo.avsc ~/ahae/src/
```

This creates the file *~/ahae/src/com/architecting/ch07/Event.java* containing the Event object that will be used to store the Event Avro object into HBase.

Implement MapReduce Transformation

As shown in Example 7-1, the first steps of the production process is to parse the received CSV file to generate HBase HFiles, which will be the input to the next step. They will map the format of the previously created table.

Our production data will be large files, so we will implement this transformation using MapReduce to benefit from parallelism. The input of this MapReduce job will be the text file, and the output will be the HFiles. This dictates the way you should configure your MapReduce job.

Example 7-1. Convert to HFiles example

```
Table table = connection.getTable(tableName);

Job job = Job.getInstance(conf, "ConvertToHFiles: Convert CSV to HFiles");

HFileOutputFormat2.configureIncrementalLoad(job, table,
                          connection.getRegionLocator(tableName)); ❶
job.setInputFormatClass(TextInputFormat.class); ❷
```

```
job.setJarByClass(ConvertToHFiles.class); ❸
job.setJar("/home/cloudera/ahae/target/ahae.jar"); ❸

job.setMapperClass(ConvertToHFilesMapper.class); ❹
job.setMapOutputKeyClass(ImmutableBytesWritable.class); ❺
job.setMapOutputValueClass(KeyValue.class); ❻

FileInputFormat.setInputPaths(job, inputPath);
HFileOutputFormat2.setOutputPath(job, new Path(outputPath));
```

❶ HBase provides a helper class that will do most of the configuration for you. This is the first thing to call when you want to configure your MapReduce job to provide HFiles as the output.

❷ Here we want to read a text file with CSV data, so we will use TextInputFormat.

❸ When running from the command line, all the required classes are bundled into a client JAR, which is referenced by the setJarByClass method. However, when running from Eclipse, it is necessary to manually provide the JAR path because the class that we are running is from the Eclipse environment, which MapReduce is not aware of. Because of that, we need to provide MapReduce with the path of an external file where the given class is also available.

❹ Defines the mapper you want to use to parse your CSV content and create the Avro output.

❺ We need to define ImmutableBytesWritable as the mapper output key class. It is the format we will use to write the key.

❻ We need to define KeyValue as the mapper output value class. This will represent the data we want to store into our HFiles.

 The reducer used to create the HFiles needs to load into memory the columns of a single row and then sort all before being able to write them all. If you have *many* columns in your dataset, it might not fit into memory. This should be fixed in a future release when HBASE-13897 will be implemented.

The operations on the mapper side are simple. The goal is just to split the line into different fields, assign them to an Avro object, and provide this Avro object to the HBase framework to be stored into HFiles ready to be loaded.

As shown in Example 7-2, the first thing we need to do is define a set of variables that we will reuse for each and every iteration of the mapper. This is done to reduce the number of objects created.

Example 7-2. Convert to HFiles mapper

```
public static final ByteArrayOutputStream out = new ByteArrayOutputStream();
public static final DatumWriter<Event> writer = new SpecificDatumWriter<Event>
                                                (Event.getClassSchema());
public static final BinaryEncoder encoder = encoderFactory.binaryEncoder(out,null);
public static final Event event = new Event();
public static final ImmutableBytesWritable rowKey = new ImmutableBytesWritable();
```

Those objects are all reused on the map method shown in Example 7-3.

Example 7-3. Convert to HFiles mapper

```
// Extract the different fields from the received line.
String[] line = value.toString().split(",");  ❶

event.setId(line[0]);
event.setEventId(line[1]);
event.setDocType(line[2]);
event.setPartName(line[3]);
event.setPartNumber(line[4]);
event.setVersion(Long.parseLong(line[5]));
event.setPayload(line[6]);  ❷

// Serialize the AVRO object into a ByteArray
out.reset();  ❸
writer.write(event, encoder);  ❹
encoder.flush();

byte[] rowKeyBytes = DigestUtils.md5(line[0]);
rowKey.set(rowKeyBytes);  ❺
context.getCounter("Convert", line[2]).increment(1);

KeyValue kv = new KeyValue(rowKeyBytes,
                    CF,
                    Bytes.toBytes(line[1]),
                    out.toByteArray());  ❻
context.write (rowKey, kv);  ❼
```

❶ First, we split the line into fields so that we can have individual direct access to each of them.

❷ Instead of creating a new Avro object at each iteration, we reuse the same object for all the map calls and simply assign it the new received values.

❸ This is another example of object reuse. The fewer objects you create in your mapper code, the less garbage collection you will have to do and the faster your code will execute. The `map` method is called for each and every line of your input file. Creating a single `ByteArrayOutputStream` and reusing it and its internal buffer for each `map` iteration saves millions of object creations.

❹ Serialize the Avro object into an array of bytes to store them into HBase, reusing existing objects as much as possible.

❺ Construct our HBase key from the sensor ID.

❻ Construct our HBase `KeyValue` object from our key, our column family, our `even tid` as the column qualifier and our Avro object as the value.

❼ Emit our `KeyValue` object so the reducers can regroup them and write the required HFiles. The row key will only be used for partitioning the data. When data will be written into the underlying files, only the `KeyValue` data will be used for both the key and the value.

 When implementing a MapReduce job, avoid creating objects when not required. If you need to access a small subset of fields in a String, it is not recommended to use the string `split()` method to extract the fields. Using `split()` on 10 million strings having 50 fields each will create 500 million objects that will be garbage collected. Instead, parse the string to find the few fields' locations and use the `substring()` method. Also consider using the `com.google.common.base.Splitter` object from Guava libraries.

Again, the example can be run directly from Eclipse or from the command line. In both cases, you will need to specify the input file, the output folder, and the table name as the parameters. The table name is required for HBase to find the region's boundaries to create the required splits in the output data, but also to look up the column family parameters such as the compression and the encoding. The MapReduce job will produce HFiles in the output folder based on the table regions and the column family parameters.

The following command will create the HFiles on HDFS (if because you are running on the standalone version you need the files to be generated on local disk, simply update the destination folder):

```
hbase -classpath ~/ahae/target/ahae.jar:`hbase classpath` \
com.architecting.ch09.ConvertToHFiles \ ❶
file:///home/cloudera/ahae/resources/ch09/omneo.csv \ ❷
hdfs://localhost/user/cloudera/ch09/hfiles/ sensors ❸
```

❶ The class called for the conversion

❷ Our input file

❸ Output folder and table name

If you start the class from Eclipse, make sure to add the parameters by navigating to Run → Run Configurations/Arguments.

Because this will start a MapReduce job, the output will be verbose and will give you lots of information. Pay attention to the following lines:

```
Map-Reduce Framework
        Map input records=1000000
        Map output records=1000000
        Reduce input groups=65536
```

The `Map input records` value represents the number of lines in your CSV file. Because for each line we emit one and only one Avro object, it matches the value of the `Map output records` counter. The `Reduce input groups` represents the number of unique keys. So here we can see that there were one million lines for 65,536 different rows, which gives us an average of 15 columns per row.

At the end of this process, your folder content should look like the following:

```
[cloudera@quickstart ~]$ hadoop fs -ls -R ch07/
drwxr-xr-x      0 2015-05-08 19:23 ch07/hfiles
-rw-r--r--      0 2015-05-08 19:23 ch07/hfiles/_SUCCESS
drwxr-xr-x      0 2015-05-08 19:23 ch07/hfiles/v
-rw-r--r-- 10480 2015-05-18 19:57 ch07/hfiles/v/345c5c462c6e4ff6875c3185ec84c48e
-rw-r--r-- 10475 2015-05-18 19:56 ch07/hfiles/v/46d20246053042bb86163cbd3f9cd5fe
-rw-r--r-- 10481 2015-05-18 19:56 ch07/hfiles/v/6419434351d24624ae9a49c51860c80a
-rw-r--r-- 10468 2015-05-18 19:57 ch07/hfiles/v/680f817240c94f9c83f6e9f720e503e1
-rw-r--r-- 10409 2015-05-18 19:58 ch07/hfiles/v/69f6de3c5aa24872943a7907dcabba8f
-rw-r--r-- 10502 2015-05-18 19:56 ch07/hfiles/v/75a255632b44420a8462773624c30f45
-rw-r--r-- 10401 2015-05-18 19:56 ch07/hfiles/v/7c4125bfa37740ab911ce37069517a36
-rw-r--r-- 10441 2015-05-18 19:57 ch07/hfiles/v/9accdf87a00d4fd68b30ebf9d7fa3827
-rw-r--r-- 10584 2015-05-18 19:58 ch07/hfiles/v/9ee5c28cf8e1460c8872f9048577dace
-rw-r--r-- 10434 2015-05-18 19:57 ch07/hfiles/v/c0adc6cfceef49f9b1401d5d03226c12
-rw-r--r-- 10460 2015-05-18 19:57 ch07/hfiles/v/c0c9e4483988476ab23b991496d8c0d5
-rw-r--r-- 10481 2015-05-18 19:58 ch07/hfiles/v/ccb61f16feb24b4c9502b9523f1b02fe
-rw-r--r-- 10586 2015-05-18 19:56 ch07/hfiles/v/d39aeea4377c4d76a43369eb15a22bff
-rw-r--r-- 10438 2015-05-18 19:57 ch07/hfiles/v/d3b4efbec7f140d1b2dc20a589f7a507
-rw-r--r-- 10483 2015-05-18 19:56 ch07/hfiles/v/ed40f94ee09b434ea1c55538e0632837
```

Owner and group information was condensed to fit the page. All the files belong to the user who has started the MapReduce job.

As you can see in the filesystem, the MapReduce job created as many HFiles as we have regions in the table.

When generating the input files, be careful to provide the correct column family. Indeed, it a common mistake to not provide the right column family name to the MapReduce job, which will create the directory structure based on its name. This will cause the bulk load phase to fail.

The folder within which the files are stored is named based on the column family name we have specified in our code—"v" in the given example.

HFile Validation

Throughout the process, all the information we get in the console is related to the MapReduce framework and tasks. However, even if they succeed, the content they have generated might not be good. For example, we might have used the wrong column family, forgotten to configure the compression when we created our table, or taken some other misstep.

HBase comes with a tool to read HFiles and extract the metadata. This tool is called the HFilePrettyPrinter and can be called by using the following command line:

```
hbase hfile -printmeta -f ch07/hfiles/v/345c5c462c6e4ff6875c3185ec84c48e
```

The only parameter this tool takes is the HFile location in HDFS.

Here we show part of the output of the previous command (some sections have been omitted, as they are not relevant for this chapter):

```
Block index size as per heapsize: 161264
reader=ch07/hfiles/v/345c5c462c6e4ff6875c3185ec84c48e,
    compression=snappy, ❶
    cacheConf=CacheConfig:disabled,
    firstKey=7778/v:03afef80-7918-4a46-a903-f6e35b629926/1432004229936/Put, ❷
    lastKey=8888/v:fc69a89f-4a78-4e2d-ae0a-b22dc93c962c/1432004229936/Put, ❸
    avgKeyLen=53, ❹
    avgValueLen=171, ❺
    entries=666591, ❻
    length=104861200 ❼
```

Let's now take a look at the important parts of this output:

❶ This shows you the compression format used for your file, which should reflect what you have configured when you created the table (we initially chose to use Snappy, but if you configured a different one, you should see it here).

❷ Key of the first cell of this HFile, as well as column family name.

❸ The last key contained in the HFile (only keys between 7778 and 8888 are present in the file; it is used by HBase to skip entire files when the key you are looking for is not between the first and last key).

❹ Average size of the keys.

❺ Average size of the values.

❻ Number of cells present in the HFile.

❼ Total size of the HFile.

Using the output of this command, you can validate that there is data in the files you have generated and that the format of the data is according to your expectations (compression, bloom filters, average key size, etc.).

Bulk Loading

Bulk loading inserts multiple pre-generated HFiles into HBase instead of performing puts one by one using the HBase API. Bulk loads are the most efficient way to insert a large quantity of values into the system. Here we will show you how to perform a bulk load.

The HDFS content of your table should look as follows (to fit the page width, file permissions and owner information was removed, and /hbase/data/default/sensors was abbreviated to .../s):

```
  0 2015-05-18 19:46 .../s/.tabledesc
287 2015-05-18 19:46 .../s/.tabledesc/.tableinfo.0000000001
  0 2015-05-18 19:46 .../s/.tmp
  0 2015-05-18 19:46 .../s/0cc853926c7c10d3d12959bbcacc55fd
 58 2015-05-18 19:46 .../s/0cc853926c7c10d3d12959bbcacc55fd/.regioninfo
  0 2015-05-18 19:46 .../s/0cc853926c7c10d3d12959bbcacc55fd/recovered.edits
  0 2015-05-18 19:46 .../s/0cc853926...3d12959bbcacc55fd/recovered.edits/2.seqid
  0 2015-05-18 19:46 .../s/0cc853926c7c10d3d12959bbcacc55fd/v
```

If your table is empty, you will still have all the region folders, because we have presplit the table. HFiles might be present in the regions folders if data already existed prior to loading. We show only one region's directory in the preceding snippet, and you can see that this region's column family v is empty because it doesn't contain any HFiles.

Our HFiles have been generated by the MapReduce job, and we now need to tell HBase to place the HFiles into the given table. This is done using the following command:

```
hbase org.apache.hadoop.hbase.mapreduce.LoadIncrementalHFiles ch07/ \
hfiles sensors
```

In this command, we provide HBase the location of the HFiles we have generated (*ch07/hfiles*) and the table into which we want to insert those files (*sensors*). If the target table splits or merges some regions before the files are bulk loaded, splits and merges of the input HFiles will be handled on the client side at that time by the application. Indeed, the application used to push the HFiles into the HBase table will validate that each and every HFile still belongs to a single region. If a region got split before we pushed the file, the load tool will split the input files the same way before pushing them into the table. On the other side, if two regions are merged, the belonging input HFiles are simply going to be pushed into the same region.

When it runs, it will produce this output in the console:

```
$ hbase org.apache.hadoop.hbase.mapreduce.LoadIncrementalHFiles \
                            ch07/hfiles sensors
2015-05-18 20:09:29,701 WARN [main] mapreduce.LoadIncrementalHFiles: Skipping
non-directory hdfs://quickstart.cloudera:8020/user/cloudera/ch07/hfiles/_SUCCESS
2015-05-18 20:09:29,768 INFO [main] Configuration.deprecation: hadoop.native.lib
is deprecated. Instead, use io.native.lib.available
2015-05-18 20:09:30,476 INFO [LoadIncrementalHFiles-0] compress.CodecPool: Got
brand-new decompressor [.snappy]
```

After completion of the bulk load, you should find your files in HDFS under the table and the regions they belong to. Looking again at HDFS should show you something like this (again, to fit the page width, file permissions and owner information was removed, /hbase/data/default/sensors was abbreviated to .../s, and the region encoded name has been truncated):

```
   0 2015-05-18 19:46 .../s/0cc...
  58 2015-05-18 19:46 .../s/0cc.../.regioninfo
   0 2015-05-18 19:46 .../s/0cc.../recovered.edits
   0 2015-05-18 19:46 .../s/0cc.../recovered.edits/2.seqid
   0 2015-05-18 20:09 .../s/0cc.../v
 836 2015-05-18 19:56 .../s/0cc.../v/c0ab6873aa184cbb89c6f9d02db69e4b_SeqId_4_  ❶
```

❶ You can see that we now have a file in our previously empty region. This is one of the HFiles we initially created. By looking at the size of this file and by comparing it to the initial HFiles created by the MapReduce job, we can match it to *ch07/hfiles/v/ed40f94ee09b434ea1c55538e0632837*. You can also look at the other regions and map them to the other input HFiles.

Data Validation

Now that data is in the table, we need to verify that it is as expected. We will first check that we have as many rows as expected. Then we will verify that the records contain what we expect.

Table Size

Looking into an HFile using the `HFilePrettyPrinter` gives us the number of cells within a single HFile, but how many unique rows does it really represent? Because an HFile only represents a subset of rows, we need to count rows at the table level. HBase provides two different mechanisms to count the rows.

Counting from the shell

Counting the rows from the shell is pretty straightforward, simple, and efficient for small examples. It will simply do a full table scan and count the rows one by one. While this works well for small tables, it can take a lot of time for big tables, so we will use this method only when we are sure our tables are small.

Here is the command to count our rows:

```
hbase(main):003:0> count 'sensors', INTERVAL => 40000, CACHE => 40000
Current count: 40000, row: 9c3f
65536 row(s) in 1.1870 seconds
```

The `count` command takes up to three parameters. The first parameter, which is mandatory, is the name of the table whose rows you want to count. The second and third parameters are optional; the second parameter tells the shell to display a progress status only every 40,000 rows, and the third parameter is the size of the cache we want to use to do our full table scan. The third parameter is used to set up the `setCaching` value of the underlying `scan` object.

Counting from MapReduce

The second way to count the number of rows in an HBase table is to use the Row Counter MapReduce tool. The benefit of using MapReduce to count your rows is HBase will create one mapper per region in your table. For a very big table, this will distribute the work on multiple nodes to perform the count operation in parallel instead of scanning regions sequentially, which is what the shell's count command does.

This tool is called from the command line by passing the table name only:

```
hbase org.apache.hadoop.hbase.mapreduce.RowCounter sensors
```

Here is the most important part of the output (some sections have been removed in order to focus attention on key information and to reduce the size of this snippet):

```
2015-05-18 20:21:02,493 INFO  [main] mapreduce.Job: Counters: 31
        Map-Reduce Framework
                Map input records=65536 ❶
                Map output records=0
                Input split bytes=1304
                Spilled Records=0
```

```
        Failed Shuffles=0
        Merged Map outputs=0
        GC time elapsed (ms)=2446
        CPU time spent (ms)=48640
        Physical memory (bytes) snapshot=3187818496
        Virtual memory (bytes) snapshot=24042749952
        Total committed heap usage (bytes)=3864526848
    org.apache.hadoop.hbase.mapreduce.RowCounter$RowCounterMapper$Counters
        ROWS=65536 ❷
```

Let's now take a look at the important fields to consider here:

❶ Because the input records of this job are the HBase rows, we will have as many input records as we have rows.

❷ The number of rows we have in the table, which will match the number of input records. Indeed, this MapReduce job simply increments a ROWS counter for each input record.

> HBase also provides a MapReduce tool called CellCounter to count not just the number of rows in a table, but also the number of columns and the number of versions for each of them. However, this tool needs to create a Hadoop counter for each and every unique row key found in the table. Hadoop has a default limit of 120 counters. It is possible to increase this limit, but increasing it to the number of rows we have in the table might create some issues. If you are working on a small dataset, this might be useful to test your application and debug it. This tool generally cannot be run on a big table. Some work have been done on the Apache repository to fix this limitation. Please refer to HBASE-15773 (*https://issues.apache.org/jira/browse/HBASE-15773*) for more details.

File Content

We have our table with the number of lines we expected and the format we asked. But what does the data in the table really look like? Are we able to read what we wrote? Let's see two ways to have a look at our data.

Using the shell

The easiest and quickest way to read data from HBase is to use the HBase shell. Using the shell, you can issue commands to retrieve the data you want. The first command is get, which will give you a single row. If you specify a column family, only the columns for that family are returned. If you specify both a column family and a column qualifier (separated with a colon), it will return only the specific value if it exists. The second option is to use scan, which will return a certain number of rows that we can limit using the LIMIT parameter or the STARTROW and STOPROW parameters. Both of the following commands will return all the columns for the row with row key value 000a:

```
get 'sensors', '000a', {COLUMN => 'v'}
scan 'sensors', {COLUMNS => ['v'], STARTROW => '000a', LIMIT => 1 }
```

Now as you will see in the output, there might be many columns for each row. If you want to limit the output to a specific column qualifier, you need to specify it in both commands the following way:

```
get 'sensors', '000a', {COLUMN => 'v:f92acb5b-079a-42bc-913a-657f270a3dc1'}
scan 'sensors', { COLUMNS => ['v:f92acb5b-079a-42bc-913a-657f270a3dc1'], \
                  STARTROW => '000a', STOPROW => '000a' }
```

The output of the get should then look like this:

```
COLUMN        CELL
 v:f9acb...   timestamp=1432088038576, value=\x08000aHf92acb5b-079a-42bc-913a...
 1 row(s) in 0.0180 seconds
```

Because the value is an Avro object, it contains some nonprintable characters, which are displayed as \x08, but most of it should still be readable. This shows us that our table contains the expected key and data that matches what we are looking for.

Using Java

Using the shell, we have been able to validate that our table contains some data resembling Avro data, but to make sure it is exactly what we are expecting, we will need to implement a piece of Java code to retrieve the value, convert it into an Avro object, and retrieve the fields from it (see Example 7-4).

Example 7-4. Read Avro object from HBase

```
try (Connection connection = ConnectionFactory.createConnection(config);
     Table sensorsTable = connection.getTable(sensorsTableName)) {  ❶
  Scan scan = new Scan ();
  scan.setCaching(1);  ❷

  ResultScanner scanner = sensorsTable.getScanner(scan);
  Result result = scanner.next();  ❸
  if (result != null && !result.isEmpty()) {
    Event event = new Util().cellToEvent(result.listCells().get(0), null);  ❹
    LOG.info("Retrived AVRO content: " + event.toString());
  } else {
    LOG.error("Impossible to find requested cell");
  }
}
```

❶ Retrieves the table from the HBase connection.

❷ Make sure we return from the scan after we get the first row. Because we don't want to print more than one row, there is no need to wait for HBase to send us back more data.

❸ Executes the scan against the table and returns the result.

❹ Transforms the cell we received as the value into an Avro object.

Once again, you can run this example from Eclipse or from the command line. You should see output similar to what is shown here:

```
2015-05-20 18:30:24,214 INFO  [main] ch07.ReadFromHBase: Retrieved Avro object
  with ID 000a
2015-05-20 18:30:24,215 INFO  [main] ch07.ReadFromHBase: Avro content: {"id":
  "000a", "eventid": "f92acb5b-079a-42bc-913a-657f270a3dc1", "docType": "FAILURE",
  "partName": "NE-858", "partNumber": "0-0000-000", "version": 1, "payload":
  "SXOAXTPSIUFPPNUCIEVQGCIZHCEJBKGWINHKIHFRHWHNATAHAHQBFRAYLOAMQEGKLNZIFM 000a"}
```

With this very small piece of code, we have been able to perform the last step of the validation process and retrieved, de-serialized, and printed an Avro object from the table. To summarize, we have validated the size of the HFiles, their format, the numbers of entries in the HFiles and in the table, and the table content itself. We can now confirm that our data has been correctly and fully loaded into the table.

Data Indexing

The next and last step of the implementation consists of indexing the table we have just loaded, to be able to quickly search for any of the records using Solr. Indexing is an incremental process. Indeed, Omneo receives new files daily. As seen in the previous chapter, data from those files is loaded into a main table, which contains data from the previous days, and an indexation table. The goal is to add the indexation result into the Solr index built from previous days' indexations. At the end, the index will reference all that has been uploaded to the main table. To implement this last example, you will need to have a Solr instance running on your environment. If you are comfortable with it, you can install and run it locally; however, HBase needs to run in pseudodistributed mode because the Solr indexer cannot work with the local jobrunner. Alternatively, you can execute this example in a virtual machine where Solr is already installed.

Most of the MapReduce indexing code has been built from the Solr examples and has been modified and simplified to index an HBase table.

After confirming that you have a working local Solr environment, running the running the following commands will create the Solr collection with a single shard and the provided schema:

```
export PROJECT_HOME=~/ahae/resources/ch07/search
rm -rf $PROJECT_HOME
solrctl instancedir --generate $PROJECT_HOME
mv $PROJECT_HOME/conf/schema.xml $PROJECT_HOME/conf/schema.old
cp $PROJECT_HOME/../schema.xml $PROJECT_HOME/conf/
solrctl instancedir --create Ch07-Collection $PROJECT_HOME
solrctl collection --create Ch07-Collection -s 1
```

In a production environment, to scale your application, you might want to consider using more shards.

The most important file to define your index is its *schema.xml* file. This file is available in the book's GitHub repository and contains many tags. The most important section of the schema is the following:

```
<field name="id" type="string" indexed="true" stored="true" required="true"
                                              multiValued="false" />
<field name="rowkey" type="binary" indexed="false" stored="true" omitNorms="true"
                                              required="true"/>
<field name="eventId" type="string" indexed="true" stored="false"
                                        omitNorms="true" required="true"/>
<field name="docType" type="string" indexed="true" stored="false"
                                              omitNorms="true"/>
<field name="partName" type="lowercase" indexed="true" stored="false"
                                              omitNorms="true"/>
<field name="partNumber" type="lowercase" indexed="true" stored="false"
                                              omitNorms="true"/>
<field name="version" type="long" indexed="true" stored="false" required="true"
                                              multiValued="false" />
<field name="payload" type="string" indexed="true" stored="false" required="true"
                                              multiValued="false" />
<field name="_version_" type="long" indexed="true" stored="true"/>
```

Because this book is focused on HBase, we won't go into all the details of this file and all its fields, but invite you to look at the Solr online documentation (*http://lucene.apache.org/solr/4_10_3/*).

The following commands will create the required index for the examples:

```
export PROJECT_HOME=~/ahae/resources/ch07/search
rm -rf $PROJECT_HOME
solrctl instancedir --generate $PROJECT_HOME
mv $PROJECT_HOME/conf/schema.xml $PROJECT_HOME/conf/schema.old
cp $PROJECT_HOME/../schema.xml $PROJECT_HOME/conf/
solrctl instancedir --create Ch07-Collection $PROJECT_HOME
solrctl collection --create Ch07-Collection -s 1
```

If, for any reason, you want to delete your collection, use the following commands:

```
solrctl collection --delete Ch07-Collection
solrctl instancedir --delete Ch07-Collection
solrctl instancedir --delete search
```

The steps to get the table indexed are pretty straightforward. The first thing we need to do is to scan the entire HBase table using MapReduce to create Solr index files. The second step is to bulk load those files into Solr similar to how we bulk loaded our HFiles into HBase. The entire code will not be shown here due to size, however there are few pieces we want to show you here.

Example 7-5 demonstrates how we need to configure our MapReduce job in the driver class.

Example 7-5. Index HBase Avro table to Solr using MapReduce driver

```
scan.setCaching(500);         ❶
scan.setCacheBlocks(false);   ❷

TableMapReduceUtil.initTableMapperJob( ❸
  options.inputTable,              // Input HBase table name
  scan,                            // Scan instance to control what to index
  HBaseAvroToSOLRMapper.class,     // Mapper to parse cells content
  Text.class,                      // Mapper output key
  SolrInputDocumentWritable.class, // Mapper output value
  job);

FileOutputFormat.setOutputPath(job, outputReduceDir);

job.setJobName(getClass().getName() + "/"
                        + Utils.getShortClassName(HBaseAvroToSOLRMapper.class));
job.setReducerClass(SolrReducer.class);  ❹
job.setPartitionerClass(SolrCloudPartitioner.class);  ❺
job.getConfiguration().set(SolrCloudPartitioner.ZKHOST, options.zkHost);
job.getConfiguration().set(SolrCloudPartitioner.COLLECTION, options.collection);
job.getConfiguration().setInt(SolrCloudPartitioner.SHARDS, options.shards);

job.setOutputFormatClass(SolrOutputFormat.class);
SolrOutputFormat.setupSolrHomeCache(options.solrHomeDir, job);

job.setOutputKeyClass(Text.class);
job.setOutputValueClass(SolrInputDocumentWritable.class);
job.setSpeculativeExecution(false);
```

❶ By default, scans cache only one row at a time. To reduce remote procedure calls (RPC) calls and improve throughput, we want to increase the size of the cache.

❷ Because we are going to scan the entire table once and only once, caching the blocks is not required and will just put pressure on the RegionServers' blockcache. It is always recommended to disable the blockcache when running a Map-Reduce job over a table.

❸ Again, we are using HBase utility classes to configure required MapReduce input formats and output formats as well as the required mapper.

❹ Use the default Apache Solr reducer class.

❺ Also use the default apache Solr partitioner class.

Everything on the class should be pretty straightforward to understand.

Now let's have a look at the mapper. The goal of the mapper is to read the content from HBase and translate it for Solr. We have already written a class to create an Avro object from an HBase cell. We reuse the same code here, as this is exactly what we want to achieve. We want to read each cell, convert it back to an Avro object, and provide to Solr the data we want to index (Example 7-6).

Example 7-6. Index HBase Avro table to Solr using MapReduce mapper

```
event = util.cellToEvent(cell, event); ❶

inputDocument.clear(); ❷
inputDocument.addField("id", UUID.randomUUID().toString()); ❸
inputDocument.addField("rowkey", row.get());
inputDocument.addField("eventId", event.getEventId().toString());
inputDocument.addField("docType", event.getDocType().toString());
inputDocument.addField("partName", event.getPartName().toString());
inputDocument.addField("partNumber", event.getPartNumber().toString());
inputDocument.addField("version", event.getVersion());
inputDocument.addField("payload", event.getPayload().toString());

context.write(new Text(cell.getRowArray()),
              new SolrInputDocumentWritable(inputDocument)); ❹
```

❶ Transform the received cell into an Avro object reusing the event instance to avoid creation of new objects.

❷ Here again we want to reuse existing objects as much as possible and therefore will simply reinitialize and reuse the Solr input document.

❸ Assign to the Solr input document all the fields we want to index or store from the Avro event object.

❹ Write the Solr document to the context for indexing.

If you want to run the indexing from the command line, you will have to use the following command:

```
hbase -classpath ~/ahae/target/ahae.jar:`hbase classpath` \
com.architecting.ch07.MapReduceIndexerTool
```

You can also execute it from Eclipse without any specific parameter.

Data Retrieval

At this point, we have generated test data, transformed it into Avro format stored into HFiles, loaded it into a table, and indexed it into Solr. The only remaining piece is to make sure we can query Solr to find what we are looking for and then retrieve the related information from HBase. The HBase retrieval part is the same as what we have already seen before. You can query Solr using the code shown in Example 7-7.

Example 7-7. Retrieve Avro data from HBase based on Solr

```
CloudSolrServer solr = new CloudSolrServer("localhost:2181/solr"); ❶
solr.setDefaultCollection("Ch09-Collection"); ❷
solr.connect();

ModifiableSolrParams params = new ModifiableSolrParams();
params.set("qt", "/select");
params.set("q", "docType:ALERT AND partName:NE-555"); ❸

QueryResponse response = solr.query(params); ❹
SolrDocumentList docs = response.getResults();

LOG.info("Found " + docs.getNumFound() + " matching documents.");
if (docs.getNumFound() == 0) return;
byte[] firstRowKey = (byte[]) docs.get(0).getFieldValue("rowkey");
LOG.info("First document rowkey is " + Bytes.toStringBinary(firstRowKey));

// Retrieve and print the first 10 columns of the first returned document
Configuration config = HBaseConfiguration.create();
try (Connection connection = ConnectionFactory.createConnection(config);
    Admin admin = connection.getAdmin();
    Table sensorsTable = connection.getTable(sensorsTableName)) {
  Get get = new Get(firstRowKey); ❺

  Result result = sensorsTable.get(get);
  Event event = null;
  if (result != null && !result.isEmpty()) { ❻
    for (int index = 0; index < 10; index++) { // Print first 10 columns
      if (!result.advance())
        break; // There are no more columns and we have not reached 10
      event = new Util().cellToEvent(result.current(), event);
      LOG.info("Retrieved AVRO content: " + event.toString());
    }
  } else {
    LOG.error("Impossible to find requested cell");
  }
}
```

❶ Connect to your Solr cluster. Adjust this if you are not running Solr on the same cluster as HBase.

❷ Define the Solr collection you want to use.

❸ Configure the request you want Solr to execute. Here we ask it for all the ALERT documents for the NE-555 part.

❹ Execute the Solr request and retrieve the response from the server.

❺ Call HBase, specifying the row key of the first document sent back by Solr.

❻ Iterate over the columns for the given key and display the first 10 Avro objects retrieved from those columns.

Going Further

If you want to extend the examples presented in this chapter, the following list offers some options you can try based on our discussions from this chapter:

Bigger input file
> To make sure examples run pretty fast, the dataset we worked with was pretty small. What about using a bigger dataset? Depending on the available disk space you have and the performance of your environment, try to create a significantly bigger input file and verify it's processed the exact same way.

Single region table
> Because it's a good practice to avoid hotspotting, we have created a table with multiple regions split based on the key we used. Therefore the different Map-Reduce jobs have generated multiple files, one per region. What if we create a table with a single region instead? Try to modify the create table statement to have a single region and load more than 10 GB of data into it. You should see the region splitting after the data is inserted; however, since we are using bulk load, you should still not see any hotspotting on this region. You can validate your table splits and the content of each region by looking in HDFS, as discussed in "Bulk Loading" on page 95.

Impact on table parameters
> We have created our table using the parameters that are good for our current use case. We recommend modifying the various parameters and rerunning the process to measure the impact.

Compression

Try to use different types of compression and compare. If you used Snappy (which is fast), try to configure LZ4 (which is slower, but compresses better), and compare the overall time it takes to process everything in relation to the size of your files.

Block encoding

Because of the format of the key we store into this table, we configured it to use the FAST_DIFF data block encoding. Here again, look at the performance and the overall data size at the end.

Bloom filter

When doing reads, Bloom filters are useful for skipping HBase store files where we can confirm the key we are looking for is not present. However, here we knew that the data we are looking for will always be present in the file, so we disabled the Bloom filters. Create a list of tens of keys and columns that you know are present in the table and measure how long it takes to read them all. Activate the Bloom filter on the table and run a major compaction, which will create the Bloom filters. There should be no noticeable performance gain on subsequent tests for this specific use case.

 It is almost always good to have Bloom filters activated. We disabled them here because this use case is very specific. If you are not sure, just keep them on.

## CHAPTER 8

Use Case: Near Real-Time Event Processing

This next use case focuses on handling claims records for the healthcare industry. The claims processor utilizes a software-as-a-service (SaaS) model to act as a bridge for patients, hospitals, and doctor's offices. Because medical claims are quite difficult to manage for many hospitals and healthcare providers, the claims processor (also known as a clearinghouse) accepts claims from customers (i.e., hospitals and doctor's offices) and then formats those claims to send to the payer. This is a difficult and tedious process, as most hospitals and doctor's offices did not traditionally use a standardized format for claims. This is where the clearinghouse comes in to submit all claims in a unified format designed specifically for the payer.

Compared to the previous use cases, the clearinghouse has a few extra layers of complexity. For example, this data is not just machine-generated data to be loaded in batch; the incoming data has to be processed inflight. In addition, because the data is classified as personally identifiable information (PII) or protected health information (PHI), and thus protected under the Health Insurance Portability and Accountability Act (HIPAA), it requires numerous layers of security. This use case focuses on electronic medical claims records and creating a system to process these records. The end objective for this system is to lower the typical claims processing time from 30 days to eventually processing the claims in real time, by optimizing the claim to ensure all of the necessary information is present, and instantly rejecting claims before sending them to the insurance provider. The ideal service-level agreement (SLA) behind a system like this is to have the claim ready for review from the system in less than 15 seconds to be available for lookup and reference from the customer, claims processor, and payers. Because the system needs to serve external requests in real time, the cluster is required to have a 99.9% uptime, which weighed heavily into the decision to use Hadoop and HBase. There is also a concept of milestones, which require the ability to update the current claims record on the fly without knowing the number of updates a single record may receive. This plays right into HBase's strengths with the ability to handle sparse data and add thousands of columns without thinking twice.

The claims provider looked at numerous other systems to solve this use case. When evaluating the technologies for this project, the provider was lucky that this was a net new project. This gave a clean slate for technologies to choose from. The first technology looked at was Oracle RAC, which was at the time the current incumbent database. The provider performed some load testing at the volumes of data expected, but unfortunately RAC was not able to keep up. Next up was Netezza, which was nixed for lack of small files and total cost of ownership. Finally, Cassandra was evaluated. Because the use case required access to different processing layers, it was ruled out in favor of the complete Hadoop ecosystem. The current cluster houses roughly 178 TB of data in HDFS with 40 TB of that data living in the HBase instance, which is sized to handle roughly 30,000 events per second, and serve roughly 10 requests per second from Solr.

As mentioned earlier, this cluster currently contains PHI data. The overall requirements for storing this type of protected data are not only limited to technology, but to process as well. We will briefly focus on the technical requirements for storing this data in the system. These strict guidelines also weighed heavily in the choice of technology. These guidelines are taken very seriously, as the administrators of the system can incur large fines as well as jail time if they are found to be in violation of the law. When dealing with PHI, the claims provider is required to offer a strong layer of authentication, authorization, and encryption.

This claims provider wanted to ensure all levels were properly met before deploying the system. For the authentication layer, the provider went with the industry standard of Kerberos. Authorization is controlled from a few different places; the first is leveraging HBase's built-in ACLs, the second is through HDFS ACLs, and finally, Sentry for the Search and Impala layer. The encryption layer started out with Vormetric, which did not seem to include a large performance hit, but later the provider moved to Gazzang encryption to leverage the integrated KeyStore and AES-NI for offloading the processing to the CPU. The claims provider also leverages Cloudera Navigator for auditing, data lineage, and metadata tagging.

Figure 8-1 illustrates the overall architecture. This diagram might be a bit daunting at first, as it contains a few Hadoop ecosystem technologies that we have not yet reviewed. Before diving into the different layers, let's spend a minute looking a little deeper into Kafka and Storm, which play a major role in the near real-time pipeline.

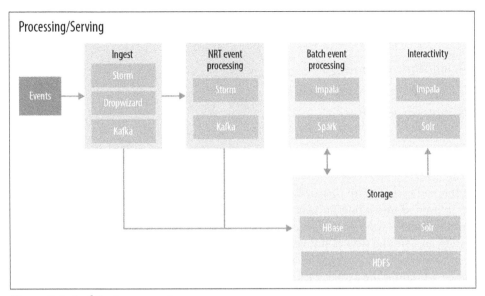

Figure 8-1. Architecture overview

Kafka is going to be a recurring component in the wonderful world of real-time ingest. Kafka maintains different streams of messages referred to as topics. The processes that publish messages to a Kafka topic are called *producers*. There are numerous pre-created producers (similar to Flume Sources), or you can always write your own producer depending on use case requirements. The processes reading from the topics are known as *consumers*. Consumers are also typically responsible for writing to the downstream applications. Kafka is traditionally run as a cluster comprised of one or more nodes, each of which is called a *broker*. These consumers are broken up into *consumer groups*, each of which handle their own offset allowing for consumers to be able to easily subscribe and unsubscribe without affecting other consumers reading for the same topic. Kafka allows for very high read and write throughput through the use of partitions that can be tuned to take advantage of numerous spindles inside the Kafka nodes.

Now that you have an understanding of the new technologies in play, let's break the architecture into three separate categories:

- Ingest/pre-processing
- Near real-time event processing
- Processing/serving

Ingest/Pre-Processing

In this use case, we are primarily looking at three different data sources. The first is an enterprise messaging aystem (EMS), the second is from Oracle RAC databases, and the third is from a custom on-premise solution. Both the on-premise and EMS system are sending new claims records, where the Oracle RAC is sending the updated milestones about each record to Kafka (Figure 8-2). Each ingest flow has roughly the same path minus the initial collection tool. In this case, there are two primary tools in place: first is Apache Storm and Dropwizard. Apache Storm is a distributed ingest system designed for processing streams of data in real time. Storm is a very popular choice for ingest as it allows for a higher level of complex event processing (CEP) than offered by Apache Flume. We will spend more time talking about Storm's CEP capabilities later in this chapter. The other initial ingest tool in place is Dropwizard, which is an open source Apache Licensed Java Framework for quickly developing web services. Dropwizard take numerous production-ready libraries and bundles them together for a quicker development cycle. It also has prebuilt integration with Kafka, eliminating the need to write a custom Kafka producer.

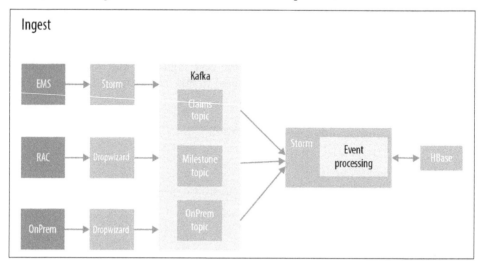

Figure 8-2. Detailed ingest pipeline

In this use case, we are using three separate topics, one for each ingest path. This allows for the end user to be able to add other systems to read from an individual topic without having to receive all of the other unwanted data. In this case, the numerous topics are being used simply for ease of management and future extensibility. From Kafka, we have a single Storm topology pulling from the three main Kafka topics.

Near Real-Time Event Processing

The main portion of the ETL work all resides inside this Storm topology. The Storm topology includes the concept of Bolts, which enable us to perform the CEP tasks that need to be done. The consumers in this case will be Kafka spouts for Storm. The Storm Bolt will receive the events from the Kafka Spout where the event enrichment will occur (Figure 8-3). We have two streams that need to be processed: the new claims records and milestones. They both need some separate processing, which Storm makes easy by allowing numerous streams to occur in a single topology. As the claims come in, they need to be enriched with previously stored data or messages. This process includes adding missing traits, such as name, doctor, hospital, address, the internal claim IDs, and the external claim ID. It is important to remember that the naming structure might differ from one claim provider to the next. It is important for claim providers to be able to identify the same claim every time. The milestones are enriching claims with updated data, and new status levels that are going to be used in the serving layer.

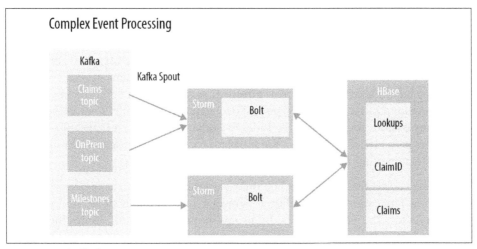

Figure 8-3. Inflight event processing

The HBase row key design has to be carefully considered when dealing with PII data. One of the most important requirements around handling healthcare information is the ability to guarantee never exposing the wrong customer information. In this case, the row key is a concatenation of the customerID and a random hash. Looking at the three relevant tables:

- Lookups - InternalID
- ClaimsID - claimsID
- Claims - CustomerID|random hash

The customer ID must be the first part of the key as this guarantees that when the application does a look up in HBase, only that record is served back. The problem is most customer IDs tend to increment in the system and are usually just a series of numbers. By adding the random hash to the end of the key, it allows for additional lexicographic sort split purposes. The most ideal row key distribution would be a simple MD5 hash, which has an astronomically low collision rate—this would spread the keys around evenly and make for a smoother write path. However, when dealing with PII data, it is a gamble to use the MD5 hash, no matter how low the risk. Remember, people win the lottery every day!

Processing/Serving

We have taken a look at the ingest and CEP layer of the pipeline. Everything we have discussed occurs outside the cluster, except for the Storm bolts calling Gets and Puts for HBase. The claims provider uses a combination of Impala, Spark, Solr, and the almighty HBase (it is the focal point of the book). HBase in this case is used in numerous ways: in addition to being the record of truth for claims, it is also used to rebuild Solr indexes and Impala tables when the data shifts, and to enrich and update incoming claims and milestones. The data coming into HBase is all being loaded through the Java API inside the Storm Bolts through the use of Gets, Puts, and check and swap operations. Once the data is written to HBase, the claims provider then leverages the Lily Indexer to write the new records and updates to Solr. The Lily Indexer is an interesting piece of software, as it allows indexing into SolrCloud without having do any custom coding. The Lily Indexer works by acting as a replication sink for HBase. As with HBase replication, the Indexer processes the write asynchronously as to not interrupt other incoming writes.

One of the coolest features of the Lily Indexer is that it piggybacks on the previously built HBase replication functionality. This means the progress is stored in ZooKeeper and it leverages the HBase HLogs. By using the previously built replication framework, the Lily Indexer is fault tolerant and can survive region and Solr Server failures without having data loss. This is very important when storing medical claims, as accuracy and data protection are two of the top concerns. As discussed in the previous chapter, Solr is not only housing the data being searched, but the HBase row key as well. This row key is going to be used later when we discuss the Spark processing layer. Once the data is in Solr, it can be accessed two different ways (Figure 8-4). The primary way the data is accessed is through Dropwizard services taking advantage of the Solr API to pull the latest claims and milestone data for the end users. The other way is from Spark, which is for running special machine learning over the data.

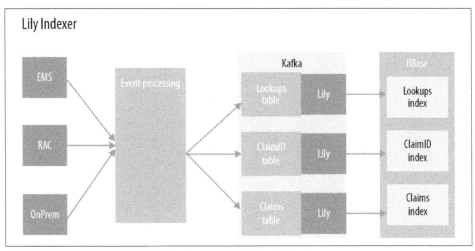

Figure 8-4. Replicating HBase to Solr using Lily

Spark is being used to identify claims that are missing key pieces of data, or have incorrect data processed in the wrong fields. Solr is perfect for this, and can act as secondary, tertiary, quarterly, etc. indexes, because by default HBase can only query the primary row key. The first thing we do is query Solr to pull the specific records that we want; these records will also contain the HBase row key. Once we have the HBase row key, we can perform gets/multigets and scans, depending on the query results from Solr. Once we have the data from HBase, a series of data models (sorry, not trying to be vague, but we do need to protect some IP!) is applied to the result set. The output of Spark is then sent over to the alerting system, which triggers milestones to alert the customer that there are missing fields, or other attributes that need to be filled in before processing can continue (Figure 8-5).

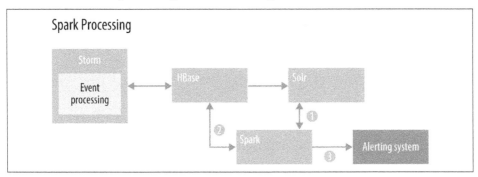

Figure 8-5. Spark processing workflow

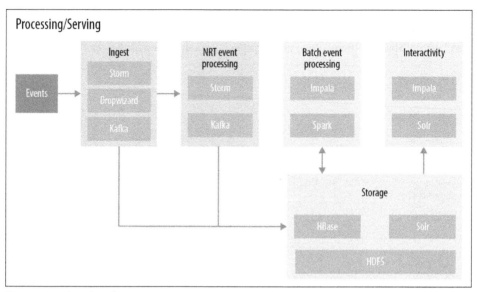

Figure 8-6. Final architecture

## CHAPTER 9

Implementation of Near Real-Time Event Processing

In the previous chapter, we introduced many tools that we did not use in the previous use case implementation, including Storm, Spark, and Kafka. This book is focused on HBase usage, so we will not review the installation of all these new tools, and we will assume that they are correctly installed and running on your environment. In addition, because Twitter decommissioned Storm and identified flaws in its design and scalability,[1] the examples here are implemented using Flume.

Because the Cloudera QuickStart VM already comes with Flume, Kafka, Spark, Solr, Lily Indexer, and HBase, we used it to develop and test this use case. Because we used only standard applications and APIs, if you are able to install all those tools locally outside of a VM, or if you have any other VM with all those tools available, it should work exactly the same way.

Keep in mind that the more services you are running, the more memory you need. We assigned 12 GB to our virtual machine to run these examples. If you are lacking memory, you can stop some of those services and run the different steps one by one with the services you have running.

Again, we will not discuss each and every implementation detail, but will cover all the required tools and examples to help you understand what is important during this phase.

Before we begin, you'll need to make sure that all services are running correctly.

---

1 *http://blog.acolyer.org/2015/06/15/twitter-heron-stream-processing-at-scale/*

If you are using Cloudera Manager, you can check the status of all the services from the web UI, as illustrated in Figure 9-1.

Figure 9-1. Cluster Services in Cloudera Manager

If you are not using Cloudera Manager, or if you don't have any web UI, you might want to make use of the sudo jps command to make sure all the services are running.

The important services are highlighted here:

```
$ sudo jps
12867 Main
5230 Main
12735 EventCatcherService
22423 DataNode
12794 Main
22920 HMaster
12813 HeadlampServer
12753 NavServer
12841 AlertPublisher
22462 SecondaryNameNode
22401 NameNode
22899 HRegionServer
22224 QuorumPeerMain
29753 Jps
12891 NavigatorMain
24098 Application
24064 Main
23055 Bootstrap
22371 Kafka
822962 ThriftServer
```

The Flume agent will appear on this list only when it will be running.

Application Flow

As described in Chapter 8, Flume will pick up data from external data sources and store that into Kafka for queuing. Then another Flume agent will read the different Kafka queues, process the data if required, then send it into HBase for storage where the Lily Indexer will pick it up and send it into Solr for indexation. This is what we are going to implement here. We will not implement all the sources nor all the real-time processing options, but we will make sure we have an entire data flow going from the initial Flume event up to the Solr indexation. To have an easy way to ingest testing events into our flow, we will make Flume read the events from a Kafka queue where we will insert test data from the `kafka-console-producer` command line.

Figure 9-2 shows a simplified version of the data flow.

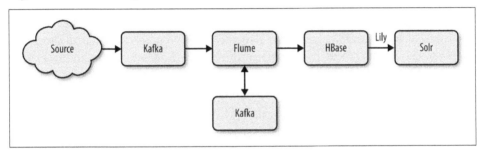

Figure 9-2. Data flow

For the purpose of this example, we will consider the incoming data to be XML files that we will transform over the process into Avro objects that we will insert into HBase and get all the fields separately indexed into Solr.

Kafka

Because Kafka will be the entry point for all our data, it is the first thing we need to get running and configured. Kafka will be used for two purposes. It will first be used to queue all the data received from the external sources and make it available for the downstream consumers. Then it will also be used for the Flume channel.

To populate the Kafka queue, we will build our own data generator script using a small Java application to create random XML documents. We will use the Kafka command line to load them into Kafka. To read and process all those events, we will configure a Flume agent that we will enhance with an interceptor to perform the XML to Avro transformation.

Flume

Flume is a stream engine commonly used to stream data from a source to a sink, applying small modifications if required. It also needs to have a channel configured. The channel is where Flume will store incoming data until it's sent to the destination.

Storm was initially selected in the original project implementation; however, we feel it is better to use Flume, which is widely adopted and used by the community.

For the examples, we will use Flume to read the events from Kafka source, transform and enrich them, and push them to HBase. We will need to use a Kafka source, a Kafka channel, an interceptor, and an HBase sink.

HBase

As we saw in Chapter 8, the HBase key has been initially designed to be the customer ID followed by a random hash. For better distribution, we also talked about the option to use an MD5 hash. In the current implementation, we will not follow exactly the same key pattern, and we will build one that will achieve the same goal, a bit differently. Here is the reasoning and how we are going to implement it.

The end goal for this use case is to get the XML documents indexed into Solr but also stored into HBase so they can easily be retrieved. Each document represents medical information for a specific person. Therefore, one person can be assigned multiple documents. A natural ID to identify a person is by insurance number or customer ID. However, the distribution of this ID cannot be guaranteed and might result in some regions being more loaded than others. For this reason (and because scanning by insurance number is untenable), we want to look at the option to hash this number. As we have seen in the previous use case, hashing a key allows it to have a better distribution. So our key can be an MD5 of the insurance number. Even if MD5s have very low risk of collisions, the risk nonetheless still exists. What if when retrieving a medical record for a patient, because of an MD5 collision, we also retrieve the records for another patient? This can create confusion, can result in bad diagnostics, and can have very dramatic consequences, including legal ramifications. Data collisions in the medical world are simply not acceptable. That means we need to find a way to preserve the distribution of the MD5 and to be absolutely certain that there will never be any collision. The easiest way to achieve this goal is to simply append the customer or insurance ID at the end of the MD5. Therefore, even if two different IDs result in the same MD5, they can still be used as a differentiator for the key and each person will then have its own row into HBase. For a row to be returned, it needs the ID and its MD5 to both match the key, which makes it unique. In comparison to the key proposed in the previous chapter, this option allows a better distribution of the data accross the table, but at the cost of a bigger footprint. Indeed, an MD5 plus the ID will be bigger than the ID plus some random bytes. However this extra cost can prove to be valuable for improving the table distribution and simplifying the splits identification.

As we already noted, the goal of the hash is to improve the distribution of the keys accross the entire table. An MD5 hash is 16 bytes. But to achieve a good distribution, just a few bytes will suffice. Thus, we will only keep the first two bytes that we will store in a string format. We chose to use MD5 hash because we already used it in the examples in Chapter 8, but any other kind of hash that offers enough distribution can be used as a replacement of MD5 (e.g., you could also use CRC32, if you prefer). Last, because we have to index the row key, it will be easier to store it as a printable string instead of a byte array. The first four characters will represent the hash, and the remaining characters of the key will represent the insurance number.

Also, even for patients undergoing treatment for a serious illness, we would not expect millions of documents per person, and a virtual limit of 10,000 documents seems reasonable. This allows us to store all those documents into the same row instead of adding the document ID to the row key and storing them as different rows.

Figure 9-3 illustrates three different approaches for the key design:

- Option 1 shows the initial key design where the key is based on the customer ID and a random hash.
- Option 2 shows the design where each document is stored in a different row.
- Option 3 shows the final design where each document for the same patient is stored into the same row.

We will implement option 3.

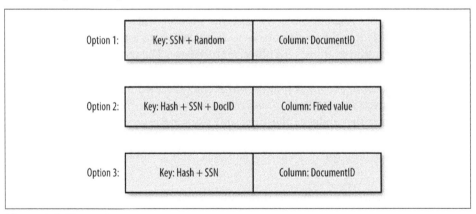

Figure 9-3. Key options

You might be wondering why we decided to go with option 3 instead of option 2. In the two last options, the document ID is stored once in the key and once as the column qualifier. Since we are storing the same information at the end whatever option is chosen, the storage size of the two options will be the same. Again, in both cases, when retrieving a document, we will query HBase given the customer ID and its MD5, and the document ID. So for both cases again, the access pattern will be direct, and identical.

The main difference here is that storing the documents together allows you to benefit from HBase row-level consistency. Indeed, if your upstream system wants to upload two documents at the same time, with the guarantee that they will both go, or both fail, having them in the same line will allow you to achieve this goal. However, having them on two different rows can potentially land the documents into two different regions. This can be problematic in case of a partial failure. If you do not have any consistency constraint, to improve the scalability, it is totally fine, and even preferred, to use the design described in version 2.

Last, keep in mind that HBase will never split within a row. So this approach works well only if your rows are a decent limited size. This is why we have estimated the maximum number of columns a row might realistically have. If we consider that we can have a maximum of 10,000 columns of small 10 KB Avro objects, this is only about 100 MB of data for this specific row. Given that HBase regions can easily grow above 10 GB, that gives us plenty of space to store those outlier rows.

Lily

The goal of the Lily Indexer is to replicate into Solr all the mutations received into HBase. We will not go into all the technical details, but Lily is built on top of the HBase replication framework. Therefore, all mutations are guaranteed to be forwarded to Solr, even in case of a node failure where the region and the related HLogs are assigned to another RegionServer. Because the indexer will receive the data that is stored into HBase, it will be accountable to *translate* it into a Solr document. In our use case, we are going to store Avro objects into HBase. The indexer will have to map the fields of the Avro objects to the fields of the Solr document we want to index. This mapping is defined using a Morphlines script. As described on the project's website (*https://github.com/kite-sdk/kite/tree/master/kite-morphlines*), "Morphlines is an open source framework that reduces the time and skills necessary to build and change Hadoop ETL stream processing applications that extract, transform and load data into Apache Solr, Enterprise Data Warehouses, HDFS, HBase or Analytic Online Dashboards."

Solr

We already discussed Solr in Chapter 8, so we will not repeat the details here. Part of the Solr schema that we will use is the following:

```
<field name="id" type="string" indexed="true" stored="true" required="true"
                                           multiValued="false" />
<field name="rowkey" type="binary" indexed="false" stored="true" omitNorms="true"
                                           required="true"/>
<field name="documentId" type="string" indexed="true" stored="true"\
                         omitNorms="true" required="true"/>
<field name="payload" type="text_general" indexed="true" stored="false"
                              required="true" multiValued="false" />
<field name="_version_" type="long" indexed="true" stored="true"/>
```

And again, the complete schema is available in the book's example files.

Implementation

Now that we have defined all of our main components (Kafka, Flume, HBase, Lily, and Solr), it is time to make sure data can flow from the entry point up to the Solr index. To allow you to test the examples as you advance into this chapter, we will implement the different required parts in the same order as the data flow.

Before going into all the details, we recommend creating the HBase table right from the beginning. Indeed, having the table available will allow you to test the examples as we describe them. Later, we will review the details of this table creation and provide a more efficient creation script, but to quickly start, simply type the following into the HBase shell:

```
create 'documents', 'c'
```

Data Generation

First of all, if we want to test our examples, we need to make sure we have data to send into our flow. Because we are going to ingest XML documents into Kafka, we will need a small XML documents generator. Because it doesn't add much value to the book, the code for this generator will not be printed here, but it is available in the example files. The generated data will follow the following format:

```
<ClinicalDocument>
  <PatientRecord>
    <FirstName></FirstName>
    <LastName></LastName>
    <SIN></SIN>
  </PatientRecord>
  <MedicalRecord>
    <Comments></Comments>
  </MedicalRecord>
</ClinicalDocument>
```

Of course, a real-world medical document will contain way more fields than what we are generating here; however, the few fields we're using here are enough to implement the examples. The social insurance number is a mandatory field, but the other fields might not always be populated. When a field is missing, at the ingestion time, HBase will try to look up the missing information.

The first thing we do to generate those documents is to create a random social insurance number (SIN). We want the same SIN to always represent the same person. Therefore, we will generate a first name and a last name based on this number. That way, the same number will always return the same name. However, because we also want to demonstrate the use of an interceptor, we are going to generate some of the messages without the first name or the last name. Leveraging a Flume interceptor, we can add missing field detection. This will not only transform the message from XML to Avro, but will allow HBase to perform a Get to retrieve previous messages that may contain the missing fields. This would allow us to fully populate the document.

To run the XML document generator, from the command line, simply use the following command:

```
java -classpath ~/ahae/target/ahae.jar com.architecting.ch09.XMLGenerator
```

Kafka

Now that we have our messages ready to enter our flow, we need to prepare Kafka to accept them.

 Make sure that Kafka is configured with the zookeeper.chroot property pointing to the /kafka zookeeper path. Indeed, by default, some distributions will keep the Kafka folder as being the root ZooKeeper path. If the default is used, you will end up with all the Kafka folders created under the root path, which could become confusing when it's time to differentiate those Kafka folders from other applications folders. Also, not setting the value could result in the following error: Path length must be > 0.

The first step is to create a Kafka queue, which can be achieved as follows:

```
[cloudera@quickstart ~]$ kafka-topics --create --topic documents --partitions 1 \
                         --zookeeper localhost/kafka --replication-factor 1
Created topic "documents".
```

 In production, you will most probably want more partitions and a bigger replication factor. However, in a local environment with a single Kafka server running, you will not be able to use any bigger number.

To learn more about the different parameters this command accepts, refer to the online Kafka documentation.

When the queue is created, there are multiple ways to add messages into it. The most efficient approach is to use the Kafka Java API. However, to keep the examples simple, we will use the command-line API for now. To add a message into the newly generated Kafka queue, use the following command:

```
java -classpath ~/ahae/target/ahae.jar com.architecting.ch09.XMLGenerator | \
kafka-console-producer --topic documents --broker-list localhost:9092
```

This method will call the XMLGenerator we have implemented earlier and will use its output as the input for the `kafka-console-producer`. At the end of this call, one new XML message will have been created and pushed into the Kafka queue.

To validate that your topic now contains the generated messages, you can make use of the following command:

```
kafka-console-consumer --zookeeper localhost/kafka --topic documents \
                           --from-beginning
```

This command will connect to the `documents` topic and will output all the events present in this topic, starting from the first available one.

The output of this last command should look like this:

```
<ClinicalDocument>\n<PatientRecord>\n<FirstName>Tom</FirstName>\n<LastName>...
```

This shows you that at least one event is available into the Kafka topic.

Also, because we configured Flume to use Kafka as a channel, we also need to create the Flume Kafka channel using the following:

```
[cloudera@quickstart ~]$ kafka-topics --create --topic flumechannel \
    --partitions 1 --zookeeper localhost/kafka --replication-factor 1
Created topic "flumechannel".
```

Flume

Now that our topic is getting events, we will need something to consume them and store them into HBase.

The configuration of Flume is done via a property file where we define all the parts to be put in place together. Flume parameters are in the following form:

```
<agent-name>.<component-type>.<component-name>.<parameter> = <value>
```

We will use `ingest` as the agent name for all the configuration.

For more details about how Flume works and all of its parameters, check out the project's online documentation (*https://flume.apache.org/FlumeUserGuide.html*) or Hari Shreedharan's book *Using Flume* (O'Reilly, 2014). For all Kafka plus Flume-specific parameters, refer to the blog post "Flafka: Apache Flume Meets Apache Kafka for Event Processing" (*http://bit.ly/291gG6a*) on the Cloudera Engineering Blog.

Flume Kafka source

Flume can be configured with many different sources, most of them being already developed. If the source you are looking for is not already built, you can develop your own. Were are looking here for a Kafka source. We will inform Flume about this source using the following parameter:

```
ingest.sources = ingestKafkaSource
```

This tells Flume that the `ingest` agent has only one source called `ingestKafka Source`. Now that we have told Flume that we have a source, we have to configure it:

```
ingest.sources.ingestKafkaSource.type = \
    org.apache.flume.source.kafka.KafkaSource
ingest.sources.ingestKafkaSource.zookeeperConnect = localhost:2181/kafka
ingest.sources.ingestKafkaSource.topic = documents
ingest.sources.ingestKafkaSource.batchSize = 10
ingest.sources.ingestKafkaSource.channels = ingestKafkaChannel
```

Again, this provides Flume with all the details about the source that we are defining.

Flume Kafka channel

A Flume channel is a space that Flume uses as a buffer between the source and the sink. Flume will use this channel to store events read from the source and waiting to be sent to the sink. Flume comes with a few different channel options. The memory channel is very efficient, but in case of server failure, data stored into this channel is lost. Also, even if servers have more and more memory, they still have a limited amount compared to what disks can store. The disk channel allows data to be persisted in case of a server failure. However, this will be slower than the other channels, and data lost still exists in case the disk used to store the channel cannot be restored. Using a Kafka channel will use more network than the other channels, but data will be persisted in a Kafka cluster and therefore cannot be lost. Kafka will store the information mainly in memory before returning to Flume, which will reduce the disk's latency impact on the application. Also, in case the source provides events way faster than what the sink can handle, a Kafka cluster can scale bigger than a single disk channel and will allow to store more of the backlogs to be processed later when the source will slow down. In our use case, we are storing healthcare information, and we cannot afford to lose any data. For this reason, we will use a Kafka queue as our Flume channel.

The channel configuration is similar to the source configuration:

```
ingest.channels = ingestKafkaChannel
ingest.channels.ingestKafkaChannel.type = org.a.f.channel.kafka
ingest.channels.ingestKafkaChannel.brokerList = localhost:9092
ingest.channels.ingestKafkaChannel.topic = flumechannel
ingest.channels.ingestKafkaChannel.zookeeperConnect = localhost:2181/kafka
```

This tells our ingest agent to use a channel called `ingestKafkaChannel` backed by Kafka.

Flume HBase sink

The goal of the Flume sink is to take events from the channel and store them downstream. Here, we are looking at HBase as the storage platform. Therefore, we will configure an HBase Flume sink. Flume comes with a few default serializers to push the data into HBase. The goal of a serializer is to transform a Flume event into an HBase event (and nothing else). However, even if they can be used most of the time, those serializers don't give you full control over the row key and the column names. We will have to implement our own serializer to be able to extract our row key from our Avro object.

The sink configuration can be done using the following:

```
ingest.sinks = ingestHBaseSink
ingest.sinks.ingestHBaseSink.type = hbase
ingest.sinks.ingestHBaseSink.table = documents
ingest.sinks.ingestHBaseSink.columnFamily = c
ingest.sinks.ingestHBaseSink.serializer = \
    com.architecting.ch09.DocumentSerializer
ingest.sinks.ingestHBaseSink.channel = ingestKafkaChannel
```

Interceptor

A Flume interceptor is a piece of code that can update a Flume event before it is sent to the sink or dropped.

In our case, we want to transform our XML source into an Avro object and perform some HBase lookups to enrich the event before sending it back to HBase. Indeed, if the first name or the last name is missing, we need to perform a lookup into HBase for already existing events to see if it is possible to enrich the current event with the information.

The interceptor is where this transformation and this enrichment takes place. This process should be executed as fast as possible to the table to return the event to Flume very quickly. Taking too much time or performing too much processing in the interceptor will result in Flume processing events performing slower than when they arrived and might end up overwhelming the channel queue.

The interceptor is configured similarly to what has been done for the source, the sink, and the channel:

```
ingest.sources.ingestKafkaSource.interceptors = ingestInterceptor
ingest.sources.ingestKafkaSource.interceptors.ingestInterceptor.type = \
                        com.architecting.ch09.DocumentInterceptor$Builder
```

Instead of building your own XmlToAvro interceptors, it is possible to apply the transformation using the Morphlines interceptor. However, for simplicity, to be able to update HBase records and to not have to go over all the Morphlines details, we chose to implement our own Java interceptor.

Conversion. The first step of the interceptor is to convert the event into an Avro object. Like in the previous chapter, we will need to define an Avro schema:

```
{"namespace": "com.architecting.ch09",
 "type": "record",
 "name": "Document",
 "fields": [
     {"name": "sin", "type": "long"},
     {"name": "firstName", "type": "string"},
     {"name": "lastName", "type": "string"},
     {"name": "comment", "type": "string"}
 ]
}
```

The related Java class is also generated the same way:

```
java -jar ~/ahae/lib/avro-tools-1.7.7.jar compile schema\
                            ~/ahae/resources/ch09/document.avsc ~/ahae/src/
```

Code similar to what has been done in the previous chapter will be used to serialize and de-serialize the Avro object. We will use the XPath method to parse the XML document to populate the Avro object. The code in Example 9-1, extracted from the complete example available on the GitHub repository, shows you how to extract those XML fields.

Example 9-1. XML extraction

```
expression = "/ClinicalDocument/PatientRecord/FirstName";
nodes = getNodes(xpath, expression, inputSource);
if (nodes.getLength() > 0) firstName = nodes.item(0).getTextContent();

expression = "/ClinicalDocument/PatientRecord/LastName";
inputAsInputStream.reset();
nodes = getNodes(xpath, expression, inputSource);
if (nodes.getLength() > 0) lastName = nodes.item(0).getTextContent();

expression = "/ClinicalDocument/PatientRecord/SIN";
inputAsInputStream.reset();
nodes = getNodes(xpath, expression, inputSource);
if (nodes.getLength() > 0) SIN =
    Long.parseLong(nodes.item(0).getTextContent());

expression = "/ClinicalDocument/MedicalRecord/Comments";
inputAsInputStream.reset();
```

```
nodes = getNodes(xpath, expression, inputSource);
if (nodes.getLength() > 0) comment = nodes.item(0).getTextContent();
```

Lookup. The second step of the interceptor is to inspect the last name and first name fields to validate that they contain the required information, and if not, to perform an HBase lookup to try to find this information. HBase might contain many records without the customer information before we find one with it. Reading all those records will consume time and resources, and will have to be performed for all the received records where this is missing. Because we want to keep all the interceptor operations as fast as possible, if the record with information we found is not the first record in HBase, we will also update the first record to get faster lookups for subsequent calls.

If the diagram in Figure 9-4 represents the data for the key 12345, because documents 1 to 4 don't have any first or last name information, when document 6 is received from Flume again without any last name and first name, the interceptor will perform an HBase lookup, scan the row to read the columns one by one, and will find the required information from document 5 only. It will then have to update document 1 to make sure that next insertions for the same row will not have to look up all the documents from 1 to 5 to find the first and last name but will find it right from the first entry.

Key:12345	Last: First: Comment:D1	Last: First: Comment:D2	Last: First: Comment:D3	Last: First: Comment:D4	Last: O'Dell First: Scottie Comment:D5

Figure 9-4. Backward update of previously inserted documents

Doing a put into HBase from a Flume interceptor is a side effect of the operation. This is something we want to avoid. Because we already have a sink for the HBase table we want to update, why don't we simply output two events from the Flume interceptor (one for the updated cell, and another for the newly inserted cell)? Flume doesn't allow this. On a Flume interceptor, you should output the exact same number of events you received, or less, but never more. However, on the serializer side, it is possible to generate two puts for the same row from one received event. Therefore, on the interceptor side, if an additional column needs to be updated for a given row, we are going to add the related information into the Flume event header. This information will be transfered to the Flume serializer in charge to build the put for the actual event. Based on this information, the serializer will generate an additional put for the same row, which will update the required cell.

Figure 9-5 shows the order of the operations.

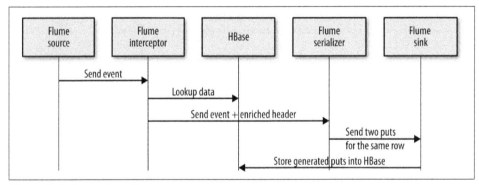

Figure 9-5. Operations flow

After all those operations, the data should now look as shown in Figure 9-6.

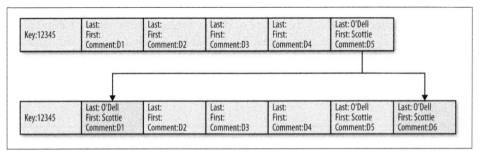

Figure 9-6. Interceptor result

Depending on your use case, this might not be optimal. Indeed, to avoid lookups, the first and last name fields might have been extracted and inserted into their own cell. However, we still did it that way for a few reasons. First, this allows us to illustrate how to correctly use the interceptor and the serializer to communicate with HBase for lookups and generate multiple HBase puts from a single Flume event. Second, combining the first and last name into the same cell as the other fields allows you at the read time to get everything in a single call, instead of having to perform a get for the document and then another get for the personal information. Third, we are here looking up the first and last name, but you might also be able to look up a doctor name (or any information about the clinic, a prescription, etc.) from the ID, and enrich the document itself again to not have to perform this lookup at the read time. Thus, in order to provide you with the most diverse and complete examples possible, we decided to still go with this table design.

Example 9-2 shows how to perform those different operations into the Flume interceptor.

Example 9-2. HBase lookup

```java
byte[] rowKeyBytes =
    Bytes.add(DigestUtils.md5("" + SIN), Bytes.toBytes((int) SIN));
if (StringUtils.isBlank(firstName) || StringUtils.isBlank(lastName)) {
  LOG.info("Some personal information is missing. Lookup required");
  Table documentsTable = connection.getTable(tableName); ❶
  Get get = new Get(rowKeyBytes);
  Result result = documentsTable.get(get); ❷
  if (!result.isEmpty()) {
    result.advance();
    Cell firstCell = result.current();
    Cell currentCell = firstCell;
    while (true) {
      document = cellToAvro(currentCell, document);
      if (document.getFirstName() != null) firstName =
          document.getFirstName().toString();
      if (document.getLastName() != null) lastName =
          document.getLastName().toString();
      if ((!"".equals(firstName) && !"".equals(lastName))
          || (!result.advance())) break; ❸
      currentCell = result.current();
    }
    if ((firstCell != currentCell) && StringUtils.isNotBlank(lastName)
        && StringUtils.isNotBlank(firstName)) { ❹
      LOG.info("Need to update first cell. Updating headers.");
      document = cellToAvro(firstCell, document);
      document.setFirstName(firstName);
      document.setLastName(lastName);
      byte[] qualifier =
          Bytes.copy(firstCell.getQualifierArray(),
            firstCell.getQualifierOffset(), firstCell.getQualifierLength());
      Map<String, String> headers = event.getHeaders();
      headers.put(COLUMN, Base64.encodeBytes(qualifier));
      headers.put(PAYLOAD, Base64.encodeBytes(avroToBytes(document))); ❺
    }
  }
}
```

❶ To improve performances, it is important to reuse a single connection to retrieve the table.

❷ Get the current customer row and prepare to iterate across all its documents.

❸ Iterate until we found both customer last and first names.

❹ If we found the information we were looking for and it is not coming from the first cell of the row, update the first cell to make subsequent requests faster.

❺ We have decided to give the entire document into the header. Doing that will allow us to not have to lookup the table again on the serializer side but just directly create the related Put object. You might want to avoid doing that if your documents are too big.

The last part of the code, shown in Example 9-3, is to make sure modified information is applied back to the Avro object, which will be serialized and sent back to Flume.

Example 9-3. Avro enrichment

```
document.setFirstName(firstName);
document.setLastName(lastName);
document.setSin(SIN);
document.setComment(comment);
```

 All those classes are going to be run by the Flume agent. Therefore, it is important for Flume to have access to the project JAR. Flume has a *plugin.d* directory where each project should create its own subdirectories with a specific structure. The Flume documentation (*http://bit.ly/291yptc*) provides more details about how this directory is structured.

Build those classes using Maven the same way you are building the other examples (using Eclipse or the command line) and copy the generated JAR into the Flume plugin directory. To simplify the process for the examples, we will just give everyone access to this directory (in a production environment, you should make sure that only required people have access to it):

```
sudo mkdir -p /var/lib/flume-ng/plugins.d/ahae/lib
sudo chmod a+rwx /var/lib/flume-ng/plugins.d/ahae/lib
cp ~/ahae/target/ahae.jar /var/lib/flume-ng/plugins.d/ahae/lib/
```

You will need to restart Flume for this JAR to be taken into consideration by the application. You will also have to restart the Flume agent each time you deploy a new version of your JAR.

Serializer

A Flume serializer is a class that given a Flume event, serializes the required output for a given sink. In our example, we will need to build an HBase Flume serializer. This serializer will receive our Avro objects generated by the interceptor plus the required headers, and will transform that into one HBase Put operation. Depending on what we will receive on the headers, our single put operations might impact one or two columns.

An HBase Flume serializer has to implement the *org.apache.flume.sink.hbase.HbaseEventSerializer* interface. This interface requires the methods shown in Example 9-4 to be implemented.

Example 9-4. Flume HBase serializer interface

```
/**
 * Initialize the event serializer.
 * @param Event to be written to HBase.
 */
public void initialize(Event event, byte[] columnFamily);

/**
 * Get the actions that should be written out to HBase as a result of this
 * event. This list is written to HBase using the HBase batch API.
 * @return List of {@link org.apache.hadoop.hbase.client.Row} which
 * are written as such to HBase.
 *
 * 0.92 increments do not implement Row, so this is not generic.
 *
 */
public List<Row> getActions();

public List<Increment> getIncrements();
/*
 * Clean up any state. This will be called when the sink is being stopped.
 */
public void close();
```

In our case, we will implement the `initialize` method and the `getActions`. We will not have anything specific to do on the `close` method, and because we do not need nor want to count our events, the `getIncrements` will stay empty, too.

Example 9-5 shows our serializer code.

Example 9-5. XML to HBase Flume serializer

```
@Override
public void initialize(Event event, byte[] cf) {
  if (LOG.isDebugEnabled()) LOG.debug("Performing initialization for a "
      + event.getBody().length + " bytes event");
  else LOG.info("Performing initialization for an event");
  this.payload = event.getBody(); ❶
  this.cf = cf;
  this.headers = event.getHeaders();
  reader = new SpecificDatumReader<Document>(Document.class);
}

@Override
public List<Row> getActions() throws FlumeException {
```

```
if (LOG.isInfoEnabled()) LOG.info("Retrieving actions.");
List<Row> actions = new LinkedList<Row>();
try {
  decoder = DecoderFactory.get().binaryDecoder(payload, decoder);
  document = reader.read(document, decoder); ❷
  byte[] rowKeyBytes =
      Bytes.add(DigestUtils.md5("" + document.getSin()),
        Bytes.toBytes(document.getSin().intValue()));
  LOG.info("SIN = " + document.getSin());
  LOG.info("rowKey = " + Bytes.toStringBinary(rowKeyBytes));
  Put put = new Put(rowKeyBytes);
  put.addColumn(cf, Bytes.toBytes(System.currentTimeMillis()), payload); ❸
  actions.add(put);
  String firstCellColumn;
  if ((firstCellColumn = headers.get(COLUMN)) != null) {
    String payload = headers.get(PAYLOAD);
    put.addColumn(cf, Base64.decode(firstCellColumn), Base64.decode(payload)); ❹
    LOG.info("Updating first cell "
        + Bytes.toStringBinary(Base64.decode(firstCellColumn)));
  }
} catch (Exception e) {
  LOG.error("Unable to serialize flume event to HBase action!", e);
  throw new FlumeException("Unable to serialize flume event to HBase action!",
      e);
}
return actions;
}
```

❶ Store the payload, the column family name, and the headers to reuse them later.

❷ Construct the document Avro object from the received payload.

❸ Create the required HBase Put object to be sent to the table.

❹ If required, add a second column of the existing Put object to overwrite the first cell with updated information.

At the end of the interceptor and serializer steps, the Flume HBase sink will receive the generated put from the serializer and will apply it against the configured table. All the steps up to this point can be run individually. You do not need to have the Lily Indexer nor the Solr service running. If you try them, you should be able to see your generated data in the input Kafka queue, your intermediate data into the Flume channel Kafka queue, and your transformed data into your HBase table, which you will need to created.

The following commands will help you to figure what has been created where.

First, to perform a lookup into the Kafka topic used as a source for the entire process, use the following command:

```
kafka-console-consumer --zookeeper localhost/kafka --topic ingest \
                        --from-beginning
```

This should show you all the events that you have inserted into the topic to be picked up by Flume. To start and to simplify the debugging, make sure to insert only few events.

If the Flume agent is running and the Flume source is correctly configured, you should also see all those events being picked up and inserted into the Flume Kafka channel topic. To inspect this specific topic, use the following command:

```
kafka-console-consumer --zookeeper localhost/kafka --topic flumechannel\
                        --from-beginning
```

If everything is working correctly, the content of this topic should be the same as the content of the ingest topic, and therefore the output of the two commands should be the same. At this point, you confirmed that both your Kafka service and your Flume service are running correctly. The next step is to validate that the interceptor and the serializer are working fine, too. Because the Flume sink is the HBase sink, the result of our operations should be visible in HBase. Performing the following scan in the HBase shell against the previously created table should show you as many cells as there was events in the ingest Kafka topic:

```
hbase(main):001:0> scan 'documents'
```

 If you have inserted millions of events into your Kafka input topic, there will be millions of entries in the two topics as well as millions of lines into HBase. If this is the case, make sure to use the LIMIT keyword of the HBase scan and use | more or | less in conjunction with the kafka-console-consumer commands.

The *produce.sh* file into the *resources/ch09/* folder will produce five events (four without last name and first name, and one with the first and last name). At the end of the process, you should see into HBase the first cell being updated, the fourth event being populated with its own first and last name, and the fifth event being enriched with the last name and first name for the other events.

There are different places where those steps might fail. If you do not see your data in the ingest topic, check the logs and the code of your data generation steps, and try to push some data from the command line. If you do not see your data in the flumechannel topic, your Flume agent might not be running or it might be incorrectly configured. Check the logs of your Flume agent and its configuration. If you do not see your data in the HBase table, there might be an issue with your interceptor or your `serializer` code. Check the logs of your Flume agent and your Java code, and make sure it has been deployed and is accessible for Flume.

HBase

Even if HBase is probably the most important part of this design, its implementation is the smallest one. Indeed, even if everything here is related to HBase, there is not any specific HBase code required. There are two things we will have to look into on the HBase side.

Table design

As usual, the first and most important one is the table and key design. As we said previously, to have a very good distribution of our keys, we are going to use an MD5 hash of the social insurance number as a prefix, followed by the number itself. An MD5 hash is represented by a byte array, values of those bytes being anything between 0 of 255. This information is what we need to correctly presplit the table and choose the correct logic to calculate the split points. Because we are going to generate binary keys, we will make use of the `UniformSplit` algorithm here. The number of regions we will create depends on the size of the cluster and on the size of the dataset we expect to have. For our example, we will create an eight-region table called `documents` with a single column family called `c`:

```
create 'documents', { NUMREGIONS => 8, SPLITALGO => 'UniformSplit' }, \
                     { NAME => 'c' }
```

Presplitting Tables

As we have suggested many times, it is always recommended to presplit your table into multiple regions. This is to avoid hotspotting a RegionServer at the time of the ingestion, and will help by reducing huge region splits and compactions. However, how many regions is a good number to start with? There are two good numbers to start with. The first is based on the expected size of your table after it is fully loaded. If the ingestion will occur over a long period (say, a few months), consider the size after a few weeks. You want to make sure you have at least 1 GB per region.

Therefore, on a 20-RegionServer cluster, if you expect your table to be only 15 GB after a month, only create 15 splits to start. The second number is based on the number of RegionServers you have. As your data becomes more distributed, the reads and writes will become more efficient. Again, on the same 20-RegionServer clusters, you would like to have, for a specific table, at least twice the number of regions as you have RegionServers. If your cluster hosts only very few tables (two or three), you might want to have at least four regions per table. However, make sure to always respect the first recommendation, which is to have at least 1 GB regions.

As another example, if you have a 30 GB table on a 20-RegionServer cluster, based on the number of RegionServers, you will want to have 40 regions for your table. But this will create regions under 1 GB, which we want to avoid. Therefore, we will use the size as our splitting factor and will presplit this table in 30 regions only.

Table parameters

The second most important part of the HBase design is the table parameters. Indeed, as we have already seen, there are many different values and parameters we can adjust on a table. First, we want to activate the compression for XML. Since XML is text based, it normally compresses quite well. Also, because the SLA regarding the read latency for this project is high (documents needs to be returned within one second), we will choose a compression algorithm that will provide a better compression ratio than the others.

To activate the compaction for this table column family, use the following command:

```
alter 'documents', { NAME => 'c', COMPRESSION => 'GZ' }
```

In addition to the compression, we want to disable the Bloom filters. All the reads done into the HBase table will be base on the key returned by Solr. Therefore, they will all always succeed. Bloom filters might still be useful if there are many files within a single region; however, major compactions being scheduled daily at night, most of the regions will have only a single file, and the Bloom filters are going to be an overhead.

If you are not sure about using Bloom filters or not, it's better to keep them activated. There are very few use cases for which it is advisable to disable them. If your reads always succeed (e.g., in cases when they are looked up from an external index) or if there is only one file (or very few files) per region, then Bloom filters can be disabled. However, for all other use cases, Bloom filters will help to skip reading some files and will improve the read latency.

To disable the Bloom filters, use the following command:

```
alter 'documents', { NAME => 'c', BLOOMFILTER => 'NONE' }
```

This example will also work very well if you keep Bloom filters activated and compression disabled.

At the end, your HBase table should look like this:

```
hbase(main):021:0> describe 'documents'
Table documents is ENABLED
documents
COLUMN FAMILIES DESCRIPTION
{NAME => 'c', DATA_BLOCK_ENCODING => 'NONE', BLOOMFILTER => 'NONE',
REPLICATION_SCOPE => '0', VERSIONS => '1', COMPRESSION => 'GZ',
MIN_VERSIONS => '0', TTL => 'FOREVER', KEEP_DELETED_CELLS => 'FALSE',
BLOCKSIZE => '65536', IN_MEMORY => 'false', BLOCKCACHE => 'true'}
1 row(s) in 0.0290 seconds
```

Java implementation

It is also possible to perform the same table create using the Java API. This might be useful if you want to keep track of how your table has been created in a version control system. Example 9-6 shows how to create a table with a single column family, the required splits and the parameters configured as we did previously using the shell.

Example 9-6. Java table creation code

```
TableName documents = TableName.valueOf("documents");
HTableDescriptor desc = new HTableDescriptor(documents);
HColumnDescriptor family = new HColumnDescriptor("c");
family.setCompressionType(Algorithm.GZ);
family.setBloomFilterType(BloomType.NONE);
desc.addFamily(family);
UniformSplit uniformSplit = new UniformSplit();
admin.createTable(desc, uniformSplit.split(8));
```

Lily

Configuring Lily is quite easy. The only thing we have to give it is a Morphlines script to describe what to do with the HBase cell and where to push it:

```
SOLR_LOCATOR : {
  # Name of solr collection
  collection : DocumentCollection

  # ZooKeeper ensemble
  zkHost : "$ZK_HOST"
}


morphlines : [
{
  id : morphline
  importCommands : ["org.kitesdk.**", "com.ngdata.**"]

  commands : [
    { logInfo{ format : "Getting something from HBase: {}", args : ["@{}"] } }
```

```
{
  extractHBaseCells {
    mappings : [
    {
      inputColumn : "c:*"
      outputField : "_attachment_body"
      type : "byte[]"
      source : value
    }
    {
      inputColumn : "c:*"
      outputField : "documentId"
      type : "string"
      source : qualifier
    }]
  }
}
{ logInfo{ format : "Reading Avro schema: {}", args : ["@{}"] } }
{
  readAvro {
    writerSchemaFile : /home/cloudera/ahae/resources/ch09/document.avsc
  }
}
{ logInfo{ format : "Extracting Avro paths: {}", args : ["@{}"] } }
{
  extractAvroPaths {
    paths : {
      sin : /sin
      firstName : /firstName
      lastName : /lastName
      comment : /comment
    }
  }
}

{ logInfo{ format : "output record: {}", args : ["@{}"] } }
{
  sanitizeUnknownSolrFields
  {
    solrLocator : ${SOLR_LOCATOR}
  }
}
    ]
  }
]
```

This says to Lily that we want to extract the column qualifier and store it into the documentId field, then extract the cell content as an Avro object and extract the specific fields we wish to replicate.

We also need an XML file to configure the indexer. This file will be given as a parameter to the command line. It defines what kind of mapper we want to use and provides some parameters for this mapper:

```
<?xml version="1.0"?>
<indexer table="documents"
 mapper="com.ngdata.hbaseindexer.morphline.MorphlineResultToSolrMapper"
 mapping-type="column" row-field="rowkey">

<!-- The relative or absolute path on the local file system to the morphline -->
<!-- configuration file. Use relative path "morphlines.conf" for morphlines  -->
<!-- managed by Cloudera Manager -->
<param name="morphlineFile" value="morphlines.conf"/>

</indexer>
```

The XML will configure Lily to use the MorphlineResultToSolrMapper. It will also configure this mapper to process the HBase cells at the column lever (instead of the default row-level mode). Last, it will also configure Lily to provide the HBase row key into the rowkey field. More information regarding the XML file content is available on the NGData GitHub page.[2]

The last step is to enable to the indexer using the following command:

```
hbase-indexer add-indexer --name myIndexer --indexer-conf indexer-config.xml \
                          --connection-param solr.zk=quickstart/solr \
            --connection-param solr.collection=DocumentCollection \
            --zookeeper localhost:2181
```

If you want to disable and remove the indexer (because you want to try another one or if something goes wrong with the configuration), use the following command:

```
hbase-indexer delete-indexer --name myIndexer
```

After this step, Lily will create a Solr document for each cell inserted into HBase by Flume. However, because Solr is not yet configured, this will probably fail. Continue to the next section to configure Solr and test Lily.

Solr

The implementation part of Solr is straightforward. We simply need to create a Solr collection based on the schema that we have defined previously. To do so, we will follow the exact same steps described in Chapter 7.

To create the collection, use the following commands:

```
export PROJECT_HOME=~/ahae/resources/ch09/search
rm -rf $PROJECT_HOME
```

---

2 *https://github.com/NGDATA/hbase-indexer/wiki/Indexer-configuration*

```
solrctl instancedir --generate $PROJECT_HOME
mv $PROJECT_HOME/conf/schema.xml $PROJECT_HOME/conf/schema.old
cp $PROJECT_HOME/../schema.xml $PROJECT_HOME/conf/
solrctl instancedir --create DocumentCollection $PROJECT_HOME
solrctl collection --create DocumentCollection -s 1
```

When this is done, the collection should be visible on the web UI: *http://quick-start.cloudera:8983/solr/#/DocumentCollection_shard1_replica1*

Testing

Now that all the parts are installed and implemented, any data inserted into the Kafka queue should be visible in both HBase and Solr. A Solr query such as the following should return all the records indexed by Solr: *http://quickstart.cloudera:8983/solr/DocumentCollection_shard1_replica1/select?q=%3A&wt=json&indent=true*. All those records should also be into HBase and can be viewed using the shell.

Inserting this XML:

```
<?xml version=\"1.0\" encoding=\"UTF-8\"?>
<ClinicalDocument>
  <PatientRecord>
    <SIN>12345</SIN>
    <FirstName>Scottie</FirstName>
    <LastName>O'Dell</LastName>
  </PatientRecord>
  <MedicalRecord>
    <Comments>Scottie is doing well.</Comments>
  </MedicalRecord>
</ClinicalDocument>
```

Will produce this entry in HBase:

```
hbase(main):002:0> get 'documents', '827c12345'
COLUMN              CELL
c:1448998062581 timestamp=1448998062683
                value=\xF2\xC0\x01\x0EScottie\x0C0'Dell6Scottie is doing well.
1 row(s) in 0.0290 seconds
```

And this output in Solr:[3]

```
{
  "responseHeader":{
    "status":0,
    "QTime":0,
    "params":{
      "indent":"true",
      "q":"rowkey: \"827c12345\"",
```

---

3 *http://quickstart.cloudera:8983/solr/DocumentCollection_shard1_replica1/select?q=rowkey%3A+%22827c12345%22&wt=json&indent=true*

```
        "wt":"json"}},
    "response":{"numFound":1,"start":0,"docs":[
        {
            "id":"827c12345-c-1448998450634",
            "lastName":"O'Dell",
            "rowkey":"827c12345",
            "firstName":"Scottie",
            "documentId":"1448998450634",
            "_version_":1519384999917256704}]
}}
```

You can now query Solr by any of the indexed fields, and using the returned information, query HBase given a specific row and a specific column qualifier to get a direct, low-latency random access to the record.

Going Further

If you want to extend the examples presented in this chapter, the following list offers some options you can try based on our discussions from this chapter:

Bigger input file

Here again we tried our workflow by ingesting one document at a time and only a few. Try to ingest way more documents. Also try to ingest documents with very big fields. When producing documents bigger than one MB, you can also even try the HBase MOB features.

Extract patient record

Extract the patient name from the document and store it separately in a specific column. Modify the lookup to populate only this column and only if information is missing. Then, instead of storing the Avro object inside of HBase, only store the comment field.

Duplicate flows

Produce two kinds of documents in two different topics and two Flume agents. Merge those two streams into a single HBase table and a single Solr index.

Row key

The row key for a new document is calculated twice (once in the interceptor, and once in the serializer). Using the event header, store, transfer, and reuse this information.

Change Solr schema

To make things easier, in the current schema, we store, index, and return the row key. However, the Solr document ID (stored in the ID field) already contains the row key as well as the column family and the column qualifier. Update the Solr schema to only index the row key and the document ID but not store them.

## CHAPTER 10

Use Case: HBase as a Master Data Management Tool

Next, we will take a look at the New York–based digital advertising company Collective. Collective is an advertising technology company that helps companies impact the bottom line by connecting brands and customers together. This approach is known as customer 360, and to execute efficiently, it requires numerous data sources and boatloads of data. Collective leverages Hadoop and HBase to help offer their clients a unified view of the consumer and allowing brands to seamlessly message across channels and devices, including PCs, tablets, and smartphones.

When looking at customer 360, Hadoop is the obvious choice. A solid customer 360 implementation gets better and better as data sources are added. Most data sources that customers interact with on a regular basis tend to create unstructured data. Some of the typical data sources seen in a customer 360 are clickstream through offerings like Adobe Omniture or IBM Tealeaf and social media data either directly through Twitter and Facebook, or more often, from curated data services providers such as Gnip and Datasift; these data sources are then joined with the all-powerful (and homegrown) customer profile. Maintaing an up-to-date, complete customer profile on an immutable filesystem like HDFS is not a trival task. Collective needed a system that could combine these numerous data sources, which fit poorly into a relational system, into a unified customer—and that's where HBase comes in.

At first, Collective tried a couple standalone relational systems and was attempting to push the data from the Hadoop ETL jobs. The company started to run into problems of serving the data to end users when the cache on a node or two became full. This caused the disks to start thrashing, and would require a major hardware overhaul to handle the data in a traditional manner. Most of these relational systems require vertical scalability as opposed to horizontal scalability. These relational systems typically require more memory and leverage expensive solid-state drives (SSDs). On the flip side, HBase utilizes commodity hardware and SATA drives. This is what led Collective to start looking at HBase. Luckily, Collective already had a Hadoop cluster in play, and had the advantage of seamlessly integrating HBase into the existing infrastructure with minor development and cost overhead.

Collective currently has 60 RegionServers deployed serving 21 TBs of data out of HBase alone. Collective's HBase deployment is pretty straightforward. For this use case, there is a single table that handles the user profile data. The table is broken into three column families consisting of visitor, export, and edge. The "visitor" CF contains the metadata about the user. This will consist of information such as date of birth, behavior information, and any third-party lookup IDs. The "export" CF contains the segment information (an example of a segment would be male, 25 years old, likes cars), and any relevant downstream syndication information needed for processing. The "edge" CF contains the activity information of the user, along with any of the additional data that may come in from the batch imported data:

```
COLUMN CELL

edge:batchimport ts=1391769526303, value=\x00\x00\x01D\x0B\xA3\xE4.
export:association:cp ts=1390163166328, value=6394889946637904578
export:segment:13051 ts=1390285574680, value=\x00\x00\x00\x00\x00\x00\x00\x00
export:segment:13052 ts=1390285574680, value=\x00\x00\x00\x00\x00\x00\x00\x00
export:segment:13059 ts=1390285574680, value=\x00\x00\x00\x00\x00\x00\x00\x00
...
visitor:ad_serving_count ts=1390371783593, value=\x00\x00\x00\x00\x00\x00\x1A
visitor:behavior:cm.9256:201401 ts=1390163166328, value=\x00\x00\x00\x0219
visitor:behavior:cm.9416:201401 ts=1390159723536, value=\x00\x00\x00\x0119
visitor:behavior:iblocal.9559:2 ts=1390295246778, value=\x00\x00\x00\x020140120
visitor:behavior:iblocal.9560:2 ts=1390296907500, value=\x00\x00\x00\x020140120
visitor:birthdate ts=1390159723536, value=\x00\x00\x01C\xAB\xD7\xC4(
visitor:retarget_count ts=1390296907500, value=\x00\x00\x00\x00\x00\x00\x00\x07
```

As already mentioned, Collective is a digital advertising company that enhances offers and profiles through consumer interactions. Each user is tracked through a custom cookie ID that is generated upstream in the process. The row key is a reverse of that cookie ID. This begs the question of why to reverse a generated UUID. There are two primary offenders that require reverse keys: websites and time series data. In this case, the beginning of the cookie ID has the timestamp on it. This would lead to monotonically increasing row keys; by simply reversing the row key, the randomly generated portion now occurs first in the row key.

Ingest

In Chapters 8 and 9, we looked at near real-time ingest pipelines and batch loading processes. Next, we are going to look at combining the two while using HBase as the system of record, which is sometimes referred to as master data management

---

(MDM); a system of record is used as the "golden copy" of the data. The records contained in HBase will be used to rebuild any Hive or other external data sources in the event of bad or wrong data. The first piece we will examine is batch processing. For this system, Collective built a tool that pulls in third-party data sources from numerous data sources covering S3, SFTP sites, and a few proprietary APIs (Figure 10-1). The tool pulls from these data sources on an hourly basis and loads the data into a new HDFS directory using the Parquet file format. A new Hive partition is then created on top of the newly loaded data, and then linked to the existing archive table.

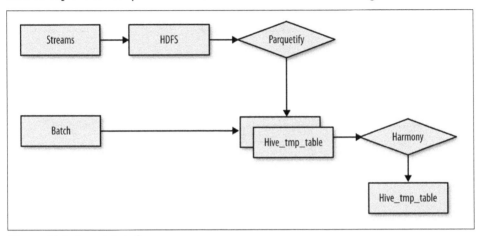

Figure 10-1. Ingest dataflow

The other side of the house is the near real-time processing, which is currently being handled by Flume. Flume brings in data from different messaging services, which is pushed into a system known as Parquetify. The Parquetify system, which runs hourly, prepares the data into a unified file format, wraps a temporary table around the data, and then inserts the data into the main archive Hive tables. In this case, the file format used for this data is Parquet files. Once the data is loaded into the system, the aptly named preprocessor Harmony is run every hour in a custom workflow from Celos (*https://github.com/collectivemedia/celos*). Harmony collects and preprocesses the necessary data from the previously listed sources. This is used to normalize the output together for the formal transformation stages. Currently this runs in a series of Flume dataflows, MapReduce jobs, and Hive jobs. Collective is in the process of porting all of this to Kafka and Spark, which will make processing both easier and faster.

Processing

Once Harmony has joined the inbound data together, it is then sent for final processing into another internal system that coordinates a series of MapReduce jobs together known as Pythia (Figure 10-2). The MapReduce jobs create a write-ahead log (WAL) for maintaining data consistency in case of failures. There are three total steps in this process:

- Aggregator
- ProfileMod
- Update MDM system

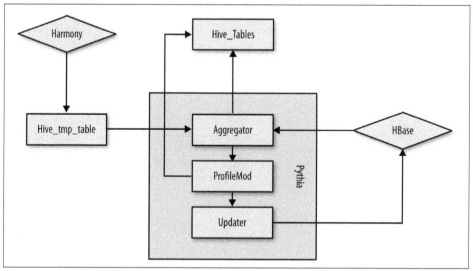

Figure 10-2. Processing dataflow

Both the Aggregator and ProfileMod steps in the pipeline also represent backed and partitioned Hive/Impala tables. The first thing done is to read the output of the Harmony job into an Avro file for our Aggregator job. Once new edits (Harmony) and previous hour of data (HDFS) are read and grouped in the mapper, they are passed to the reducer. During the Reduce phase, numerous HBase calls are made to join the full profile together for the next hourly partition. The reducer will pull the full HBase record for each record that has an existing profile. The Aggregator job then outputs a set of differences (typically known as diffs) that is applied during the ProfileMod stage. These diffs are used as a sort of WAL that can be used to rectify the changes if any of the upstream jobs fail.

Next, the ProfileMod job is executed. ProfileMod will be a Map job because we already extracted the data we needed from HBase in the reducer from the Aggregator flow. The mapper will read all of the data from the previous output and rectify the diffs. Once the diffs are all combined together, ProfileMod will use these as the actual diffs that need to be written back to HBase. The final output of this job is a new hourly partition in the ProfileMod Hive table.

Finally, the MDM system of record (HBase) needs to get updated. The final step is another MapReduce job. This job (the Updater) reads the output of the profile mode data and then builds the correct HBase row keys based off the data. The reducer then updates the existing rows with the new data to be used in the next job. Figure 10-3 shows the complete dataflow from the different inputs (stream and bach) up to the destination Hive table.

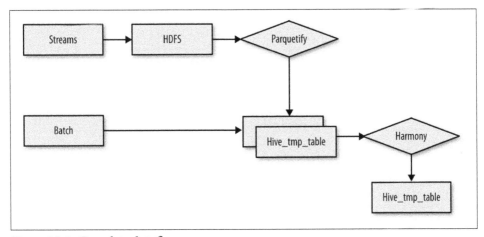

Figure 10-3. Complete dataflow

## CHAPTER 11

Implementation of HBase as a Master Data Management Tool

In Chapter 10, we reviewed the implementation of a customer 360 solution. In addition to HBase, it uses several different applications, including MapReduce and Hive. On the HBase side, we described how MapReduce is used to do lookups or to generate HBase files. In addition, as discussed in the previous chapter, Collective plans to improve its architecture by using Kafka. None of this should be new for you, as we covered it in detail in previous chapters. However, Collective is also planning to use Spark, and this is where things start to be interesting. Indeed, over the last several years, when applications needed to process HBase data, they have usually used MapReduce or the Java API. However, with Spark becoming more and more popular, we are seeing people starting to implement solutions using Spark on top of HBase.

Because we already covered Kafka, MapReduce, and the Java API in previous chapters, instead of going over all those technologies again to provide you with very similar examples, we will here focus on Spark over HBase. The example we are going to implement will still put the customer 360 description in action, but as for the other implementation examples, this can be reused for any other use case.

MapReduce Versus Spark

Before we continue, we should establish the pros and cons of using Spark versus using MapReduce. Although we will not provide a lengthy discussion on this topic, we will briefly highlight some points for you to consider as you narrow down your choice.

Spark is a recent technology, while MapReduce has been used for years. Although Spark has been proven to be stable, you might be more comfortable with a technology deployed in hundreds of thousands of production applications—if so, you should build your project around MapReduce. On the other hand, if you prefer to rely on recent technologies, then Spark will be a good fit.

For companies with good MapReduce knowledge that already have many MapReduce projects deployed, it might be easier, faster, and cheaper to stay with something they know well. However, if they start a brand-new project and are planning many projects, they might want to consider Spark.

Some use cases require fast and efficient data processing. MapReduce comes with a big overhead. It gives you reliability and many other benefits, but at the price of a performance hit. If your use case has tight SLAs, you might want to consider Spark. Otherwise, MapReduce is still a good option.

One last consideration is the development language. Spark is compatible with both Java and Scala code, while MapReduce is mostly for Java developers.

So which one should you choose? If you are still deciding between the two, we recommend trying Spark, as it has nice benefits over MapReduce.

Get Spark Interacting with HBase

As with MapReduce, there are two main ways for Spark to interact with HBase. The first is to run a Spark application on top of an HBase table. The second is to interact with HBase while running Spark on other data. We will assume that you have at least basic spark knowledge. Refer to the Spark website (*http://spark.apache.org/*) for more information.

Run Spark over an HBase Table

When we are running a MapReduce job on top of an HBase table, each mapper process a single region. You can also run a simple Java application that will scan the entire HBase table. This will be very similar with Spark. The HBase Spark API can return you an RDD representing your entire HBase table. But you partition this RDD to get it processed over multiple executors where each of them will process a single region

Calling HBase from Spark

The HBase Java API is accessible from the Spark code. Therefore, you can perform lookups like what we did when implementing our Flume interceptor. You can also use Spark to enrich and store data into HBase leveraging Puts and Increments. Last, the same way you can use MapReduce to generate HFiles for BulkLoads, you can use Spark to generate the same kind of files that you will later BulkLoad into HBase.

Implementing Spark with HBase

To illustrate using Spark with HBase, we will begin by implementing a Spark job to process a text file where each line is a record that we will use to enrich HBase data. Later, we will process another source of data that we will use to create HFiles to Bulk-Load into HBase tables. Finally, we will implement a Spark job over the same HBase table to perform data aggregation.

 You might find different versions of the Spark HBase API. The one we will use here is extracted from the Apache HBase 2.0 project. If you are using another version of the Spark HBase API, you might face some compilation issues, but the logic behind it will still be the same. You might be able to adjust the examples to compile with your code and run them.

All the operations we are going to implement will be done over the same table. Use the following command to create this table:

```
create 'user', {NAME => 'edge', BLOOMFILTER => 'NONE',\
                COMPRESSION => 'SNAPPY', DATA_BLOCK_ENCODING => 'FAST_DIFF'},\
                {NAME => 'segment', BLOOMFILTER => 'NONE',\
                COMPRESSION => 'SNAPPY', DATA_BLOCK_ENCODING => 'FAST_DIFF'},\
                {NAME => 'visitor', BLOOMFILTER => 'NONE',\
                COMPRESSION => 'SNAPPY', DATA_BLOCK_ENCODING => 'FAST_DIFF'}
```

Let's take a closer look at the table creation command and the reason for the different options we have chosen. First, we disabled the Bloom filters. Indeed, every time we query HBase for a row, we will use its rowID so that we can be sure that it exists. Also, most of the time, the entire dataset will be processed and not just a single line. Therefore, having to look at the Bloom filter just to confirm that the row exists is an overhead. Most of the time, it is a good idea to keep the Bloom filters on. If you are not sure, just keep them.

Second, we enabled the Snappy compression. Even if the compression ratio it gives is less efficient compared to some other algorithm, Snappy allows quick compression with very small impact on the CPU. Unless you are storing data like compressed images or sound, it is always a good idea to enable it.

Last, we enabled data block encoding. Data block encoding is very useful to reduce the overhead of storing the key for every column of the same row. Given that a user can have many columns, and given that the row key can be pretty long, activating the FAST_DIFF block encoding will provide us with extra savings.

Spark and HBase: Puts

There are two ways to enrich HBase data while processing an input file. The first way is to do that in "real time," where we update data into HBase as we are parsing the input file. This allows you to see the results in HBase as soon as they are read by Spark. You can also implement a stream processing pipeline using similar code and Spark streaming. Now, if you don't have the requirement to get the data in real time in HBase, you can process it to generate HBase HFiles to be bulk loaded. While the streaming approach will give you a more real-time way of updating HBase, the bulk load approach provides better throughput, as it doesn't need to interact with HBase.

The very first thing we will need is a text file big enough to get a sense of Spark's performance capabilities. As in "Kafka" on page 117, we will create a small utility to generate this file. This utility can be called as follows:

```
java -classpath ~/ahae/target/ahae.jar:`hbase classpath`\
    com.architecting.ch11.DataGenerator 100000 > ~/ahae/resources/ch11/data.txt
```

After the file has been generated, it must be pushed into HDFS for processing:

```
hdfs dfs -put  ~/ahae/resources/ch11/data.txt
```

Running Spark over a text file doesn't require any specific HBase API. The code in Example 11-1 simply reads a file from HDFS and processes all the lines. To keep it simple, we will only count those lines here, but later on we will enrich this example.

Example 11-1. Simple line count using Spark

```
SparkConf sparkConf = new SparkConf().setAppName("JavaHBaseBulkGetExample ")
                                              .setMaster("local[2]");
JavaSparkContext jsc = new JavaSparkContext(sparkConf);
JavaRDD<String> textFile = jsc.textFile("hdfs://localhost/user/cloudera/data.txt");
JavaPairRDD<String, Integer> pairs = textFile.
                          mapToPair(new PairFunction<String, String, Integer>() {
  public Tuple2<String, Integer> call(String s) {
    return new Tuple2<String, Integer>(s.substring(0, s.indexOf("|")), 1); }
  });
JavaPairRDD<String, Integer> counts = pairs.
                          reduceByKey(new Function2<Integer, Integer, Integer>() {
  public Integer call(Integer a, Integer b) { return a + b; }
  });
System.out.println ("We have generaged " + counts.count() + " users");
```

This example should be straightforward—from each line, we extract the user ID only, then we group them together for a count. Because this is a very basic example, we will simply run it from Eclipse using the local environment.

Despite all the long DEBUG and INFO logs, what you are looking for is something like this:

```
We have generaged 999952 users
```

Now that we have a skeleton for our application, everything else will be standard HBase Java API calls mixed with Spark. As you might have figured, each entry in the input file represents information for someone. What we want to do is to update HBase with this information. There are two different ways to do that. The first option, illustrated in Example 11-2, has the benefit of being very easy to read and to understand. It will create one mutation per row on the input file and will buffer that to be sent to the HBase table.

Example 11-2. Performing HBase BulkPut using Spark

```
SparkConf sparkConf = new SparkConf().setAppName("IngestLines ")
                                     .setMaster("local[2]");
JavaSparkContext jsc = new JavaSparkContext(sparkConf);
Configuration conf = HBaseConfiguration.create();
JavaHBaseContext hbaseContext = new JavaHBaseContext(jsc, conf);
JavaRDD<String> textFile =
                  jsc.textFile("hdfs://localhost/user/cloudera/data.txt");

hbaseContext.bulkPut(textFile, TABLE_NAME, new Function<String, Put>() {
  @Override
  public Put call(String v1) throws Exception {
    String[] tokens = v1.split("\\|");
    Put put = new Put(Bytes.toBytes(tokens[0]));
    put.addColumn(Bytes.toBytes("segment"),
                  Bytes.toBytes(tokens[1]),
                  Bytes.toBytes(tokens[2]));
    return put;
  }
});
jsc.close();
```

This code creates one mutation (a Put) for each and every column and simply returns it to the HBase Spark BulkPut framework. If we ignore the duplicates, we only have a maximum of seven columns per row, so it is acceptable to have one mutation for each. However, if you have tens of columns, you might improve performance by regrouping them first, and then creating the related Puts and emitting them directly to HBase. This approach is illustrated in Example 11-3, and if you are new to Spark, the code will be much more difficult to read and to understand. However, running on a local VM environment, with seven columns and one million lines, the code in Example 11-3 is about 10% faster than the code in Example 11-2. If you increase the number of columns, the difference will be even more significant.

Example 11-3. Text file to HBase Spark processing

```java
SparkConf sparkConf = new SparkConf().setAppName("IngestLines ")
                                     .setMaster("local[2]");
JavaSparkContext jsc = new JavaSparkContext(sparkConf);
Configuration conf = HBaseConfiguration.create();
JavaHBaseContext hbaseContext = new JavaHBaseContext(jsc, conf);
JavaRDD<String> textFile =
                   jsc.textFile("hdfs://localhost/user/cloudera/data.txt");

PairFunction<String, String, String> linesplit = ❶
new PairFunction<String, String, String>() {
  public Tuple2<String, String> call(String s) {
    int index = s.indexOf("|");
    return new Tuple2<String, String>(s.substring(0, index),
                                      s.substring(index + 1));
  }
};

JavaPairRDD<String, String> pairs = textFile.mapToPair(linesplit);
Function<String, List<String>> createCombiner =
new Function<String, List<String>>() {
  public List<String> call(String s) {
    List<String> list = new ArrayList<String>();
    list.add(s);
    return list;
  }
};

Function2<List<String>, String, List<String>> mergeValue =
new Function2<List<String>, String, List<String>>() {
  @Override
  public List<String> call(List<String> v1, String v2) throws Exception {
    v1.add(v2);
    return v1;
  }
};

Function2<List<String>, List<String>, List<String>> mergeCombiners =
new Function2<List<String>, List<String>, List<String>>() {
  @Override
  public List<String> call(List<String> v1, List<String> v2) throws Exception {
    v2.addAll(v1);
    return v2;
  }
};

JavaPairRDD<String, List<String>> keyValues = ❷
         pairs.combineByKey(createCombiner, mergeValue, mergeCombiners);

JavaRDD<Put> keyValuesPuts = keyValues.map( ❸
new Function<Tuple2<String, List<String>>, Put>() {
```

```
  @Override
  public Put call(Tuple2<String, List<String>> v1) throws Exception {
    Put put = new Put(Bytes.toBytes(v1._1));
    ListIterator<String> iterator = v1._2.listIterator();
    while (iterator.hasNext()) {
      String colAndVal = iterator.next();
      int indexDelimiter = colAndVal.indexOf("|");
      String columnQualifier = colAndVal.substring(0, indexDelimiter);
      String value = colAndVal.substring(indexDelimiter + 1);
      put.addColumn(COLUMN_FAMILY, Bytes.toBytes(columnQualifier),
                                   Bytes.toBytes(value));
    }
    return put;
  }
});

hbaseContext.foreachPartition(keyValuesPuts, ❹
  new VoidFunction<Tuple2<Iterator<Put>, Connection>>() {
    @Override
    public void call(Tuple2<Iterator<Put>, Connection> t) throws Exception {
      Table table = t._2().getTable(TABLE_NAME);
      BufferedMutator mutator = t._2().getBufferedMutator(TABLE_NAME);
      while (t._1().hasNext()) {
        Put put = t._1().next();
        mutator.mutate(put);
      }

      mutator.flush();
      mutator.close();
      table.close();
    }
  });
jsc.close();
```

❶ Extract the key from the lines to create pairs that can be regrouped together.

❷ Combine all the entries based on the key so each key will have a list of "column qualifier|value" strings associated.

❸ Transform one key and all its related "column qualifier|value" strings to a single HBase put object.

❹ Emit all the puts to HBase.

Basically, what we are doing here is regrouping all the lines based on the key that we extract from the string, then we transform them into a single put for this line that we then send to HBase.

You can run this example directly from Eclipse.

Because of the way it is configured, this example only runs with two local threads. If you want to run it on YARN, remove the `.set Master("local[2]")` parameter from the code and run the example again adding `--master yarn-cluster` and `--deploy-mode client` parameters.

Because the output of this example is quite verbose, we will not reproduce it here. However, when it is done, you can query your HBase table to make sure data has been processed:

```
hbase(main):005:0> scan 'user', LIMIT => 2
ROW                    COLUMN+CELL
 0000003542a7-... column=segment:postalcode, ts=1457057812022, value=34270
 0000013542a7-... column=segment:birthdate, ts=1457057756713, value=20/05/1946
2 row(s) in 0.0330 seconds
```

Similarly to what we have done in Chapter 9 to enrich data as we ingest it into HBase, you can use the default HBase API to perform lookups before creating the mutations and enrich them with the required information.

Spark on HBase: Bulk Load

In the previous section, we discussed a real-time approach of updating an HBase table. If this is not required for your use case, you will achieve a better throughput by using the HBase bulk load option. Let's reuse the same example, but this time, instead of interacting directly with HBase, we will generate HBase HFiles that we will upload later on.

The data will remain the same. The main difference will be on the Spark side. HBase split the tables in regions based on the keys boundaries. Each HFile that we will create will have to belong to one of those regions and will have to contain keys only within those regions boundaries.

At the time of writing, the Java API to perform bulk loads in Spark is not completed. This is tracked by the JIRA HBASE-14217 (*https://issues.apache.org/jira/browse/ HBASE-14217*). Until this JIRA is resolved, only Scala can be used to perform this operation. Therefore, the code in Example 11-4 will be done in Scala.

Example 11-4. HBase BulkLoad example in Scala using Spark

```
import org.apache.hadoop.fs.Path
import org.apache.hadoop.hbase.mapreduce.LoadIncrementalHFiles
import org.apache.spark.SparkContext
import org.apache.hadoop.hbase.HBaseConfiguration
import org.apache.hadoop.hbase.TableName
import org.apache.hadoop.hbase.client._
import org.apache.hadoop.hbase.spark._
import org.apache.hadoop.hbase.spark.HBaseContext
```

```
import org.apache.hadoop.hbase.util.Bytes
import org.apache.spark.SparkConf
import org.apache.hadoop.hbase.spark.HBaseRDDFunctions._

object SparkBulkLoad {
  def main(args: Array[String]) {

    val columnFamily1 = "segment"
    val stagingFolder = "/tmp/user"
    val tableNameString = "user"
    val tableName = TableName.valueOf(tableNameString)

    val sc = new SparkContext(new SparkConf().setAppName("Spark BulkLoad")
                                      .setMaster("local[2]"))
    val config = HBaseConfiguration.create
    val hbaseContext = new HBaseContext(sc, config)

    val textFile = sc.textFile("hdfs://localhost/user/cloudera/data.txt")
    val toByteArrays = textFile.map(line => { ❶
      val tokens = line.split("\\|")
      (Bytes.toBytes(tokens(0)), (Bytes.toBytes(columnFamily1),
                                  Bytes.toBytes(tokens(1)),
                                  Bytes.toBytes(tokens(2))))
    })

    toByteArrays.hbaseBulkLoad(hbaseContext, tableName, ❷
      t => { ❸
        val rowKey = t._1
        val family:Array[Byte] = t._2._1
        val qualifier = t._2._2
        val value = t._2._3

        val keyFamilyQualifier= new KeyFamilyQualifier(rowKey, family, qualifier)

        Seq((keyFamilyQualifier, value)).iterator
      },
      stagingFolder)

    val load = new LoadIncrementalHFiles(config)
    load.run(Array(stagingFolder, tableNameString)) ❹
  }
}
```

❶ Apply transformation on the input file to transform each line into byte arrays representing the key, the column family, the column qualifier, and the value.

❷ Based on the transformed input, make us of the Spark HBase API to generate the related HFiles.

❸ Describe how bytes arrays are going to be transformed into the format required by the bulk load.

❹ After HFiles are generated, make use of the `LoadIncrementalHFiles` API to load generated files into the target table.

There are a few steps required to run this application. First, because you will most probably not run this application as the Spark user, you will need permission to write in the *applicationhistory* directory. Use the following command to help you with this (you might need to set a password for HDFS):

```
sudo -u hdfs hadoop fs -chmod 1777 /user/spark/applicationHistory
```

Another important consideration to keep in mind is that, on a nonsecured cluster, HBase `LoadIncrementalHFiles` has to run with the HBase user. Indeed, it will push files into the */hbase* tree, which will be read and written by the HBase processes. Pushing a file there with another user will end up with HBase not able to delete this file after compaction and fail.

You can run this small example using the following command:

```
su -l hbase -- spark-submit --class com.architecting.ch11.SparkBulkLoad \
        --master local ~/ahae/target/ahae.jar
```

Then add the following content into your HBase table:

```
hbase(main):013:0> scan 'user', LIMIT =>
ROW                COLUMN+CELL
 0000123542a7-... column=segment:postalcode, ts=1457567998199, value=34270
 0000153542a7-... column=segment:lastname, ts=1457567998199, value=Smith
 0000173542a7-... column=segment:birthdate, ts=1457567998199, value=06/03/1942
 0000173542a7-... column=segment:status, ts=1457567998199, value=maried
```

 Spark stream is typically viewed as a micro batch processing engine. It will process a couple of entries at a time, then take the next batch, and so on. The bulk load approach creates HFiles. The bigger the files, the better throughput we will have. Because it will create HFiles for each small batch, using Spark streaming with bulk load will not make sense and is not recommended.

Spark Over HBase

The final example we will look at for using Spark and HBase will process the content of an HBase table using Spark. As we have done MapReduce over an HBase table, we will do Spark over an HBase table. The concept for Spark is similar; it will process the different regions in parallel.

The examples we'll look at in this section are very simple, and they achieve the same goal—that is, they count the lines of an HBase table. Although this is very simple, you will see later how it can be extended for more complex use cases.

We'll break the example down into a few pieces. The most important part is shown in Example 11-5.

Example 11-5. HBase Spark over HBase initialization

```
// SparkConf sc = new SparkConf().setAppName("ProcessTable").setMaster("local[2]");
SparkConf sc = new SparkConf().setAppName("ProcessTable");
JavaSparkContext jsc = new JavaSparkContext(sc);
Configuration conf = HBaseConfiguration.create();

JavaHBaseContext hbaseContext = new JavaHBaseContext(jsc, conf);

Scan scan = new Scan();
scan.setCaching(100);
KeyOnlyFilter kof = new KeyOnlyFilter();
scan.setFilter(kof);

JavaRDD<Tuple2<ImmutableBytesWritable, Result>> data =
                    hbaseContext.hbaseRDD(TABLE_NAME, scan);
```

This is where all the magic happens. We start with the normal Spark and HBase initialization calls. If you are used to HBase, and as we have seen when we have done MapReduce over an HBase table, we have to initialize a scan that will help us to filter the rows that we do not want and return the one we are looking at. Here we just want to get all the rows. However, because we want to count them, we do not need to get the value so we will filter it and keep only the keys. This should already be familiar to you. The last line is the interesting part. Using the HBaseContext and given the table name and the scan object, you will get an RDD representation of your HBase table. Processing this RDD will handle the entire HBase table. Example 11-6 is a very basic count operation on the table rows.

Example 11-6. Spark HBase RDD count

```
System.out.println("data.count() = " + data.count());
```

This simple line of code will trigger a count on the Spark RDD. The Spark RRD representing the entire HBase table, it will simply count all the rows in the table. This is very simple, but it doesn't really let you do any specific operation on the rows.

Examples 11-7 and 11-8 also perform a count on the HBase table, however, as you will see, even if they just count the rows, it will be very easy to modify these examples to perform any manipulation of the row you might want.

Example 11-7. HBase Spark over HBase partitions reduce count

```
FlatMapFunction<Iterator<Tuple2<ImmutableBytesWritable, Result>>, Integer> setup =
new FlatMapFunction<Iterator<Tuple2<ImmutableBytesWritable, Result>>, Integer>() {
  @Override
  public Iterable<Integer>
                    call(Iterator<Tuple2<ImmutableBytesWritable, Result>> input) {
    int a = 0;
    while (input.hasNext()) {
      a++; ❶
      input.next();
    }
    ArrayList<Integer> ret = new ArrayList<Integer>();
    ret.add(a);
    return ret;
  }
};
Function2<Integer, Integer, Integer> combine =
new Function2<Integer, Integer, Integer>() {
  @Override
  public Integer call(Integer a, Integer b) {
    return a+b; ❷
  }
};

System.err.println("data.mapPartitions(setup).reduce(combine) = " +
    data.mapPartitions(setup).reduce(combine));
long time3 = System.currentTimeMillis();
System.err.println("Took " + (time3 - time2) + " milliseconds");
```

❶ For each Spark partition, we simply increment a counter for each line we found. Here, it will be very easy to accumulate a value extracted from the HBase cell or do any other kind of aggregation we want.

❷ Now that all the partitions are aggregated, to combine them, we simply need to sum all the values.

Example 11-7 looks very close to what we were doing in previous chapters with Map-Reduce. Because it doesn't really map by partition, Example 11-8 is a bit different, but the output will again be the same.

Example 11-8. HBase Spark over HBase aggregate count

```
Function2<Integer, Tuple2<ImmutableBytesWritable, Result>, Integer> aggregator =
new Function2<Integer, Tuple2<ImmutableBytesWritable, Result>, Integer>() {
  @Override
  public Integer call(Integer v1, Tuple2<ImmutableBytesWritable, Result> v2)
      throws Exception {
    return v1 + 1; ❶
  }
```

```
  };
  Function2<Integer, Integer, Integer> combiner =
  new Function2<Integer, Integer, Integer>() {
    @Override
    public Integer call(Integer v1, Integer v2) throws Exception {
      return v1 + v2; ❷
    }
  };

  System.err.println("data.aggregate(0, aggregator, combiner) = " +
                                     data.aggregate(0, aggregator, combiner));
  long time4 = System.currentTimeMillis();
  System.err.println("Took " + (time4 - time3) + " milliseconds");
  // end::PROCESS1[]

  jsc.close();
}

public static void main(String[] args) {
  processVersion1();
}

}
```

❶ Because we just want to count the rows, we simply emit 1 for each one. However, think about something more complicated. Imagine that the cell contains an Avro object representing an order. If you want to sum all the order's amounts, this is the place where you will do that. Simply extract the Avro object from the parameter and aggregate its amount.

❷ Again, to combine the values together, we simply have to sum them.

Examples 11-7 and 11-8 can very easily be modified to achieve way more processing on the data you have:

- Think about doing data correlation where you perform an HBase lookup on the map side to enrich an output file that will generate Parquet data for analytic quests.

- Think about doing aggregation to enrich your HBase table with daily, weekly, and monthly values.

- Think about feeding a Kafka key to allow subsequent systems to receive and process the HBase data.

Everything you were previously doing with MapReduce can now be achieved using Spark.

Going Further

If you want to extend the examples presented in this chapter, the following list offers some options you can try based on our discussion:

Partitions
> To clearly see the benefit of partitioning the RRDs, create a bigger HBase table with multiple regions and try to create two version of your Spark code: one that runs over all the data with a single executor, and another that partitions the data to run it over multiple executors. Instead of a single executor processing the entire table, you should see one executor per HBase region on your table. The difference in execution time should be significant.

Streaming
> Try to convert the put example into Spark streaming. Instead of processing the entire file at once, try to process it by micro batches. This should allow you to start seeing results into HBase sooner than with the entire puts bulked at once.

Scan modification
> Try to modify the scanner initialization to sort only certain rows, or extract only certain columns from your table. The scan object you give to your Spark RDD will determine what data you are going to receive on the subsequent calls.

## CHAPTER 12

Use Case: Document Store

The final use case focuses on leveraging HBase as a document store. This use case is implemented by a large insurance company, which will henceforth be referred to as "the firm." The information the firm collects is used to determine accident at faults, payouts, and even individual net worth. This particular use case involves data management and curation at a massive scale.

The firm needed to build a document store that would allow it to serve different documents to numerous business units and customers. A company of this size will end up having hundreds to thousands of different business units and millions of end users. The data from these different business units creates massive amounts of information that needs to be collected, aggregated, curated, and then served to internal and external consumers. The firm needed the ability to serve hundreds of millions of documents over thousands of different logical collections. That is a challenge for any platform, unless that platform is HBase.

Leveraging HBase as a document store is a relatively new use case for HBase. Previously, documents larger than a few 100 KB were not recommended for consumption. The competition to earn the production deployment was against a major RDBMS system. In this bake off, reads, writes, and file sizes were tested. The incumbent vendor performed well against HBase. HBase writes were slightly faster on smaller documents (ranging in size from 4 to 100 KB). Yet, the incumbent vendor managed to outperform HBase on larger documents by showing almost twice the write throughput with large documents of 300+ MB. HBase shined through with the reads, which is most important to the end users for this use case. HBase was 4 times faster when reading small files and 3.5 times faster with the large documents over 300 MB in size. Finally, HBase was tested with documents up to 900 MB in size and performed well, though the production deployment will not have any 900 MB cells floating around.

This use case would have been problematic in earlier versions of HBase. Luckily, the Medium Object (MOB) storage feature was introduced in HBASE-11339. Originally HBase struggled with cells up to 100 KB to 1 MB or larger in size. When using these larger sized cells without the MOB feature enabled, HBase suffered from something known as write amplification. This occurs when HBase compactions have to rewrite these larger cells over and over again potentially causing flush delays, blocked updates, disk I/O to spike, and latencies to shoot through the roof. This may be fine in batch-based systems using HBase as a system of record, updating large sets of data in Spark or MR jobs, but real-time systems with SLAs would suffer the most.

The MOB feature allowed HBase to accommodate larger cells with an official recommendation of 100 KB to 10 MB, but we have seen reasonable success with documents over 100 MB. MOB solves this issue by writing the MOB files into a special region. The MOB files are still written to the WAL and block cache to allow for normal replication and faster retrieval. Except when flushing a memstore containing a MOB file, only a reference is written into the HFile. The actual MOB file is written into an offline MOB region to avoid being compacted over and over again during major compactions causing write amplification. Figure 12-1 highlights the read path when leveraging MOB.

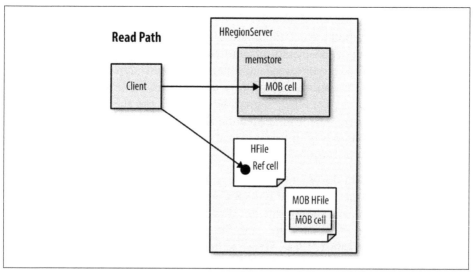

Figure 12-1. Understanding the MOB read path

To accomplish the deployment, the firm needed to have the ability to store 1 PB on the primary cluster and 1 PB on the disaster recovery cluster, while maintaining the ability to stay cost-effective. Staying cost-effective means enabling greater vertical scalability to keep the total node count down. To achieve this, we had to push HBase beyond the known best practices. We leveraged 40 GB for our region size and had roughly 150 regions per RegionServer. This gave us about 6 TB of raw data in HBase alone, not including scratch space for compactions or Solr Indexes. The MOB feature enabled us to take better advantage of the I/O system by isolating the larger files. This allowed the firm to deploy on denser nodes that offered over 24 TB of storage per node. For this use case, we will be focused on serving, ingest, and cleanup.

Serving

We are going to reverse the usual order and start with the serving layer to better understand the key design before getting into how the data is broken up. In step 1, the client (end user) reaches out to the application layer that handles document retrievals (Figure 12-2). In this case, the end client is not going to know how to represent the HBase row key when looking up specific documents. To accomplish this, the firm uses Solr to look up the specific document information. The search engine contains the metadata about the documents needed to construct the HBase row key for the gets. Clients send their search terms to Solr, and based on search results, can request an entire document or numerous documents from HBase based on information from the search result, including:

GUID
This is a hashed document ID.

Partner ID
Identifier for location of document's originating point (e.g., US, Canada, France, etc.).

Version ID
Version of the document that corresponded to the search.

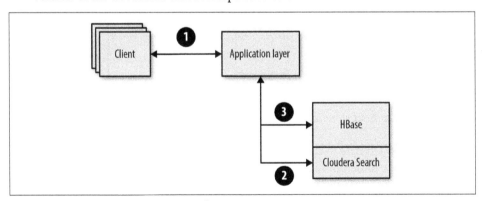

Figure 12-2. Document store serving layer

The application layer will then take retrieved pieces of information from the search engine to construct the row key:

```
GUID+PartnerID+VersionID
```

After the application layer has constructed the row key from the search engine, it will then execute a get against HBase. The get is against the entire row, as each row represents the entire document. The application layer is then responsible for reconstructing the document from the numerous cells that document has been chunked into. After the document is reconstructed, it is passed back to the end user to be updated and rewritten back to the document store.

Ingest

The ingest portion is very interesting, because all of the documents will be of varying size (Figure 12-3). In step 1, the client passes an updated or new document to the application layer. The application layer then takes the document and creates the necessary metadata for future document retrieval:

- GUID
- Partner ID
- Version ID

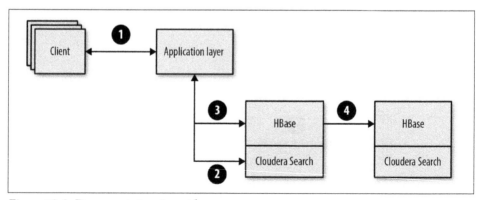

Figure 12-3. Document store ingest layer

To create the new update to the search engine, the application will first do a lookup in the search engine to determine the correct version ID, and then increment to the next level to ensure the latest document is served and that older versions of documents can be retained. Once the search engine has been updated, the application will then determine the document size and break the document up into the correct number of 50 MB cells to be written to HBase. This means a 250 MB document will look like Figure 12-4.

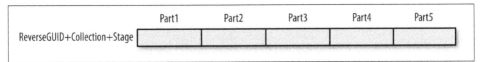

Figure 12-4. Cell layout while chunking large documents

The final HBase schema was different than what was tested during the bake off. HBase showed the best performance when the documents were broken out into chunks, as illustrated in Figure 12-4. The chunking also helps to keep total memstore usage under control, as we can flush numerous chunks at a time without having to buffer the entire large document. Once the HBase application has written the data to both the search engine and HBase, the document is the made available for retrieval from the client.

Once the data has been written to HBase, the Lily Indexer picks up the metadata about each document and writes it into Cloudera Search. While the search engine is indexing some metadata in step 4, HBase is also replicating the data to the disaster recovery cluster, which in turn is also writing the metadata to Cloudera Search through the Lily Indexer (Figure 12-5). This is actually a very clever way to do very quick document counts without having to utilize HBase resources to issue scans to count the total number of documents. Cloudera Search can quickly give back a total count of documents in both sites, ensuring that the document counts stays the same.

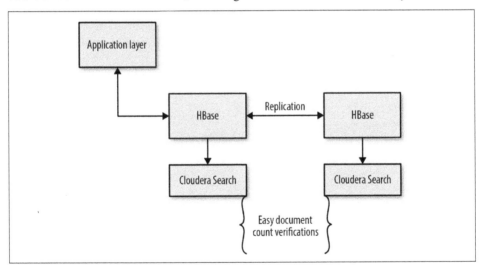

Figure 12-5. Disaster recovery layout

Clean Up

For those of you following along at home, you may be thinking "Hey! Great schema, but how do you control versions?" Normally versions are handled through individual HBase cells and are configurable on the column family level. However, the portion of the row key known as "VersionID" is used to control the versioning. This allows the client to be able to easily pull the latest, or the last X versions with a single scan. If the firm wished to keep all copies of a single document, this would be fine; but depending on the delta rate of the documents, this could balloon out of control fast. Seriously, think about how many times you have changed a sentence, got busy and saved the document, then came changed another sentence, then repeat. To combat this, the firm has written a clean up job that will iterate through the table and delete unneeded versions of their documents.

For the current RDBMS-based solution, the cleanup process runs constantly in order to minimize storage and contain costs on their expensive RDBMS. Because HBase is lower cost, storage is less of an issue, and cleanups can run less frequently. To do this, the firm fires off a Spark job daily.

The Spark job has two primary tasks. First, it collects the version count of each document from the search system. This is an easy way to eliminate the documents that do not exceed the maximum version count. In this case, the firm retains up to the last 10 versions of a document. Once the document list has been built, the Spark job will use the response to build the necessary row keys to issue the deletes. Finally, the job will fire off a series of deletes to HBase, followed by a major compaction to age off all of the tombstones.

## CHAPTER 13

Implementation of Document Store

As you might have guessed, this use case again utilizes most if not all of what we have seen before—that is, replication for backup, Lily and Solr for real-time indexing and search, Spark for fast processing, and of course the Java API. The only thing that we don't really have look at is the MOB aspect. Therefore, we will focus on that over the next sections. Because consistency is also one important aspect of the use case, we will also address it.

As you will see next, there is not that much to do on the implementation side, but we will mostly focus on the key concepts to keep in mind when designing your own application.

MOBs

HBase works very well with small to average size cell values, but bigger ones, because of the compactions, create write amplification. MOBs have been implemented to avoid this.

 MOBs require HFiles format v3. You will have to make sure your HBase version is configured for that. The Apache version of HBase has HFile configured to v3 since version 1.0. However, for compatibility purposes, some distributions still keep the v2. To make sure your version is configured to v3, add `hfile.format.version` parameter to your config file and set it to 3.[1]

---

1 *http://blog.cloudera.com/blog/2015/06/inside-apache-hbases-new-support-for-mobs/*

In the following section, we will see how to configure a table to use the MOB feature and how to push some data into it. You will need to decide the cut off point for when data will be considered a regular cell, or if the entry is too large and needs to be moved into a MOB region.

For testing purposes, we will keep this value pretty small:

```
create 'mob_test', {NAME => 'f', IS_MOB => true, MOB_THRESHOLD => 104857}
```

 MOB have been implemented as part of HBASE-11339, which has been commited into the HBase 2.0 branch. Is had not been backported into the 1.0 branch by the community. Therefore, if you want to try the MOB feature, you have to use a 2.0+ version of HBase or a distribution where this has been backported. Because the Cloudera QuickStart VM includes this implementation, we will use it for testing in this chapter.

This command will create a table called mod_test with a single column family called f where all cells over tens of a megabyte will be considered to be a MOB. From the client side, there is no specific operation or parameter to add. Therefore, the Put command will transfer the entire cell content to the RegionServer. Once there, the RegionServer will decide whether to store the document as a normal cell or a MOB region.

The following two puts against our mob_test table are very similar from a client point of view, but will be stored differently on the server side:

```
byte[] rowKey = Bytes.toBytes("rowKey");
byte[] CF = Bytes.toBytes("f");
byte[] smallCellCQ = Bytes.toBytes("small");
byte[] bigCellCQ = Bytes.toBytes("big");
byte[] smallCellValue = new byte(1024);
byte[] bigCellValue = new byte(110000);
Put smallPut = new Put(rowKey);
smallPut.addColumn(CF, smallCellCQ, smallCellValue);
table.put (smallPut);

Put bigPut = new Put(rowKey);
bigPut.addColumn(CF, bigCellCQ, bigCellValue);
table.put (bigPut);
```

Those two puts for the same row key of the same table will both go into the same region. However, after flushing the memstore, the small one will go in a regular HFile while the big one will go as a separate MOB file.

Being pretty new, MOBs are a bit sensitive to the version of HBase you are running. Indeed, building the preceding example with CDH5.7, it will not run against CHD5.5 nor against HBase master branch. Make sure you adjust your POM file to compile with the same version of the HBase you will run.

Storage

In Part I, we saw how HBase stores the data into HFile. Each table is split into regions, each region will be a directory on HDFS, and each column family is a subdirectory of the region directory. For the table we're looking at here, after everything has been flushed from memory, if we consider we did not use any specific namespace, the following directory structure will be created on HDFS:

```
├── data
│   ├── default
│   │   └── mob_test
│   │       └── 4ef02a664043021a511f4b4585b8cba1
│   │           ├── f
│   │           │   └── adb1f3f22fa34dfd9b04aa273254c773
│   │           └── recovered.edits
│   │               └── 2.seqid
```

This looks exactly like what we had for any other regular table. However, we now also have a MOB directory created under the HBase folder:

```
├── mobdir
│   └── data
│       └── default
│           └── mob_test
│               └── 0660f699de69e8d4c52e4a037e00a732
│                   └── f
│                       └── d41d8cd98f00b204e9800998ecf8427e20160328fa75df3f...0
```

As you can see here, we still have our regular HFile that contains the small cells that are not filtered as MOB, but we also have an additional file that contains the MOB values. This new file will not be handled the same way as the regular files. Indeed, when HBase has to compact files together, it has to read the entire HFiles and create a new one containing the merged content. The goal of the compaction is to reduce the number of small files and create bigger ones. Because MOB cells are already big, storing them in separate will reduce the read and write amplification caused by the compactions. Only references to those MOB cells will be read and rewritten each time there is a compaction.

MOB files still have to be compacted. You might have deleted a value that was stored as a MOB. There is a shell command for that, but HBase will also automatically trigger those compactions when required.

If most of what you are doing with HBase is writes of big cells and almost no deletes, MOB will give you a very good improvement compared to the regular format.

Usage

At this point, you might be wondering what constitutes a big cell versus a small one. HBase performs very well with cells up to 1 MB. It is also able to process cells up to 5 MB. However, above that point, regular write path will start to have some performance challenges. The other thing you have to consider is how many times you are going to write big cells versus regular ones. MOBs required some extra work for HBase. When you are reading a cell, we first need to lookup into the related HFile and then into the MOB file. Because of this extra call, latency will be slightly impacted. Now, if your MOB is 50 MB, the time to transfer it to the client versus the extra read access on HBase might not be significant. The extra read access on the HBase side will add few milliseconds to your call. But transferring 50 MB of data to your client might take more than that and might just hide the extra milliseconds for the additional read.

The main question you will need to ask yourself is how often are you going to insert big cells into HBase. If you expect to do so only, once in a while, and not more than once per row, a cell that might be a big bigger than the others, like up to 5 MB, you might just be able to use the regular put API. That will save you the extra management of the MOB files and HBase will be able to handle that. Because there will be only a few big cells, the read and write amplification will be limited. However, if you are planning to have multiple big cells per row, if some of your cells are going to be bigger than 5 MB, or if most of your puts are big, you might want to consider using the MOBs.

 Keep in mind that even if MOB reduces the rewrite amplification of the regular HFiles, if you have to perform many puts and deletes of big cells, you will still have to perform many compactions of the MOB files.

Too Big

As we have just seen, it's fine for regular HBase cells to occasionally grow up to 5 MB cells. MOBs will allow you to easily handle cells up 20 MB. Even if it is not necessarily recommended, some people have pushed it a bit further and are using MOBs with 50 MB cells.

Now, if your use case is to store only very big cells, like 100 MB cells or more, you are better off using a different approach.

There are two best practices around this. First, if your cells are bigger than 100 MB (and you know for sure that they will continue to be over that limit), a better approach is to store the content as a file on HDFS and store the reference of this file into HBase. Keep in mind that it's inadvisable to store millions of files in the same directory, so you should devise a directory structure based on your use case (e.g., you might create a new folder every month or every day, or for every source).

The second approach is the one described in the previous chapter. If only some of your cells will be very big, but some will be smaller, and you don't know in advance the distribution of the size, think about splitting your cell into multiple smaller cells. Then when writing the data, check its size and split it if required, and when reading it, perform the opposite operation and merge it back.

The best design to do this is to abstract that from the client application. Indeed, if the client has to split the content itself, it will add complexity and might hide some business logic. However, if you extend the existing HBase API to parse the Puts before they are sent to HBase, you can silently and easily perform the split operations. The same thing is true for the Get where you can, again, parse the content retrieved from HBase and merge it back to one single object.

Example 13-1 gives you an example of how to perform that.

To keep things simple and illustrate how it should work, we are not extending the client API.

Example 13-1. Split one HBase cell to many pieces

```
public static void putBigCell (Table table, byte[] key, byte[] value)
            throws IOException {
  if (value.length < 10 * MB) {
    // The value is small enough to be handled as a single HBase cell.
    // There is no need to split it in pieces.
    Put put = new Put(key).addColumn(columnFamily, columnQualifierOnePiece, value);
    table.put(put);
  } else {
    byte[] buffer = new byte[10*MB];
    int index = 0;
    int piece = 1;
    Put put = new Put(key);
    while (index < value.length) {
      int length = Math.min((value.length - index), buffer.length);
      byte[] columnQualifier = Bytes.toBytes(piece);
      System.arraycopy(value, index, buffer, 0, length);  ❶
      KeyValue kv = new KeyValue(key, 0, key.length,  ❷
                                 columnFamily, 0, columnFamily.length,
                                 columnQualifier, 0, columnQualifier.length,
                                 put.getTimeStamp(), KeyValue.Type.Put,
                                 buffer, 0, length);
      put.add(kv);
```

```
            index += length + 1;
            piece ++;
        }
        table.put(put);
    }
}
```

❶ We do not want to create a new 10 MB object each time we read a new slice, so we keep reusing the same buffer array.

❷ The HBase `Put` object doesn't allow you to give a byte array or to specify the length of your value, so we have to make use of the `KeyValue` object.

 To make sure you don't create rows that are too big, HBase validates the size of the cells you are trying to store. If you are trying to start 10 MB cells, you might want to make sure *hbase.client.key-value.maxsize* is not set to a lower number. This is a relatively unknown setting that can cause lots of headaches when dealing with large cells.

Consistency

Let's take a small example to really get the sense of what is the consistency in HBase. Imagine you are writing a website order into HBase. Let's consider you are writing all the entries one by one with a different key formed by the order ID and the entry ID. Each line in the order will have a different entry ID and so will be a different HBase row. Most of the time, it will all go well and at once into HBase. But what if this is split over two different regions hosted on two different servers? And what if the second server just failed before storing the entries? Some will make it, and some others will have to be retried until the region is reassigned and the data finally makes it in. If a client application tries to read the entire order while this is happening, it will retrieve a partial view of the order. If we use Lily to index the data coming into this table, a query to the index will return partial results.

This is where consistency awareness is important.

Let's see how this applies to the current use case.

Documents are received by the application where a modified HBase client split them in 10 MB slices and sends all the slices plus the metadata into HBase. All the slices and the metadata have to go together. If you send the slices as different HBase rows, it may take some time for each part to make its way into HBase and therefore an application trying to read it might get only a partial file. Because it is important for all the slices to be written in a single write and be read at once, they will have to be stored into a single row. Metadata also needs to be part of the consistency equation. Because it will be indexed and used for the document retrieval, the metadata is tightly coupled to the file. It will have to go with the same row, at the same time.

There are cases where consistency is not an issue. As an example, if you receive a list of tweets from a user, all those tweets are not linked together. Therefore, retrieving just a subset of them might not impact your results.

Consistency is a *very* important concept in HBase. It's not always required to have consistency within an operation. But if you have to, it is very important to keep your data together to make sure it makes it together into HBase, or not at all.

 Stay away from cross-references. Let's imagine you have a row A where you store the key and the value of a reference called row B When you will update the value of row B, you will also have to update the value of row A. However, they can be on different regions, and consistency of those update operations cannot be guaranteed. If you need to get the value of row B when reading row A, you are much better off keeping row B key in row A values and doing another call based on that. This will require an extra call to HBase, but will save you the extra burden of having to rebuild your entire table after a few failures.

Going Further

If you want to extend the examples presented in this chapter, the following list offers some options you can try based on our discussions from this chapter:

Single cell
> Try to push HBase to its maximum capability. Instead of splitting cells into 10 MB chunks, try to create bigger and bigger chunks and see how HBase behaves. Try to read and write those giant cells and validate their content.

Deletes impacts
> To gain a better understanding of how deletes are handled with MOBs, update the example to generate some big MOB cells, flush them onto disk, and then execute a delete. Then look at the underlying filesystem storage. Later, flush the table again and run a compaction to see what happens.

Read
> This chapter illustrated how to split a huge cell into a smaller one and write it to HBase. But we leave it to you to write the read path. Based on how we have split the cell into multiple pieces, build a method that will read it, back and re-create the initial document. To help you get started, you will have to find the last column, read it and get its size. The size of the document will be the number of columns minus one, multiplied by 10 MB plus the size of the last one. As an

example, if you have three columns and the last one is 5 MB, the document size will be (3 - 1) * 10 MB + 5 MB, which is 25 MB.

## PART III

Troubleshooting

There are many different gotchas that can occur when deploying an HBase use case. This upcoming section is all about HBase issues we have run into over the years of using it. Ideally, you should read this section before deploying HBase, as recovering from some of these mistakes in production can be quite difficult.

This section will cover the typical issues we run into, such as too many regions or column familes, hotspotting, issues with region time outs, or worst-case scenario, having to recover from metadata or filesystem corruption. We will go over the typical cause and recovery from these issues. We will also highlight some best practices around Java tuning that can enable greater vertical scalability.

## CHAPTER 14

Too Many Regions

Consequences

Having too many regions can impact your HBase application in many ways.

The most common consequence is related to HFile compactions. Regions are sharing the memstore memory area. Therefore, the more regions there are, the smaller the memstore flushes will be. When the memstore is full and forced to flush to disk, it will create an HFile containing data to be stored in HDFS. This means the more regions you have, the smaller the generated HFiles will be. This will force HBase to execute many compaction operations to keep the number of HFiles reasonably low. These compactions will cause excessive churn on the cluster, affecting performance. When specific operations are triggered (automatic flush, forced flush, and user call for compactions), if required, HBase will start compactions. When many compactions run in tandem, it is known as a *compaction storm*.

 Compactions are normal HBase operations. You should expect them, and there is nothing to worry about when minor compactions are running. However, it is recommended to monitor the number of compactions. The compaction queue should not be constantly growing. Spikes are fine, but the key needs to stay close to zero most of the time. Constant compactions can be a sign of poor project design or a cluster sizing issue. We call constant compactions a situation where the compaction queue for a given RegionServer never goes down to zero or is constantly growing.

Certain operations can timeout as a result of having too many regions. HBase commands like splits, flushes, bulkloads, and snapshots (when using flush) perform operations on each and every region. As an example, when the flush <table> command is called, HBase needs to store a single HFile into HDFS for each column family in each region of <table> where there are pending writes in the memstore. The more regions you have, the more files will be created in the filesystem. Because all of those new file creations and data transfers will occur at the same time, this can overwhelm the system and impact SLAs. If the time taken to complete the operation is greater than the configured timeout for your operation, you will start to see some timeout failures.

Here is a quick summary of the problems you might encounter on your cluster as a result of having too many regions:

- Snapshots timeout
- Compaction storms
- Client operations can timeout (like flush)
- Bulk load timeouts (might be reported as `RegionTooBusyException`)

Causes

There are multiple root causes for having too many regions, ranging from misconfiguration to misoperation. These root causes will be discussed in greater detail in this section:

- Maximum region size set too low
- Configuration settings not updated following an HBase upgrade
- Accidental configuration settings
- Over-splitting
- Improper presplitting

Misconfiguration

In previous HBase versions, 1 GB was the default recommendation for region size. HBase can now easily handle regions ranging in size from 10 to 40 GB, thanks to optimizations in HBase and ever-increasing default memory size in hardware. For more details on how to run HBase with more memory, refer to Chapter 17. When an older HBase cluster is migrated into a recent version (0.98 or greater), a common mistake is to retain previous configuration settings. As a result, HBase tries to keep regions under 1 GB when it will be better letting them grow up to 10 GB or more. Also, even if the cluster has not been migrated from an older version, the maximum region size configuration might have been mistakenly modified to a smaller value, resulting in too many regions.

Misoperation

There are also multiple manual operations that might cause HBase to have too many regions to serve.

Over-splitting

The first one is a misuse of the split feature. HBase's "Table Details" Web UI allows administrators to split all the regions of a given table. HBase will split the regions even if they are small, as long as the amount of data in the region meets the minimum size required to qualify for manual splitting. This option can sometimes be very useful, but abusing it can easily create too many regions for a single table. Take as an example a 128 region table on a four-node cluster where each RegionServer hosts only 32 regions. This is a correct load for a cluster of that size. The use of the split option three times will create up to 1,024 regions, which represents 256 regions per server!

Improper presplitting

It is also possible to create too many regions when using the presplit HBase feature. Presplitting is very important to help spread the load across all the RegionServers in the cluster; however, it needs to be well thought out beforehand. There should be a fundamental understanding of row key design, HBase writes, and desired region count to correctly presplit a table. A poorly split table can result in many regions (hundreds or even thousands) with only a few of them being used.

Solution

Depending on the HBase version you use, there are different ways to address the issue of having too many regions. But in both scenarios, the final goal is to reduce the total number of regions by merging some of them together. What differs between the HBase versions is the ways to achieve this.

Before 0.98

Before version 0.98, there are two main options to merge regions together: copying the table to a new presplit table or merging regions. Before HBase 0.98, regions could be merged offline only.

The first option is to create a new table with the same definitions as the existing table but with a different table name. Copy the data from the original table into this table. To complete the process, drop the original table and then rename the new table to the original table name. In this method, we will use the HBase snapshot feature so HBase 0.94.6 or above is required. Also, you will need to run the MapReduce CopyTable job on top of the HBase cluster, so you will need to make sure that the MapReduce framework is available and running. Last, this method will require a temporary suspension of data ingestion. This interruption will be short but is the important part of the process.

 Because this method will duplicate the initial table, it will consume space on your cluster equal to the original tables size. Ensure the extra space is available before starting. It is also important to understand the impact of running MapReduce on the HBase cluster.

The new table should be presplit with the expected newly merged region boundaries. Figure 14-2 illustrates this. Once the presplit step is completed, use the CopyTable command to copy data from the original table to the new table. The CopyTable tool accepts a date range as an argument and will then copy data from time t0 to t1 directly into the target table, into the correct regions. This will allow you to transfer the oldest data first and rerun the tool again to transfer newly created data. CopyTable also allows you to rename or drop unnecessary column families, which can be very useful in case of table redesign.

 As illustrated in Figure 14-1, if you are doing puts and deletes with modified timestamps, you might want to avoid this method, as some of your deletes and puts might not be copied correctly if any compaction occurs on the source side between the two CopyTable calls. It is almost never a good idea to be modifying internal HBase timestamps. In Figure 14-1, CopyTable is done between t0 and t1 to copy data from one table to another. By the time CopyTable is run for data between t1 and current time, some data with old time-stamps is inserted into the source table. Because only data with a timestamp greater than t1 will be consider by the second run of CopyTable, this newly inserted data in the past will be ignored (i.e., it will not be copied over to the new table and will be lost if the source table is dropped).

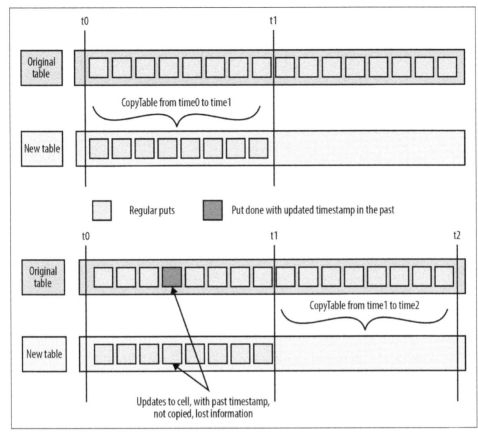

Figure 14-1. Risk when performing updates with timestamp of cells in the past

Figure 14-2 is an example to better understand how this can be done. Consider that you built an application that stores transactions into a table using the transaction ID as the row key. Your initial assumption was that the transaction ID would be a unique randomly generated readable string. Based on this assumption, the initial table was split into 26 regions from A to Z. However, after running the application for a few weeks, you notice that the transaction ID is a hexadecimal ID. Therefore, instead of going from A to Z, it goes from 0 to F. With the new distribution, regions greater than F will never be used, while the first region will get way more data than the others (puts from 0 to A) and will split into many new regions as it grows. In this case, we're only moving 26 region to 8 regions; but if you scale this example, you can easily see how hundreds of regions may have been initially created to handle more load and how the same issue of data balancing can occur.

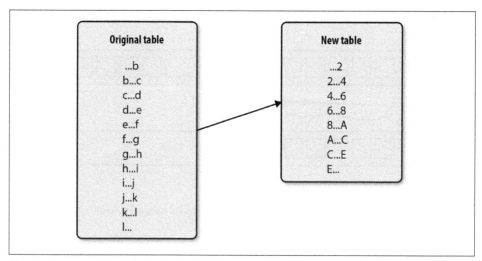

Figure 14-2. Regions redesign

In order to fix this, we will create a new table where regions are already presplit on hexadecimal boundaries. Using the `CopyTable` command, we will copy data from the existing table to the new table, from t0 to the current day:

```
hbase org.apache.hadoop.hbase.mapreduce.CopyTable --starttime=0 \
--endtime=1411264757000 --new.name=new_table previous_table
```

The goal of the `starttime` and `endtime` parameters is to make sure we copy a specific and controlled section of the source table. Because this operation might take some time, before going to the next steps, and to reduce the input table downtime, we want to copy as much data as possible; but we also want to make sure we will be able to restart the copy from a specific point in time.

Depending on the size of your dataset, this copy might take several hours to a few days. While the copy is running, normal operations can continue on the cluster and on the initial table.

Once the first `CopyTable` operation is done, the new table contains almost all of the existing data except what has been added between when your previous operation was started (t=141126475700, in this example) and now. Depending on the time it takes to run the first copy, this can represent a considerable amount of data. Because of that, and to make sure the next steps are going to be as short as possible, we will rerun the `CopyTable` command again. Because the `endtime` parameter that we used in the previous command is exclusive, we will use it for our current `starttime`:

```
hbase org.apache.hadoop.hbase.mapreduce.CopyTable --starttime=1411264757000 \
--endtime=1411430414000 --new.name=new_table previous_table
```

This second operation should be faster, as most of the data was copied in the initial operation. When the two `CopyTable` operations are done and before doing the last run, to not lose any data, you will have to stop the ingestion to your existing table while you are performing the following operations. In production environments, it is sometimes very sensitive to stop data ingestion. If that is the case, you can think about mitigation solutions. One of them consists of pushing the data into the newly created table. Another is to design the ingestion such that it can accept those pauses. Applications such as Kafka and Flume can be used to queue the data being ingested to HBase and can be paused without losing any information. Typically, the remaining steps might be accomplished in less than one hour. It is hard to quantify how long it will take to bring in the delta. It can be computed from the previous runs, but it can vary widely.

Finally, you will need to do one last run of the `CopyTable` tool to copy the remaining data. The time between the end of the last run and when you disabled the data ingestion is only a couple minutes, so it should run even faster. This time, because we want to copy all the remaining data, we will again use the last `endtime` value as the `starttime` parameter, but we will not specify any `endtime`:

```
hbase org.apache.hadoop.hbase.mapreduce.CopyTable --starttime=1411264757000 \
--new.name=new_table previous_table
```

This should run for a few seconds up to a few minutes. At the end of this operation, we will have a duplicate of the original table in our new table, with the new regions boundaries. The last step is to run some snapshot commands to rename the newly created table:

```
disable 'events_table'
drop 'events_table'
disable 'new_events_table'
snapshot 'new_events_table', 'snap1'
clone_snapshot 'snap1', 'events_table'
delete_snapshot 'snap1'
drop 'new_events_table'
```

At the end of all those operations, you will have a table containing the exact same data but with a reduced number of regions.

Offline merges

The second option to reduce the number of regions you have is to perform offline merges. To be able to perform the following steps, you will need to run HBase 0.94.13 or higher. Offline merge before 0.94.13 can fail and can leave corrupted files in your system (see HBASE-9504 (*https://issues.apache.org/jira/browse/HBASE-9504*)). One major constraint with offline merges is that they require total cluster downtime.

The steps to perform offline merges are as follows (we'll look at the details momentarily):

1. Stop the cluster.

2. Perform one or more merge operations.

3. Start the cluster.

To stop and start your HBase cluster, you can use the *bin/stop-hbase.sh* and *bin/start-hbase.sh* commands. If you are using a management tool such as Cloudera Manager, you will find the HBase actions in the HBase service management page.

Using HBase command

Performing an offline merge is done using the HBase `Merge` class called from the command line:

```
bin/hbase org.apache.hadoop.hbase.util.Merge testtable \
        "testtable,,1411948096799.77873c05283fe40822ba69a30b601959."\
        "testtable,11111111,1411948096800.e7e93a3545d36546ab8323622e56fdc4."
```

This command takes three parameters: the first is the table name, and the other two are the regions to merge. You can capture the region names from the HBase web interface. However, depending on the key design, it can be very difficult to run from the command line. Your key may contain some reserved characters (e.g., $, ^, etc.), which can make the formatting a bit difficult. If that's the case and you are not able to format the command, it may be prudent to use the Java API method described next. Once the command has been run, HBase will first test that the cluster is stopped. HBase will then perform many operations to merge all the content of those two regions into a single region. This will also create a new region with the new boundaries, create the related directory structure, move content into this new region, and update the HBase `.META.` information. The duration of the operation will depend on the size of the regions you are merging.

Using the Java API

To perform the same operation using the Java API, we will make use of the HBase merge utility class and call it while giving the correct parameters. This example is specific to HBase 0.94 and 0.96, and will not compile with later HBase versions. We have omitted parts of this code here, but provide a snippet in Example 14-1.

Example 14-1. Java merge for HBase 0.94

```
public int mergeRegion (Configuration config, String tableName,
                        String region1, String region2) {
    String[] args = {tableName, region1, region2};
    int status = -1;
```

```
try {
    status = ToolRunner.run(config, \
    new org.apache.hadoop.hbase.util.Merge(), args);
} catch (Exception e) {
    e.printStackTrace();
}
return status;
}
```

This method allows you to bypass the command line parsing challenge by directly passing the table and region names. It is still available in HBase 1.0, but because online merge is also available, it is no longer the recommended approach.

 Because this method requires a running ZooKeeper instance, you will not be able to test the offline merge operation with an HBase 0.94 standalone server. You will need to run it in a pseudodistributed or distributed mode.

Starting with 0.98

HBASE-7403 introduces online merge into HBase starting at version 0.98. Online merge allows you to concatenate two regions into a single one without having to shut down the HBase cluster or disable the target table. This is a big improvement in the merge process. Assuming a high enough version of HBase, this is currently the preferred way to solve the issue of too many regions.

Using HBase shell

Using the HBase shell, you will need to use the `merge_region` command. This command simply takes the two region-encoded names as parameters:

```
merge_region 'ENCODED_REGIONNAME', 'ENCODED_REGIONNAME'
```

The region-encoded name is the last token of the entire region name. From the region `testtable,22222222,1411566070443.aaa5bdc05b29931e1c9e9a2ece617f30.` "testtable" is the table name, "22222222" is the start key, "1411566070443" is the timestamp, and finally, "aaa5bdc05b29931e1c9e9a2ece617f30" is the encoded name (note that the final dot is part of the encoded name and is sometimes required, but not for the `merge` command).

Command call and output should look like this:

```
hbase(main):004:0> merge_region 'cec1ed0e20002c924069f9657925341e',\
                                 '1d61869389ae461a7971a71208a8dbe5'
0 row(s) in 0.0140 seconds
```

At the end of the operation, it is possible to validate from the HBase web UI that regions were merged and a new region has been created to replace them, including the boundaries of the two initial regions.

Using the Java API

The same merge operation is available from the HBase Java API. Example 14-2 will look up a table, retrieve the list of regions, and merge them two by two. At the end of the execution, the original table will have half the number of regions.

Example 14-2. Online Java merge

```
Configuration conf = HBaseConfiguration.create();
Connection connection = ConnectionFactory.createConnection(conf);
HBaseAdmin admin = (HBaseAdmin)connection.getAdmin();
List<HRegionInfo> regions = admin.getTableRegions(TableName.valueOf("t1")); ❶
LOG.info("testtable contains " + regions.size() + " regions.");
for (int index = 0; index < regions.size() / 2; index++) {
  HRegionInfo region1 = regions.get(index*2);
  HRegionInfo region2 = regions.get(index*2+1);
  LOG.info("Merging regions " + region1 + " and " + region2);
  admin.mergeRegions(region1.getEncodedNameAsBytes(),
                     region2.getEncodedNameAsBytes(), false); ❷
}
admin.close();
```

❶ Retrieves the existing regions for a given table

❷ Performs the merge operation

Output of this example over a nine-region table will look like the following (some of the output has been truncated to fit the width of this page):

```
2014-09-24 16:38:59,686 INFO  [main] ch18.Merge: testtable contains 9 regions.
2014-09-24 16:38:59,686 INFO  [main] ch18.Merge: Merging regions ... and ...
2014-09-24 16:38:59,710 INFO  [main] ch18.Merge: Merging regions ... and ...
2014-09-24 16:38:59,711 INFO  [main] ch18.Merge: Merging regions ... and ...
2014-09-24 16:38:59,713 INFO  [main] ch18.Merge: Merging regions ... and ...
```

Each region will print the following information in the output:

- The encoded region name in the form of a 32-character long hexadecimal string: 4b673c906173cd99afbbe03ea3dceb15

- The region name formed by the table name, the start key, the timestamp, and the encoded name, comma separated: testtable,aaaaaaa8,1411591132411,4b673c906173cd99afbbe03ea3dceb15

- The start key: aaaaaaa8

- The end key: `c71c71c4`

Keys used in the example table are string based and can be printed by HBase. However, when your keys contain nonprintable characters, HBase will format them in hexadecimal form. A key containing a mix of printable and nonprintable characters, represented by the byte array [42, 73, 194] will be printed *I\xC2.

Prevention

There are multiple ways to prevent an HBase cluster from facing issues related to the number of regions.

 Keep in mind that you need to consider not only the number of regions, but also the number of column families in each of those regions. Indeed, for each column family within a region, HBase will keep track of it in memory and in the `hbase:meta` table. Therefore, having 400 regions of two column families is not better than having 800 regions of a single column family. Having too many column families in a table also creates problems, as we will explore in Chapter 15.

Regions Size

First, you will want to make sure the maximum file size is set to at least 10 GB. It is not an issue to have regions smaller than that, but you want to make sure that when required, regions can get as big as 10 GB. Presplitting is discussed later in this section. It is recommended to monitor region sizes using a visualization tool such as Hannibal (*https://github.com/sentric/hannibal*). Watch for regions that are growing faster than others, and look to split them during off-peak usage times. Figure 14-3 illustrates how Hannibal helps you to view the size of each region.

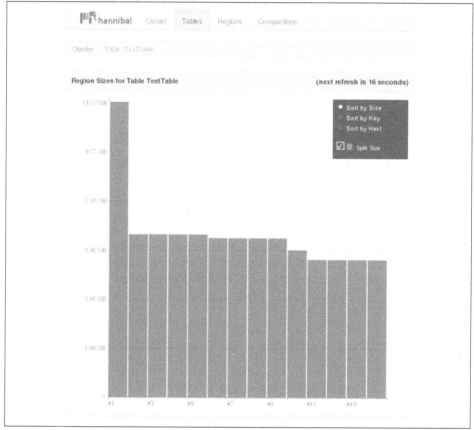

Figure 14-3. Visual overview of region sizes courtesy of Hannibal

HBase default split policy (org.apache.hadoop.hbase.regionserver.Increasing
ToUpperBoundRegionSplitPolicy) ensures that regions never go above the configured maximum file size (hbase.hregion.max.filesize). However, it might create
many smaller regions when cluster load is small (fewer than 100 regions). To make
sure your regions can grow to a decent size, validate that hbase.hregion.max.file
size property is configured to at least 10 GB. This property is represented in bytes;
therefore it should be 10737418240. However, it is also a common practice to set the
maximum file size value to a higher number up to 100 GB. When using larger region
sizes, it is important to manage the splits manually. This will make sure the splits
occur at the right time and have a minimum impact on the HBase cluster operations
and SLAs.

We do *not* recommend disabling splits or setting the split size to very big values like 200 GB or more. A region can easily grow to an unwieldy size if there's a spike in volume, if there are uncleansed records, or if the admin takes a vacation. If a region does not get split and continues to grow up to a very big size, it might crash the RegionServer. Upon failure, all regions from the server will be reassigned to another server, which will cause a cascading effect of crashes because of the size. From RegionServer to RegionServer, the culprit region will be reassigned and each time it will cause the target host to fail. If this is not recognized early, the entire cluster might go down.

Even if you expect your table to be small, you can still presplit it to increase distribution across RegionServers or manually trigger the splits to make sure you have up to as many regions as you have RegionServers. However, because HBase works better with bigger regions, make sure all your regions are at least 1 GB.

Key and Table Design

The second thing you want to look at is how your application has been designed. One of the most common mistakes in HBase application design is to abuse the number of column families. Because a memstore for a specific region will be divided between the different column families, having too many of them will reduce the size of the memory available for each and might result in very small flushes for some column families. Also, because of the size of the flushed files, it will generate extra compactions. Reducing the number of column families will allow more memory per region for the remaining column families, will reduce the required flushes and compactions, and will allow you to host more regions per server.

Another common mistake on table design is related to presplitting. Based on your key design and the size of the dataset, you will want to make sure that the table is correctly presplit before starting to inject data into the cluster. If the table has not been presplit correctly, you may end up with many unused or underutilized regions. Unused and underutilized regions still require resources such as memory and CPU, and still require periodic compactions. If your data is not evenly distributed but the table is evenly split, you will also end up with some regions being heavily used and some others being almost not used.

Too Many Column Families

Many HBase users start to design HBase tables before reading about it and before knowing about all the HBase features and behaviors. People coming from the RDBMS world, with no knowledge of the differences between a column family and a column qualifier, will be tempted to create a column family for each column they have of a table they want to migrate to HBase. As a result, it is common to see tables designed with too many column families.

For years, it has been recommended to keep the number of column families under three. But there is no magic number like this. Why not two? Why not four? Technically, HBase can manage more than three of four column families. However, you need to understand how column families work to make the best use of them. The consequences explained here will give you a very good idea of what kind of pressure column families are putting on HBase. Keep in mind that column families are built to regroup data with a similar format or a similar access pattern. Let's look at these two factors and how they affect the number of column families:

Regarding the format

> If you have to store large text data, you will most probably want to have this column family compressed. But if for the same row you also want to store a picture, then you most probably do not want this to be compressed because it will use CPU cycles to not save any space so will have negative impact on the performances. Using separate column families make sense here.

Regarding the access pattern

> The best way to describe this is to consider a real-world example. Imagine you have a table storing customer information. A few huge columns store the customer metadata. They contain a lot and are a few kilobytes in size. Then another column is a counter that stores each time the customer clicks on a page on the website. The metadata columns will almost never change, while the counter col-

umn will be updated many times a day. Over time, because of all the operations on the counters, the memstore will be flushed into disk. This will create files that mostly contain only counter operations, which at some point will be compacted. However, when the compaction is performed, it will most probably select HFiles that contain customer metadata. The compaction will rewrite all those huge cells of customer metadata as well as the small counters. As a result, the vast majority of the I/O will be wasted rewriting files with little to no change just to update or compact the small counters. This creates an overhead on the I/Os. HBase triggers compactions at the column family level. By separating the customer metadata and the customer counters into two different columns families, we will avoid unnecessarily rewriting the static information. It will lower the total IOPs on the RegionServers and therefore will improve the overall performances of the applications.

So how many column families is too many? We will not be able to give you a magic number. If it makes sense to separate them from the access pattern or from the format, separate them. But if you read and write them almost the same way and data has almost the same format, then simply keep it together in the same column family.

Consequences

Abusing column families will impact your application's performance and the way HBase reacts in different ways. Depending how hard you are pushing HBase, it might also impact its stability because timeouts can occur, and RegionServers can get killed.

Memory

The first impact of too many column families is on the memory side. HBase shares its memstore (write cache) among all the regions. Because each region is allowed a maximum configurable cache size of 128 MB, this section has to be shared between all the column families of the same region. Therefore, the more column families you have, the smaller the average available size in the memstore will be for each of them. When one column family's bucket is full, all of the other column families in that region must be flushed to disk as well, even if they have relatively little data. This will put a lot of pressure on the memory, as many objects and small files will get created again and again, but it will also put some pressure on the disks because those small files will have to be compacted together.

 Some work over HBASE-3149 and HBASE-10201 has been done to flush only the column families that are full instead of flushing all of them. However, this is not yet available in HBase 1.0. Once this feature is available, the memory impact of having too many column families will be drastically reduced, as will the impact on the compactions.

Compactions

The number of column families affects the number of store files created during flushes, and subsequently the number of compactions that must be performed. If a table has eight column families, and region's 128 MB memstore is full, the data from the eight families is flushed to separate files. Over time, more flushes will occur. When more than three store files exist for a column family, HBase considers those files for compaction. If a table has one column family, one set of files would need to be compacted. With eight column families, eight sets of files need to be compacted, affecting the resources of the RegionServers and HDFS. Configuring fewer column families allows you to have larger memstore size per family; therefore fewer store files need to be flushed, and most importantly, fewer compactions need to occur, reducing the I/Os on the underlying HDFS system. When a table needs to be flushed (like before taking a snapshot, or if administrators trigger flushes from the shell), all the memstores are flushed into disk. Depending on the previous operations, it is possible that doing this will make HBase reach yet another compaction trigger and will start compactions for many if not all the regions and column families. The more column families, the more compactions will go into the queue and the more pressure will be put on HBase and HDFS.

Split

HBase stores columns families' data into separate files and directories. When one of those directories become bigger than the configured region size, a split is triggered.

Splits affect all column families in a region, not only the column family whose data grew beyond the maximum size. As a result, if some column families are pretty big while others are pretty small, you might end up with column families containing only a few cells. RegionServers allocate resources like memory and CPU threads per region and column family. Very small regions and column families can create unnecessary pressure on those resources. The HBase master will also need to manage more entries in the `hbase:meta` table and the underlying HDFS system. The HDFS DataNodes and NameNodes will also need to manage more I/Os for the small column family files. If you expect some column families to contain much more data than others, you might want to separate that data into other tables, producing fewer but larger files.

Causes, Solution, and Prevention

The cause of having too many column families is always related to schema design. HBase will not create too many column families on your behalf; there's no automatic-split behavior that can cause too many column families. Thus, to prevent this problem, you need to carefully consider HBase principles before you begin designing your schema so that you can determine an appropriate number of column families.

Several solutions exist for the issue of having too many column families. Understanding the data in the column families and the access pattern is critical. Sometimes the column families are not required and can simply be dropped—for example, if the data is duplicated/denormalized and is available in another table. Sometimes the column family is present due to the access pattern (i.e., rollups or summary column-families). In that case, maybe the column family can simply be de-coupled from the table and moved to its own table. Other times, the data in the separate column family can be merged together with larger column families.

All the operations in the next sections can be done using the Java API, but they can also very simply be done using the HBase shell or the command line. Because the Java API will not really add any benefit to those operations, we have not documented it.

Delete a Column Family

If you have decided that you don't need a specific column family, simply remove this column family from the table META information. The following method will delete the picture column family from the sensors table:

```
alter 'sensors', NAME => 'picture', METHOD => 'delete'
```

This operation might take some time to execute because it will be applied in all the regions one by one. At the end, related files in HDFS will be removed, and the hbase:meta table will be updated to reflect the modification.

Merge a Column Family

Because of a flaw in the original schema design, or a shift in scope in the original use case, you might have separated the data in two different column families but now want to merge it back into a single column family. As we discussed in "Solution" on page 179, CopyTable allows you to copy data from one table into another one. CopyTable will help us in the current situation. The idea is that CopyTable will require a source table and a destination table; however, those two tables don't necessarily need to be different. Also, CopyTable allows us to rename one column family into a new one (Figure 15-1).

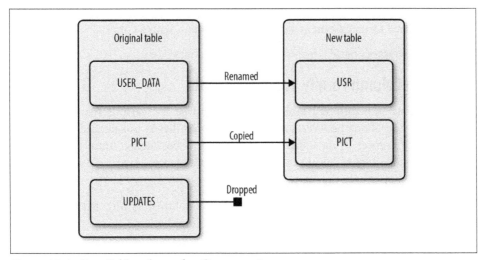

Figure 15-1. CopyTable column families operations

`CopyTable` will run a MapReduce job over the data you want to read and will emit puts based on what you asked. If for a given table called `customer` you want to transfer the data present in the column family `address` into the column family `profile`, you simply need to set both the input and the output table to be the `customer` table, the input column family to be `address` and the output to be `profile`. This operation can be achieved by running the following command:

```
hbase org.apache.hadoop.hbase.mapreduce.CopyTable --new.name=customer \
                                    --families=address:profile customer
```

At the end of the MapReduce job, all the data in that you had into the `address` column family will also be present in the `profile` column family. You can now delete the address column family using the `alter` command seen in the preceding code snippet.

 There are few things to keep in mind when using the `CopyTable` method of merging column families. Data may be overwritten in the destination column family. If data with the same row/column qualifier exists in both the source and destination column family, the data in the destination column family will be overwritten. When copying a column family, there will need to be enough free space in HDFS to hold both copies temporarily. Before starting this operation, estimate this additional space usage and account for it. If you run this on a live production table, make sure any updates made to the source column family are also made to the destination column family. If you are using a supplied or custom timestamp on your puts or deletes, avoid this method on a live table, as there might be unexpected results.

It is also possible to merge back multiple column families into a single column family. You simply need to specify them all by separating them with a comma:

```
--families=address:profile,phone:profile,status:profile
```

Separate a Column Family into a New Table

Separating data into different tables might be desired for various reasons. Perhaps atomicity of operations between a table's column families is not needed or there are significant differences in data size or access patterns between column families. Perhaps it just makes more logical sense to have separate tables. Again, we will make use of CopyTable to perform the operations.

The following command copies the data from column family picture of the customer table to the map table in the same column family:

```
hbase org.apache.hadoop.hbase.mapreduce.CopyTable --families=picture \
                  --new.name=map customer
```

Here again, as long as you want to transfer multiple column families into the same destination table, you can specify each desired column family by separating them with a comma.

Both the destination table and the destination column family should exist before you start the MapReduce job.

 All the warnings from the previous paragraph also apply to the current one.

Hotspotting

As previously discussed, to maintain its parallel nature, HBase takes advantage of regions contained in RegionServers distributed across the nodes. In HBase, all read and write requests should be uniformly distributed across all of the regions in the RegionServers. Hotspotting occurs when a given region serviced by a single Region-Server receives most or all of the read or write requests.

Consequences

HBase will process the read and write requests based on the row key. The row key is instrumental for HBase to be able to take advantage of all regions equally. When a hotspot occurs, the RegionServer trying to process all of the requests can become overwhelmed while the other RegionServers are mostly idle. Figure 16-1 illustrates a region being hotspotted. The higher the load is on a single RegionServer, the more I/O intensive and blocking processes that will have to be executed (e.g., compactions, garbage collections, and region splits). Hotspotting can also result in increased latencies, which from the client side create timeouts or missed SLAs.

Table Regions					
Name	Region Server	Start Key	End Key	Locality	Requests
TestTable,,1427677218929.c808f8d56f78c3c41fb9617c95c5d8fc.	t430s:16201		010094234	0.0	2209665
TestTable,010094234,1427677218929.979d5f6ed7859d60cf67973ae83747d3.	t430s:16201	010094234	020223584	0.0	667
TestTable,020223584,1427677269908.f9d413e1a9df96f0eccb4f24428ef71e.	t430s:16201	020223584	030929104	0.0	686
TestTable,030929104,1427677269908.a8c98da26de9c3138a00e1b2876cdf0b.	t430s:16201	030929104	050013975	0.0	1238
TestTable,050013975,1427677280538.6c053ebc240abea285ea800e09c82c0e.	t430s:16201	050013975	06007249	0.0	588
TestTable,06007249,1427677280538.5ba5a5cfb4660c2717ecf49cf5880098.	t430s:16201	06007249	07015627	0.0	630
TestTable,07015627,1427677283513.efdb955f394be47dac15bb0745631d13.	t430s:16201	07015627	080419479	0.0	655
TestTable,080419479,1427677283513.4a1ea52a4e57617067bbc879b11f8a25.	t430s:16201	080419479		0.0	1238

Figure 16-1. Region being hotspotted

Causes

The main cause of hotspotting is usually an issue in the key design. In the following sections, we will look at some of the most common causes of hotspotting, including monotonically incrementing or poorly distributed keys, very small reference tables, and applications issues.

Monotonically Incrementing Keys

Monotonically incrementing keys are keys where only the last bits or bytes are slowly incrementing. This means that most of the new key being written to or read from HBase is extremely similar to the previously written or read key. The most commonly seen monotonically incrementing key occurs when the timestamp is used as the key. When timestamp is used as the row key, the key will slowly increment from the first put. Let's take a look at a quick example: in HBase, keys are stored ordered in lexicographical order. Our row keys will update as shown here:

```
1424362829
1424362830
1424362831
1424362832
...
1424362900
1424362901
1424362902
1424362903
1424362904
```

If requests are writes, each of the preceding updates is going to go into the same region until it reaches the key of the next region or its maximum configured size. At that point, the region will split, and we will begin incrementally updating the next region. Notice that most of the write operations are against the same region, thereby burdening a single RegionServer. Unfortunately, when this issue is detected after a deployment, there is nothing you can do to prevent hotspotting. The only way to avoid this kind of issue is to prevent it with a good key design.

Poorly Distributed Keys

As stated before, key design is very important, as it will impact not only the scalability of your application, but also its performance. However, in the first iteration of schema design in a use case, it is not uncommon for keys to be poorly designed and therefore wrongly distributed. This can occur due to a lack of information at the time of the schema design but also because of issues when implementing the application. A good example of a poorly distributed key is when you expect the source data to send you keys with digits distributed between "0" and "9"; but you end up receiving keys always prefixed with value before the expected "0" to "9" values. In this case, the application expects to receive "1977" and "2001" but gets "01977" and "02001" instead. In this example, if you had properly presplit the table into 10 regions (up to "1", "1" to "2", "2" to "3", etc.), then all the values you received and stored in HBase would be written to the first region (up to "1") while all of the other regions would remain un-touched. In this case, even though we had the right intentions with the schema design, the data will never get fully distributed. This issue should be discovered during proper testing, but if you discover this issue after the application has been deployed, don't despair—all is not lost. It is recommended to split the hotspotting region into multiple regions. This should restore the expected distribution. In this example, you will have to split the first region into 10 regions to account for the leading zero. The new region range distribution being "00", then "00" to "01", "01 to "02", and so on. The other regions, after "1", will not be used if the keys are always prefixed by "0" and can be merged together one by one through region "10".

Small Reference Tables

This common hotspotting issue refers to the bottleneck that results from the use of small reference tables typically to perform joins in HBase. For this example, we have two reference tables consisting of a single region defining postal codes and city names. In this case, we perform a MapReduce join over a billion-row orders table. All the generated mappers are going to query those two tables to perform the lookups. As a result, the two RegionServers hosting the two reference regions will be overwhelmed by calls from all the other servers in the cluster. If you are really unlucky, those two regions will be served by the same RegionServer. This kind of contention/bottleneck will increase latency and create delays that can lead to job failures due to timeouts. The good news is that there are multiple ways to avoid this situation. The first and easiest option is to presplit your reference tables. The goal would be to have close to as many regions as you have RegionServers. Presplitting the reference table may not be an option if the table is too small or if you have too many RegionServers on HBase at the current time.

The other option here would be to distribute this table to all the nodes before performing the join. The distribution of this data will be done using the MapReduce distributed cache mechanism. The distributed cache framework will copy the data to the slave node before any tasks are executed. The efficiency of this approach stems from the fact that the files are copied only once per job.

When all servers have a local copy of the data, and if the data is small enough to fit into memory, it can then be loaded from the setup method of the MapReduce code, and lookups can now be performed into memory instead of reading from the disk.

This will increase performance, while also fixing the hotspotting issue.

If MapReduce also updates or enriches the reference table, the distributed cache is not a viable option. Indeed, distributing a copy of the table at the beginning means the content is fixed for the duration of the job. If updates to the reference table are required in your use case, then the best option is to presplit your reference table to ensure even distribution of the table across the RegionServers.

Applications Issues

The final example of region hotspotting is related to application design or implementation issues. When a region is hotspotting, it is very important to identify the root cause. To accomplish this, we need to determine the source of the offending calls. If the data is very well distributed into the table, the hotspotting may be coming from a bug causing writes to always land in the same region. This is where mistakenly added prefix fields, double or triple writes, or potentially badly converted data types can manifest themselves as application issues. Let's imagine the system is expected to receive a four-byte integer value, but the backend code converts that to a height byte value. The four initial bytes might have been very well distributed over the entire range of data, however, adding four empty bytes to this value will create a never incrementing prefix of four empty bytes [0x00, 0x00, 0x00, 0x00] all landing into the same HBase region and creating the hotspot.

Meta Region Hotspotting

Another commonly seen issue is applications hotspotting the META region. When creating a connection to an HBase cluster, the application's first stop is ZooKeeper to acquire HBase Master and the META region location. The application will cache this information, and will then query the META table to send read and write requests to the proper region. Each time a new connection is created, the application will again go to ZooKeeper, and to META. To avoid having all those calls to ZooKeeper and the META table each time you perform a request to HBase, it is recommended to create a single connection and to share it across your application. For a web service application, it is recommended to create a pool of a few HBase connections and share them with all the threads on the application side.

Prevention and Solution

The best way to solve hotspotting is to prevent it from happening. This starts right at the beginning of the project with a well-tested key design (refer back to "Key and Table Design" on page 189 if you need a refresher on how to do this). It is also important to keep an eye on all your region metrics to have early detection of potential hotspotting. On the HBase Master web interface, the table page shows the number of requests received for each of the table's regions. Requests column represents the number of read and write requests received by the region since it has been online. When regions are moved to other RegionServers, or when a table is disabled, the region metrics are reset. So when a region shows a very high number compared to the others, it might be hotspotting but could also be due to very recent balancing of the region between two servers. The only way to determine if it is from hotspotting or region transitions is by looking through the logs or monitoring the suspect region over time. The best way to avoid these issues in production is to put your application through proper testing and development cycles.

Timeouts and Garbage Collection

Garbage collection (GC) is the process that cleans up the memory no longer refer-enced by Java objects. This is done to free up the memory and make it available again to the application. Garbage collections are a normal, unavoidable occurrence in Java, but they can be managed. Depending on the garbage collection algorithm used, there might be one or more garbage collection events going. The most impactful garbage collection event for an HBase server is when the Java Virtual Machine needs to per-form a full garbage collection (full GC). Such an operation is known as a "stop-the-world pause" and will pause the JVM while it is cleaning enough memory to allocate required objects. During this operation, the current running threads are in a holding pattern until the JVM completes its GC. Long-running GC pauses are usually the main cause of timeouts on an HBase server, but we will also look at a few other risks.

Consequences

As stated before, full GCs are a "stop-the-world pause," meaning any operation run-ning on an HBase server will be paused until GC completion. These pauses can mani-fest themselves externally as visible big spikes in the reads and writes latencies, or even in the worst cases as false server failures. There are other issues that can reflect similar performance spikes in the RegionServer. The sources of these spikes should always be clearly identified before starting to treat GC issues. The JVM will be paused while performing the garbage collection cleanup, during this time all read and write operations will be queued by the client, which must wait for the server to become responsive again. Garbage collection should always complete before the configured timeout values. Once complete, the reads and writes will resume to the server and be processed. However, if the Java tunings are not properly configured, the garbage col-lection can last longer than the configured timeouts. There are a few different actions that can occur when the garbage collection exceeds the configured timeout values. If

the timeout occurs on the client side before the operations were processed by the
server, the client will receive an exception and operation will not be processed:

```
Tue Mar 17 12:23:03 EDT 2015, null, java.net.SocketTimeoutException:\
callTimeout=1, callDuration=2307: row '' on table 'TestTable' at\
region=TestTable,,1426607781080.c1adf2b53088bef7db148b893c2fd4da.,\
hostname=t430s,45896,1426609305849, seqNum=1276
    at o.a.h.a.client.RpcRetryingCallerWithReadReplicas.throwEnrichedException\
    (RpcRetryingCallerWithReadReplicas.java:264)
    at o.a.h.a.client.ScannerCallableWithReplicas.call\
    (ScannerCallableWithReplicas.java:199)
    at o.a.h.a.client.ScannerCallableWithReplicas.call\
    (ScannerCallableWithReplicas.java:56)
    at o.a.h.a.client.RpcRetryingCaller.callWithoutRetries\
    (RpcRetryingCaller.java:200)
    at o.a.h.a.client.ClientScanner.call(ClientScanner.java:287)
    at o.a.h.a.client.ClientScanner.next(ClientScanner.java:367)
    at DeleteGetAndTest.main(DeleteGetAndTest.java:110)
Caused by: java.net.SocketTimeoutException: callTimeout=1, callDuration=2307:\
row '' on table 'TestTable' at region=TestTable,,1426607781080.\
c1adf2b53088bef7db148b893c2fd4da., hostname=t430s,45896,\
1426609305849, seqNum=1276
    at o.a.h.a.client.RpcRetryingCaller.callWithRetries\
    (RpcRetryingCaller.java:159)
    at o.a.h.a.client.ScannerCallableWithReplicas$RetryingRPC.call\
    (ScannerCallableWithReplicas.java:294)
    at o.a.h.a.client.ScannerCallableWithReplicas$RetryingRPC.call\
    (ScannerCallableWithReplicas.java:275)
    at java.util.concurrent.FutureTask.run(FutureTask.java:262)
    at java.util.concurrent.ThreadPoolExecutor.runWorker\
    (ThreadPoolExecutor.java:1145)
    at java.util.concurrent.ThreadPoolExecutor$Worker.run\
    (ThreadPoolExecutor.java:615)
    at java.lang.Thread.run(Thread.java:745)
Caused by: java.io.IOException: Call to t430s/10.32.0.23:45896 failed on local\
exception: o.a.h.a.ipc.CallTimeoutException: Call id=2, waitTime=2001,\
operationTimeout=2000 expired.
    at o.a.h.a.ipc.RpcClientImpl.wrapException(RpcClientImpl.java:1235)
    at o.a.h.a.ipc.RpcClientImpl.call(RpcClientImpl.java:1203)
    at o.a.h.a.ipc.AbstractRpcClient.callBlockingMethod\
    (AbstractRpcClient.java:216)
    at o.a.h.a.ipc.AbstractRpcClient$BlockingRpcChannelImplementation.\
    callBlockingMethod(AbstractRpcClient.java:300)
    at o.a.h.a.protobuf.generated.ClientProtos$ClientService$BlockingStub.scan\
    (ClientProtos.java:31751)
    at o.a.h.a.client.ScannerCallable.call(ScannerCallable.java:199)
    at o.a.h.a.client.ScannerCallable.call(ScannerCallable.java:62)
    at o.a.h.a.client.RpcRetryingCaller.callWithRetries\
    (RpcRetryingCaller.java:126)
    ... 6 more
Caused by: o.a.h.a.ipc.CallTimeoutException: Call id=2, waitTime=2001,\
operationTimeout=2000 expired.
```

```
at o.a.h.a.ipc.Call.checkAndSetTimeout(Call.java:70)
at o.a.h.a.ipc.RpcClientImpl.call(RpcClientImpl.java:1177)
... 12 more
```

Before timing out, operations will be retried a few times with an increasing delay between each of the retries.

The timeout can also occur on the server side, which can cause false RegionServer failures. From time to time, HBase RegionServers need to report back to ZooKeeper to confirm they are still alive. By default, to confirm they are still alive, the HBase regions servers need to report back to ZooKeeper every 40 seconds when using an external ZooKeeper, or every 90 seconds when HBase manages ZooKeeper service. Timeouts and retries can be configured using multiple parameters such as `zookeeper.session.timeout`, `hbase.rpc.timeout`, `hbase.client.retries.number`, or `hbase.client.pause`.

When a server is too slow to report, it can miss the heartbeat and report to Zoo-Keeper too late. When the RegionServer misses a heartbeat, it is considered as lost by ZooKeeper and will be reported to the HBase Master because it's not possible to determine if the RegionServer is responding too slow, or if the server has actually crashed. In the event of a crash, the HBase master will reassign all the regions previously assigned to the server to the other RegionServers. While reassigning the regions, the previously pending operations will be reprocessed to guarantee consistency. When the slow RegionServer recovers from the pause and finally reports to ZooKeeper, the RegionServer will be informed that it has been considered dead and will throw a `YouAreDeadException` which will cause the RegionServer to terminate itself.

Here's an example of a `YouAreDeadException` caused by a long server pause:

```
2015-03-18 12:29:32,664 WARN  [t430s,16201,1426696058785-HeapMemoryTunerChore]
      util.Sleeper: We slept 109666ms instead of 60000ms, this is likely due
      to a long garbage collecting pause and it's usually bad, see
      http://hbase.apache.org/book.html#trouble.rs.runtime.zkexpired
2015-03-18 12:29:32,682 FATAL [regionserver/t430s/10.32.0.23:16201] regionserver.
      HRegionServer: ABORTING RegionServer t430s,16201,1426696058785:
      o.a.h.h.YouAreDeadException: Server REPORT rejected; currently
      processing t430s,16201,1426696058785 as dead server
    at o.a.h.h.m.ServerManager.checkIsDead(ServerManager.java:382)
    at o.a.h.h.m.ServerManager.regionServerReport(ServerManager.java:287)
    at o.a.h.h.m.MasterRpcServices.regionServerReport(MasterRpcServices.java:278)
    at o.a.h.h.p.g.RegionServerStatusProtos$RegionServerStatusService$2.
          callBlockingMethod(RegionServerStatusProtos.java:7912)
    at o.a.h.h.i.RpcServer.call(RpcServer.java:2031)
    at o.a.h.h.i.CallRunner.run(CallRunner.java:107)
    at o.a.h.h.i.RpcExecutor.consumerLoop(RpcExecutor.java:130)
    at o.a.h.h.ic.RpcExecutor$1.run(RpcExecutor.java:107)
    at java.lang.Thread.run(Thread.java:745)
```

Causes

When dealing with Java-based platforms, memory fragmentation is typically the main cause of full garbage collection and pauses. In a perfect world, all the objects would be the same size, and it would be very easy to track, find, and allocate free memory without causing heavy memory fragmentation. Unfortunately, in the real world this is not the case, and puts received by the servers are almost never the same size. Also, the compressed HFiles blocks and many other HBase objects are also almost neither never the same size. The previously mentioned factors will create fragmentation of the available memory. The more the JVM memory is fragmented, the more it will need to run garbage collection to release unused memory. Typically, the larger the heap is, the longer a full GC will take to complete. This means raising the heap too high without (or even sometimes) with proper tuning can lead to timeouts.

Garbage collection is not the only contributing factor to timeouts and pauses. It is possible to create a scenario where the memory is overallocated (giving to HBase or other applications more memory than available physical memory), the operating system will need to swap some of the memory pages to the disks. This is one of the least desirable situations in HBase. Swapping is guaranteed to cause issues with cluster, which in turn will create timeouts and drastically impact the latencies.

The final risk is improper hardware behaviors or failures. Network failures and hard drives are good examples of such risks.

Storage Failure

For multiple reasons, a storage drive can fail and become unresponsive. When this occurs, the operating system will try multiple times before reporting the error to the application. This might create delays and general slowness, which again will impact the latency and might trigger timeouts or failures. HDFS is designed to handle such failures and no data will be lost, however failures on the operating system drive my impact the entire host availability.

Power-Saving Features

To reduce energy consumption, some disks have energy-saving features. When this feature is activated, if a disk is not accessed for a certain period of time, it will go on sleep and will stop spinning. As soon as the system needs data stored on that disk, it needs first to start spinning the disk back, wait for it to reach its full speed, and then only start to read from it. When HBase makes any request to the I/O layer, the total time it takes the energy-saving drives to spin back up can contribute to timeouts and latency spikes. In certain circumstances, those timeouts can even cause server failures.

Network Failure

On big clusters, servers are assigned into racks, connected together using top-of-the-rack switches. Such switches are powerful and come with many features, but like any other hardware they can have small failures and can pause because of them. Those pauses will cause communications between the servers to fail for a certain period of time. Here again, if this period of time extends beyond the configured timeout, HBase will consider those servers as lost and will kill them if they come back online, with all the impacts on the latencies that you can imagine.

Solutions

When a server crashes or has been closed because of a timeout issue, the only solution is to restart it. The source of such a failure can be a network, configuration, or hardware issue (or something else entirely). Whatever the source of this failure is, it needs to be identified and addressed to avoid similar issues in the future. When your server fails for any reason, if not addressed, the chances of this occurring again on your cluster are very high and other failures are to be expected. The best place to start with to identify issues are the servers logs, both HBase Master and the culprit Region-Server; however, it might also be good to have a look at the system logs (*/var/log/messages*), the network interfaces statistics (in particular, the drop packages), and the switch monitoring interface. It is also a very good practice to validate your network bandwidth between multiple nodes at the same time across different racks using tools like iperf. Testing the network performances and stability will allow you to detect bottleneck in the configuration, but will miss configured interfaces (like, configured to be 1 Gbps instead of 10 Gbps, etc.).

Hardware duplication and new generation network management tools like Arista products can help to avoid network and hardware issues and will be looked at in the following section.

Last, Cloudera Manager and other cluster management applications can automatically restart the services when they exit (RegionServers, Masters, ThriftServers, etc.), however, it might be good to not activate such features, as you want to identify the root cause of the failures before restarting the services.

There are multiple ways to prevent such situations from occurring, and the next section will review them one by one.

Prevention

As we have just seen, timeouts and garbage collection can occur for multiple different reasons. In this section, we identify what those situations might be, and provide ways to prevent them from happening.

Reduce Heap Size

The bigger the heap size, the longer it takes for the JVM to do a garbage collection (GC). Even if more memory can be nice to increase cache size and improve latency and performance, you might face some long pauses because of the GC. With the JVM's default garbage collection algorithms, a full garbage collection will freeze the application and is highly probable to create a ZooKeeper timeout, which will result in the RegionServer being killed. There is very little risks to face GC pauses on the HBase Master server. Using the default HBase settings, it is recommended to keep the HBase heap size under 20 GB. Garbage collection can be configured inside the *conf/hbase-conf.sh* script. The default setting is to use the Java CMS (Concurrent Mark Sweep) algorithm: `export HBASE_OPTS="-XX:+UseConcMarkSweepGC"`.

Additional debugging information for the GC processes is avalable in the configuration file, and is ready to use. In the following example, we are adding only one of these options (we recommend taking a look at the configuration file to understand all of the available options):

```
# This enables basic GC logging to its own file with automatic log rolling.
# Only applies to jdk 1.6.0_34+ and 1.7.0_2+.
# If FILE-PATH is not replaced, the log file(.gc) would still be generated in
# the HBASE_LOG_DIR .
# export CLIENT_GC_OPTS="-verbose:gc -XX:+PrintGCDetails -XX:+PrintGCDateStamps\
# -Xloggc:<FILE-PATH> -XX:+UseGCLogFileRotation -XX:NumberOfGCLogFiles=1\
# -XX:GCLogFileSize=512M"
```

Starting with Oracle JDK 1.7, the JVM comes with a new garbage collection algorithm called G1 for Garbage First. Details about G1 can be found in "Using the G1GC Algorithm" on page 209 .

Off-Heap BlockCache

HBase 1.0 or more recent allows you to configure off-heap `BlockCache` using what is called `BucketCache`. Using off-heap memory allows HBase to manage the fragmentation on its own. Because all HBase blocks are supposed to be the same size (except if specifically defined differently at the table level), it is easy to manage the related memory fragmentation. This reduces the heap memory usage and fragmentation and therefore, the required garbage reduction. When using off-heap cache, you can reduce the default heap size memory, which reduces the time required for the JVM to run a full garbage collection. Also, if HBase is getting a mix load of reads and writes, as only the `BlockCache` is moved off heap, you can reduce the heap `BlockCache` to give more memory to the memstore using `hbase.regionserver.global.memstore` and `hfile.block.cache.size` properties. When servers have a limited amount of memory, it is also possible to configure the bucket cache to use specific devices such as SSD drives as the memory storage for the cache.

Using the G1GC Algorithm

The Default JVM garbage collection algorithm in Java 6, 7, and 8 tends to struggle with large heaps running full GC. These full GCs will pause the JVM until memory is cleaned. As seen in the previous section, this might negatively impact the server availability. Java 1.7_u60+ is the first stable release of the G1GC algorithm. G1GC is a garbage collection algorithm that stands for garbage first collection. G1 breaks memory into 1–32 MB regions depending on the heap size. Then when running cleanup attempts to clean the regions that are no longer being used first, G1 frees up more memory without having to perform stop-the-world pauses. G1GC also heavily leverages mixed collections that occur on the fly, again helping to avoid the stop-the-world pauses that can be detrimental to HBase latency.

Tuning the G1GC collector can be daunting and require some trial and error. Once properly configured, we have used the G1GC collector with heaps as large as 176 GB. Heaps that large are beneficial to more than just read performance. If you are looking for strictly for read performance, off-heap caching will offer the performance bump without the tuning headaches. A benefit of having large heaps with G1GC is that it allows HBase to scale better horizontally by offering a large memstore pool for regions to share.

Must-use parameters

- `-XX:+UseG1GC`
- `-XX:+PrintFlagsFinal`
- `-XX:+PrintGCDetails`
- `-XX:+PrintGCDateStamps`
- `-XX:+PrintGCTimeStamps`
- `-XX:+PrintAdaptiveSizePolicy`
- `-XX:+PrintReferenceGC`

Additional HBase settings while exceeding 100 GB heaps

`-XX:-ResizePLAB`
    Promotion local allocation buffers (PLABs) avoid the large communication cost among GC threads, as well as variations during each GC.

`-XX:+ParallelRefProcEnabled`
    When this flag is turned on, GC uses multiple threads to process the increasing references during young and mixed GC.

`-XX:+AlwaysPreTouch`
Pre-touch the Java heap during JVM initialization. That means every page of the heap is demand-zeroed during initialization rather than incrementally during application execution.

`-XX:MaxGCPauseMillis=100`
Max pause will attempt to keep GC pauses below the referenced time. This becomes critical for proper tuning. G1GC will do its best to hold to the number, but will pause longer if necessary.

Other interesting parameters

`-XX:ParallelGCThreads=X`
Formula: 8 + (logical processors – 8) (5/8)

`-XX:G1NewSizePercent=X`
Eden size is calculated by (heap size * `G1NewSizePercent`). The default value of `G1NewSizePercent` is 5 (5% of total heap). Lowering this can change the total time young GC pauses take to complete.

`-XX:+UnlockExperimentalVMOptions`
Unlocks the use of the previously referenced flags.

`-XX:G1HeapWastePercent=5`
Sets the percentage of heap that you are willing to waste. The Java HotSpot VM does not initiate the mixed garbage collection cycle when the reclaimable percentage is less than the heap waste percentage. The default is 10%.

`-XX:G1MixedGCLiveThresholdPercent=75`
Sets the occupancy threshold for an old region to be included in a mixed garbage collection cycle. The default occupancy is 65%. This is an experimental flag.

The primary goal from the tuning is to be running many mixed GC collections and avoiding the full GCs. When properly tuned, we should see very repeatable GC behavior assuming the workload stays relatively uniform. It is important to note that overprovisioning of the heap can help avoid the full GCs by leaving headroom for the mixed GCs to continue in the background. For further reading, check out Oracle's comprehensive documentation (*http://bit.ly/28LUPkI*).

Configure Swappiness to 0 or 1

HBase might not be the only application running on your environment, and at some point memory might have been over allocated. By default, Linux will try to anticipate the lack of memory and will start to swap to disk some memory pages. This is fine because it will allow the operating system to avoid being out of memory; however, writing such pages into disk takes time and will, here again, impact the latency. When a lot of memory need to be written to disk that way, a significant pause might occur into the operating system, which might cause the HBase server to miss the ZooKeeper heartbeat and die. To avoid this, it is recommended to reduce the swappiness to its minimum. Depending of the version of your kernel, this value will need to be set to 0 or 1. Starting with kernel version 3.5-rc1, `vm.swappiness=1` simulates `vm.swappiness=0` from earlier kernels. Also, it is important to not over commit the memory. For each of the applications running in your server, note the allocated memory, including off heap usage (if any), and sum them. You will need this value to be under the available physical memory after you remove some memory reserved for the operating system

---

Example of Memory Allocation for a 128 GB Server

- Reserve 2 GB for the OS.
- Reserve 2 GB for local applications you might have (Kerberos client, SSSD, etc.).
- Reserve 2 GB for the DataNode.
- Reserve 2 GB for the OS cache.
- The remaining 120 GB can be allocated to HBase.

However, because garbage collection can be an issue when more than 20 GB of heap is allocated, you can configure HBase to use 20 GB of Heap memory plus 100 GB of off-heap `BlockCache`.

Disable Environment-Friendly Features

As we discussed earlier in this chapter, environment-friendly features such as power saving can impact your server's performance and stability. It is recommended to disable all those features. They can usually be disabled from the bios. However, sometimes (like for some disks) it is simply not possible to deactivate them. If that's the case, it is recommended to replace those disks. In a production environment, you will need to be very careful when ordering your hardware to avoid anything including such features.

Hardware Duplication

It is a common practice to duplicate hardware to avoid downtime. Primary examples would be: running two OS drives in RAID1, leveraging dual power supplies, and bonding network interfaces in a failover setting. These duplications will remove numerous single points of failure creating a cluster with better uptime and less operations maintenance. The same can be applied to the network switches and all the other hardware present in the cluster.

HBCK and Inconsistencies

HBase Filesystem Layout

Like any database or filesystem, HBase can run into inconsistencies between what it believes its metadata looks like and what its filesystem actually looks like. Of course, the inverse of the previous statement can be true as well. Before getting into debugging HBase inconsistencies, it is important to understand the layout of HBase's metadata master table known as hbase:meta and the how HBase is laid out on HDFS. Looking at the meta table name hbase:meta, the hbase before the : indicates the namespace the table lives in, and after the : is the name of the table, which is meta. Namespaces are used for logical grouping of similar tables, typically utilized in multitenant environments. Out of the box, two namespaces are used: default and hbase. default is where all tables without a namespace specified are created, and hbase is used for HBase internal tables. For right now, we are going to focus on hbase:meta. HBase's meta table is used to store important pieces of information about the regions in the HBase tables. Here is a sample output of an HBase instance with one user table named odell:

```
hbase(main):002:0> describe 'hbase:meta'
DESCRIPTION
 'hbase:meta', {TABLE_ATTRIBUTES => {IS_META => 'true', coprocessor$1 =>
 '|org.apache.hadoop.hbase.coprocessor.MultiRowMutation Endpoint|536870911|'},
 {NAME => 'info', DATA_BLOCK_ENCODING => 'NONE', BLOOMFILTER => 'NONE',
 REPLICATION_SCOPE => '0', COMPRESSION => 'NONE', VERSIONS => '10', TTL =>
 'FOREVER', MIN_VERSIONS => '0', KEEP_DELETED_CELLS => 'false', BLOCKSIZE =>
 '8192', IN_MEMORY => 'true', BLOCKCACHE => 'true'}
```

The important pieces of information to glean from the this output are as follows:

IS_META => *true*

This means that the table you are describing is the meta table. Hopefully this comes as no surprise!

NAME => *info*

There is only one column family in the meta table called info. We look deeper into what is stored in this column family next.

IN_MEMORY => *true*, BLOCKCACHE => *true*

The metatable and HBase indexes are both stored in block cache, and it's important to never set the block cache below the necessary amount (usually 0.1 or 10% of the heap is sufficient for this).

Reading META

Looking at the following block of data, it is clear that meta is not very fun to read natively, but it is a necessary evil when troubleshooting HBase inconsistencies:

```
hbase(main):010:0> scan 'hbase:meta', {STARTROW => 'odell,,'}
ROW                                                      COLUMN+CELL

odell,,1412793323534.aa18c6b576bd8fe3eaf71382475bade8.
 column=info:regioninfo, timestamp=1412793324037, value={ENCODED => aa18c6b576b...
 column=info:seqnumDuringOpen, timestamp=1412793324138, value=\x00\x00\x00\x00\...
 column=info:server, timestamp=1412793324138, value=odell-test-5.ent.cloudera.c...
 column=info:serverstartcode, timestamp=1412793324138, value=1410381620515


odell,ccc,1412793397646.3eadbb7dcbfeee47e8751b356853b17e.
 column=info:regioninfo, timestamp=1412793398180, value={ENCODED => 3eadbb7dcbf...
 column=info:seqnumDuringOpen, timestamp=1412793398398, value=\x00\x00\x00\x00\...
 column=info:server, timestamp=1412793398398, value=odell-test-3.ent.cloudera.c...
 column=info:serverstartcode, timestamp=1412793398398, value=1410381620376

...truncated
```

The first column of the output is the row key:

```
odell,,1412793323534.aa18c6b576bd8fe3eaf71382475bade8.
```

and:

```
odell,ccc,1412793397646.3eadbb7dcbfeee47e8751b356853b17e.
```

The meta row key is broken down into table name, start key, timestamp, encoded region name, and . (yes, the . is necessary). When troubleshooting, the most important aspects are table name, encoded region name, and start key because it is important these match up expectedly. The next column are all of the key value pairs for this row—in this case, there is one column family named `info` and four column qualifiers named `regioninfo`, `seqnumDuringOpen`, `server`, and `serverstartcode`. There are a few main values to make particular note of when looking at the meta table for a particular region:

`info:regioninfo`
> Contains the encoded region name, the row key, the start key, and the stop key.

`info:seqnumDuringOpen`
> Used for later HBase features such as shadow regions, but is currently not important for troubleshooting.

`info:server`
> Contains the information about the RegionServer the region is assigned to (this will become quite useful when troubleshooting unassigned regions).

`info:serverstartcode`
> Contains the start times for the particular region in the RegionServer.

Reading HBase on HDFS

Looking at the layout of `meta` can be a good indicator of what the HBase region structure should look like, but there are times when `meta` can misleading or incorrect. In these cases, HDFS is the source of truth for HBase. It is just as important to be able to read the HDFS file layout of HBase as it is the meta table. We are now going to explore the HDFS layout on disk:

```
-bash-4.1$ hadoop fs -ls /hbase
Found 9 items
drwxr-xr-x   - hbase hbase          0 2014-10-08 12:14 /hbase/.hbase-snapshot
drwxr-xr-x   - hbase hbase          0 2014-08-26 10:36 /hbase/.migration
drwxr-xr-x   - hbase hbase          0 2014-09-30 06:48 /hbase/.tmp
drwxr-xr-x   - hbase hbase          0 2014-09-10 13:40 /hbase/WALs
drwxr-xr-x   - hbase hbase          0 2014-10-10 21:33 /hbase/archive
drwxr-xr-x   - hbase hbase          0 2014-08-28 08:49 /hbase/data
-rw-r--r--   3 hbase hbase         42 2014-08-28 08:53 /hbase/hbase.id
-rw-r--r--   3 hbase hbase          7 2014-08-28 08:49 /hbase/hbase.version
drwxr-xr-x   - hbase hbase          0 2014-10-14 06:45 /hbase/oldWALs
```

The first set of directories that begin with a `.` are all internal HBase directories that do not contain any data. The *.hbase-snapshot* directory is fairly self-explanatory—it contains all of the current HBase snapshots. Next is the *.migration* directory, which is utilized in upgrades from one HBase version to the next. The *.tmp* directory is where files are temporarily created. Also, FSUtils and HBCK will take advantage of this space. For example, the *hbase.version* file is created here and then moved to */hbase* once fully written. *HBCK* will use the space when merging regions or any other operations that involve changing the FS layout. The WALs directory will contain all of the currently active WALs that have not yet been rolled or need to be split during a restart. The *archive* directory is related directly to the *.hbase-snapshots* and is reserved for snapshot use only. The *archive* directly holds the HFiles that are being protected by the HBase snapshot, rather than being deleted. The *hbase.id* file contains the unique ID of the cluster. The *hbase.version* file holds a string representation of the current version of HBase. The *oldWALs* directory is used in direct correlation with HBase replication. Any WALs that still need to be replayed to the destination cluster are written here rather than deleted when rolled. This backup typically happens whenever there is communication issues between the source and destination cluster. For the exercise of troubleshooting inconsistencies, we will be focused on the *data* directory. The *data* directory is aptly named—it contains the data for HBase. Let's take a deeper look at the the the directory structure for data:

```
-bash-4.1$ hadoop fs -ls /hbase/data
Found 2 items
drwxr-xr-x   - hbase hbase          0 2014-10-08 11:31 /hbase/data/default
drwxr-xr-x   - hbase hbase          0 2014-08-28 08:53 /hbase/data/hbase
```

The next layer is where the namespaces for the HBase are contained. In the preceding example, there are only two namespaces—default and hbase:

```
-bash-4.1$ hadoop fs -ls /hbase/data/default
Found 1 items
drwxr-xr-x   - hbase hbase          0 2014-10-08 11:40 /hbase/data/default/odell
-bash-4.1$ hadoop fs -ls /hbase/data/hbase
Found 2 items
drwxr-xr-x   - hbase hbase          0 2014-08-28 08:53 /hbase/data/hbase/meta
drwxr-xr-x   - hbase hbase          0 2014-08-28 08:53 /hbase/.../namespace
```

The next level down will show the tables' names. As in the preceding code snippet, we have a table called odell in our default namespace, and we have two tables, meta, and namespace, in the hbase namespace. We are going to focus on what odell looks like going forward:

```
-bash-4.1$ hadoop fs -ls /hbase/data/default/odell
Found 5 items
drwxr-xr-x 2014-10-08 11:31 /hbase/data/default/odell/.tabledesc
drwxr-xr-x 2014-10-08 11:31 /hbase/data/default/odell/.tmp
drwxr-xr-x 2014-10-08 11:36 /hbase/data/default/odell/3eadbb7dcbfeee47e875...
drwxr-xr-x 2014-10-08 11:36 /hbase/data/default/odell/7450bb77ac287b9e77ad...
drwxr-xr-x 2014-10-08 11:35 /hbase/data/default/odell/aa18c6b576bd8fe3eaf71...
```

The *.tabledesc* directory contains a file typically named *.tableinfo.000000xxxx* where *x* is a count for the number of tables. The *tableinfo* file contains a listing of the same information presented when running a describe from the HBase shell. This includes information such as meta, data block encoding type, bloomfilter used, version count, compression, and so on. It is important to maintain the *tableinfo* file when attempting to duplicate tables using distcp (we highly recommend using snapshots instead). The *.tmp* directory is used to write the *tableinfo* file which is then moved to the *.tabledesc* when it is complete. Next, we have the encoded region name; glancing back at the meta output you will notice that the encoded region names should match up to the output of meta especially in the `info:regioninfo` under ENCODED. Under each encoded region directory is:

```
-bash-4.1$ hadoop fs -ls -R /hbase/data/default/odell/3ead...
-rwxr-xr-x 2014-10-08 11:36 /hbase/data/default/odell/3ead.../.regioninfo
drwxr-xr-x 2014-10-08 11:36 /hbase/data/default/odell/3ead.../.tmp
drwxr-xr-x 2014-10-08 11:36 /hbase/data/default/odell/3ead.../cf1
-rwxr-xr-x 2014-10-08 11:36 /hbase/data/default/odell/3ead.../cf1/5cadc83fc35d...
```

The *.regioninfo* file contains information about the region's <INFORMATION>. The *.tmp* directory at the individual region level is used for rewriting storefiles during major compactions. Finally there will be a directory for each column family in the table, which will contain the storefiles if any data has been written to disk in that column family.

General HBCK Overview

Now that we have an understanding of the HBase internals on meta and the filesystem, let's look at what HBase looks like logically when everything is intact. In the preceding example we have one table named `odell` with three regions covering "–aaa, aaa–ccc, ccc–eee, eee–". It always helps to be able to visualize that data:

Table 18-1. HBCK data visualization

Region 1	Region 2	Region 3	...	Region 24	Region 25	Region 26
"	aaa	bbb	...	xxx	yyy	zzz
aaa	bbb	ccc	...	yyy	zzz	"

Table 18-1 is a logical diagram of a fictitious HBase table covering the alphabet. Every set of keys is assigned to individual regions, starting and ending with absolute quotation marks which will catch anything before or after the current set of row keys.

Earlier versions of HBase were prone to inconsistencies through bad splits, failed merges, and incomplete region cleanup operations. The later versions of HBase are quite solid, and rarely do we run into inconsistencies. But as with life, nothing in this world is guaranteed, and software can have faults. It is always best to be prepared for anything. The go-to tool for repairing inconsistencies in HBase is known as the HBCK tool. This tool is capable of repairing most any issues you will encounter with HBase. The HBCK tool can be executed by by running `hbase` hbck from the CLI:

```
-bash-4.1$ sudo -u hbase hbase hbck
14/10/15 05:23:24 INFO Client environment:zookeeper.version=3.4.5-cdh5.1.2--1,...
14/10/15 05:23:24 INFO Client environment:host.name=odell-test-1.ent.cloudera.com
14/10/15 05:23:24 INFO Client environment:java.version=1.7.0_55
14/10/15 05:23:24 INFO Client environment:java.vendor=Oracle Corporation
```

```
14/10/15 05:23:24 INFO Client environment:java.home=/usr/java/jdk1.7.0_55-clou...
...truncated...
Summary:
hbase:meta is okay.
Number of regions: 1
Deployed on: odell-test-5.ent.cloudera.com,60020,1410381620515
odell is okay.
Number of regions: 3
Deployed on: odell-test-3.ent.cloudera.com,60020,1410381620376
hbase:namespace is okay.
Number of regions: 1
Deployed on: odell-test-4.ent.cloudera.com,60020,1410381620086
0 inconsistencies detected.
Status: OK
```

The preceding code outlines a healthy HBase instance with all of the regions assigned, META is correct, all of the region info is correct in HDFS, and all of the regions are currently consistent. If everything is running as expected, there should be 0 inconsistencies detected and status of OK. There are a few ways that HBase can become corrupt. We will take a deeper look at some of the more common scenarios:

- Bad region assignments
- Corrupt META
- HDFS holes
- HDFS orphaned regions
- Region overlaps

Using HBCK

When dealing with inconsistencies, it is very common for false positives to be present and cause the situation to look more dire than it really is. For example, a corrupt META can cause numerous HDFS overlaps or holes to show up, when the underlying FS is actually perfect. The primary flag to run in HBCK with only the -repair flag. This flag will execute every repair in a row command:

```
-fixAssignments
-fixMeta
-fixHdfsHoles
-fixHdfsOrphans
-fixHdfsOverlaps
-fixVersionFile
-sidelineBigOverlaps
-fixReferenceFiles
-fixTableLocks
```

This is great when you are working with an experimental or development instance, but might not be ideal when dealing with production or pre-production instances. One of the primary reasons to be careful with executing just the -repair flag is the -sidelineBigOverlaps flag. If there are overly large overlaps, HBase will sideline regions outside of HBase, and they will have to be bulk loaded back into the correct region assignments. Without a full understanding of every flag's implication, it is possible to make the issue worse than it is. It is recommended to take a pragmatic approach and start with the less impactful flags.

Log Everything

Before you start running any HBCK, make sure you are either logging to an external file or your terminal is logging all commands and terminal outputs

The first two flags we typically prefer to run are -fixAssignments and -FixMeta. The -fixAssignments flag repairs unassigned regions, incorrectly assigned regions, or regions with multiple assignments. HBase uses HDFS as the underlying source of truth for the correct layout of META. The -fixMeta flag removes meta rows when corresponding regions are not present in HDFS and adds new meta rows if the regions are present in HDFS while not in META. In HBase, the region assignments are controlled through the Assignment Manager. The Assignment Manager keeps the current state of HBase in memory, if the region assignments were out of sync with HBase and META, it is safe to assume they are out of sync in the Assignment Manager. The fastest way to update the Assignment Manager to the correct values provided by HBCK is to rolling restart your HBase Master nodes. After restarting the HBase Master nodes, it is time to run HBCK again.

If after rerunning HBCK the end result is not "0 inconsistencies detected," then it is time to use some heavier-handed commands to correct the outstanding issues. The three other major issues that could still be occurring are HDFS holes, HDFS overlaps, and HDFS orphans.

If running the -FixMeta and the -FixAssignments flag, we would recommend contacting your friendly neighborhood Hadoop vendor for more detailed instructions. If, on the other hand, you are handling this yourself, we would recommend using the -repair flag at this point. It is important to note that numerous passes may need to be run. We recommend running the -repair flag in a cycle similar to this:

```
-bash-4.1$ sudo -u hbase hbase hbck

-bash-4.1$ sudo -u hbase hbase hbck -repair

-bash-4.1$ sudo -u hbase hbase hbck
```

```
-bash-4.1$ sudo -u hbase hbase hbck -repair

-bash-4.1$ sudo -u hbase hbase hbck

-bash-4.1$ sudo -u hbase hbase hbck -repair

-bash-4.1$ sudo -u hbase hbase hbck
```

If you have run through this set of commands and are still seeing inconsistencies, you may need to start running through individual commands depending on the output of the last HBCK command. Again, at this point, we cannot stress enough the importance of contacting your Hadoop vendor or the Apache mailing lists—there are experts available who can help with situations like this. In lieu of that, here is a list of other commands that be found in HBCK:

-fixHdfsHoles
> Try to fix region holes in HDFS.

-fixHdfsOrphans
> Try to fix region directories with no *.regioninfo* file in HDFS.

-fixTableOrphans
> Try to fix table directories with no *.tableinfo* file in HDFS (online mode only).

-fixHdfsOverlaps
> Try to fix region overlaps in HDFS.

-fixVersionFile
> Try to fix missing *hbase.version* file in HDFS.

-sidelineBigOverlaps
> When fixing region overlaps, allow to sideline big overlaps.

-fixReferenceFiles
> Try to offline lingering reference store files.

-fixEmptyMetaCells
> Try to fix hbase:meta entries not referencing any region (empty REGION INFO_QUALIFIER rows).

-maxMerge <n>
> When fixing region overlaps, allow at most <n> regions to merge (n=5 by default).

-maxOverlapsToSideline <n>
> When fixing region overlaps, allow at most <n> regions to sideline per group (n=2 by default).

The preceding list is not inclusive, nor is it meant to be. There are lots of dragons ahead when messing with Meta and the underlying HDFS structures. Proceed at your own risk!

Index

HFile validation, 94
implementation, 83-106
table design, 83-88
testing options, 105
use cases
    document store, 161-174
    master data management tool, 141-145,
        147-160
    near real-time event processing, 107-113,
        115-140
    system of record, 73-81
    underlying storage engine implementation,
        83-106
user tables, 7

V

version count, compactions and, 16

virtual Linux environment, 58
virtual machine
    environment setup, 50-52, 56-57
    Hadoop distribution, 51
    Linux environment, 51
    local mode vs., 57
    local virtual distribution, 51
    local vm, 50
    modes, 50
    public cloud, 51

W

weekly major compaction, 17

About the Authors

Jean-Marc Spaggiari, an HBase contributor since 2012, works as an HBase specialist Solutions Architect for Cloudera to support Hadoop and HBase through technical support and consulting work. He has worked with some of the biggest HBase users in North America.

Jean-Marc's prime role is to support HBase users over their HBase cluster deployments, upgrades, configuration and optimization, as well as to support them regarding HBase-related application development. He is also a very active HBase community member, testing every release from performance and stability standpoints.

Prior to Cloudera, Jean-Marc worked as a Project Manager and as a Solution Architect for CGI and insurance companies. He has almost 20 years of Java development experience. In addition to regularly attending HBaseCon, he has spoken at various Hadoop User Group meetings and many conferences in North America, usually focusing on HBase-related presentations and demonstration.

Kevin O'Dell has been an HBase contributor since 2012 where he has been active in the community. Kevin has spoken at numerous Big Data conferences and events including Hadoop User Groups, Hadoop Summits, Hadoop Worlds, and HBaseCons. Kevin currently works at Rocana serving in a Sales Engineering position. In this role, Kevin specializes in solving IT monitoring issues at scale while applying inflight advanced anomaly detection. Kevin previously worked as a Systems Engineer for Cloudera, building Big Data applications with a specialization in HBase. In this role Kevin worked to architect, size, and deploy Big Data applications across a wide variety of verticals in the industry. Kevin was also on the Cloudera support team where he was the team lead for HBase and supported some of the largest HBase deployments in the known universe.

Prior to Cloudera, Kevin worked at EMC/Data Domain and was the Global Support Lead for Hardware/RAID/SCSI where he ran a global team and supported many of the Fortune 500 customers. Kevin also worked at Netapp, where he specialized in performance support on NetApp SAN and NAS deployments, leveraging the WAFL file system.

Colophon

The animal on the cover of *Architecting HBase Applications* is a killer whale or orca (*Orcinus orca*). Killer whales have black and white coloring, including a distinctive white patch above the eye. Males can grow up to 26 feet in length and can weigh up to 6 tons. Females are slightly smaller, growing to 23 feet and 4 tons in size.

Killer whales are toothed whales, and feed on fish, sea mammals, birds, and even other whales. Within their ecosystem they are apex predators, meaning they have no natural predators. Groups of killer whales (known as pods) have been observed specializing in what they eat, so diets can vary from one pod to another. Killer whales are highly social animals, and develop complex relationships and hierarchies. They are known to pass knowledge, such as hunting techniques and vocalizations, along from generation to generation. Over time, this has the effect of creating divergent behaviors between different pods.

Killer whales are not classified as a threat to humans, and have long played a part in the mythology of several cultures. Like most species of whales, the killer whale population was drastically reduced by commercial whaling over the last several centuries. Although whaling has been banned, killer whales are still threatened by human activities, including boat collisions and fishing line entanglement. The current population is unknown, but is estimated to be around 50,000.

Many of the animals on O'Reilly covers are endangered; all of them are important to the world. To learn more about how you can help, go to *animals.oreilly.com*.

The cover image is from *British Quadrapeds*. The cover fonts are URW Typewriter and Guardian Sans. The text font is Adobe Minion Pro; the heading font is Adobe Myriad Condensed; and the code font is Dalton Maag's Ubuntu Mono.

Get even more for your money.

Join the O'Reilly Community, and register the O'Reilly books you own. It's free, and you'll get:

- $4.99 ebook upgrade offer
- 40% upgrade offer on O'Reilly print books
- Membership discounts on books and events
- Free lifetime updates to ebooks and videos
- Multiple ebook formats, DRM FREE
- Participation in the O'Reilly community
- Newsletters
- Account management
- 100% Satisfaction Guarantee

Signing up is easy:

1. Go to: oreilly.com/go/register
2. Create an O'Reilly login.
3. Provide your address.
4. Register your books.

Note: English-language books only

To order books online:
oreilly.com/store

For questions about products or an order:
orders@oreilly.com

To sign up to get topic-specific email announcements and/or news about upcoming books, conferences, special offers, and new technologies:
elists@oreilly.com

For technical questions about book content:
booktech@oreilly.com

To submit new book proposals to our editors:
proposals@oreilly.com

O'Reilly books are available in multiple DRM-free ebook formats. For more information:
oreilly.com/ebooks

©2014 O'Reilly Media, Inc. O'Reilly logo is a registered trademark of O'Reilly Media, Inc. 14373

Have it your way.

O'Reilly eBooks

- Lifetime access to the book when you buy through oreilly.com
- Provided in up to four, DRM-free file formats, for use on the devices of your choice: PDF, .epub, Kindle-compatible .mobi, and Android .apk
- Fully searchable, with copy-and-paste, and print functionality
- We also alert you when we've updated the files with corrections and additions.

oreilly.com/ebooks/

Safari Books Online

- Access the contents and quickly search over 7000 books on technology, business, and certification guides
- Learn from expert video tutorials, and explore thousands of hours of video on technology and design topics
- Download whole books or chapters in PDF format, at no extra cost, to print or read on the go
- Early access to books as they're being written
- Interact directly with authors of upcoming books
- Save up to 35% on O'Reilly print books

See the complete Safari Library at safaribooksonline.com

O'REILLY®

©2014 O'Reilly Media, Inc. O'Reilly logo is a registered trademark of O'Reilly Media, Inc. 14373

Lightning Source UK Ltd.
Milton Keynes UK
UKHW031112180521
383929UK00003B/17

9 781491 915813